Jesus Hospital
Rothwell

A Schoolmaster's Legacy

William Franklin

STAPLOE

S

HISTORICAL
PUBLISHING

Published in the United Kingdom in 2019 by
STAPLOE HISTORICAL PUBLICATIONS,
69 North Street, Burwell, Cambridgeshire , CB25 0BA

ISBN 978-0-9930834-4-0

Printed by Akcent Media, P.O. Box 10, St Neots, Cambridgeshire, PE19 6WR.

Front Cover: The forecourt and entrance of Jesus Hospital in the Summer of
2013 showing the Tudor building with its later north facing wings.
(photograph William Franklin)

Back Cover: Photograph of the residents and staff in the hospital courtyard circa
1900.

Contents

Figures

Abbreviations and Conventions

Abbreviations

NRO	Northamptonshire Record Office
NRO JHR	Northamptonshire Record Office Jesus Hospital Records Collection
TNA	The National Archives
BL	British Library

Conventions

All transcriptions and quotations from original source material are given in italics. Transcriptions retain the original spelling and abbreviations as given in the original document, which the exception of the use of 'ff' which has been transcribed as 'f'. Where a contraction is given in the original document, an apostrophe has been used to make reading easier.

Acknowledgements

I am grateful for the help and support given to me, without which this book would not have been possible. In particular I would like to thank:

The staff at the Northamptonshire Record Office for their assistance in accessing the Jesus Hospital Collection and for allowing me to photograph various documents in that collection.

The staff at the National Archives for their assistance in accessing state papers and other collections.

The governors of Jesus Hospital for allowing contact with their estate managers, and Kettering Borough Council for assisting with a plan of the hospital before conversion.

My special thanks go to Professor John Morrill who read my initial draft and agreed to provide the Preface, and after I failed to find a publisher, urged me not to give up. Without his support, the content of this publication may have remained as a draft hidden away in a drawer, never to see the light of day.

William Franklin

March 2019

Preface

The Reformation not only blighted the English landscape, leaving us with the 'bare ruined quires ', to use Shakespeare's term: it also destroyed almost all the centres of philanthropy. For the abbeys, monasteries and convents, together with the chantries attached to most parish churches, provided for the vulnerable members of medieval society: the sick, the aged, the orphan, the destitute. At a stroke, Henry VIII's paranoia and greed took it all into his own possession, to squander it for the most part on pointless wars against France and Scotland It took generations for a welfare system to emerge. A system of mandatory parish poor rates and 'outdoor' relief administered by churchwardens and overseers in all 9,324 English parishes was supplemented by a burgeoning number of charitable trusts set up under the wills of men and women grateful for the long and prosperous lives God had granted them. Amongst the most enduring of these charitable bequests are several hundred free schools and hospitals. William Franklin offers us in this book, an extraordinarily rich and vivid account of one quite unusual hospital. To understand the word 'hospital' we should not think of a modern 'hospital' (what the Tudor age would have known as an infirmary) but think instead of the modern word 'hospitality: What Owen Ragsdale founded in Rothwell in 1591 was a hospitalis pauperum (a guest house for the poor). It was the second of eleven such hospitals founded in Northamptonshire by between 1556 and 1700 and it is the only one of the eleven not named after its benefactor. He explicitly asked for it to be called the Jesus Hospital. He almost certainly got the idea from his uncle and probably his godfather (given Ragsdale's baptismal name), Owen Oglethorpe, the Marian Bishop of Carlisle deprived by Elizabeth in 1559. In his will, Oglethorpe made ample provision for the establishment and endowment of a school and a hospital in his birth town of Tadcaster. It would provide for twelve old people and another twelve young scholars. Twelve, of course, is the number of Christ's Apostles and I am sure that is significant. It is also surely pertinent that Oglethorpe wanted it to be called Christ's Hospital. His will described his Hospital with £500 allocated for its construction.

Calling it not 'Ragsdales Hospital but Jesus Hospital is simply one of its distinctive features. Ragsdale was a closet Catholic and he ensured that those who would set up the hospital and realise his ambitious plans were all or principally Catholics. Indeed at least some of the early inmates were Catholics. On the other hand, consistent with his one outward show of conformity, the Principal and inmates were to walk 'in orderly and decent fashion' and in a hospital uniform every Sunday from the hospital to Holy Trinity Church - and significantly also on every Holy Day and Festival which no self-respecting puritan would consent to do. One of their tasks was to be the care and maintenance of the founder's tomb. Piety towards both God and towards the memory of the founder were characteristic of these charities. The particular forms at Jesus Hospital were distinctive.

Ragsdale made startling and, as far as I know, unusual provision for governance. The governors took it in turn, a different governor each time, to elect the Principal, himself a single man of modest means in need of support, and also take it in turn to fill vacancies amongst the inmates. The Board of Governors or their deputies would be a self-perpetuating group, filling vacancies in their own number by cooption.

It was a system that worked and the proof of that is of course that the Hospital still exists as a charity 420 years later. It exists because Ragsdale and his wife had no children (his step-children being modestly provided for from his estate and more lavishly from her jointure): because of his troubled conscience - as his will makes clear, he was 'right sorry that I have not continued a faithful and fruitful member' of the Catholic Church; from the inspiration of his uncle/godfather; very probably, because of his friendship with Sir Thomas Tresham with whom he had collaborated in the rebuilding of the market house adjacent to the hospital and whose unflinching suffering with his faith was surely both an inspiration and a rebuke; and his gratitude for life of comfort made possible by the major benefaction he had received from an Oglethorpe uncle.

The records of the hospital are at once voluminous and forbidding. William Franklin has done an exemplary job in unpacking the very early history - the bequest, the royal charter, the establishment of the hospital and its statutes - and with piecing together the later financial history of the hospital during periods of rapid economic change. It is a story of effective attentiveness by generations of governors and trustees. The records allow us to get a stronger sense of those who ran the hospital than of those who inhabited it, and it is sad that the records simply do not allow a sense of what daily life was like across the centuries. But Franklin unpacks the detail and makes sense of some very dry financial records in a way which makes us recognise how much more humane English society was before the era of the New Poor Law and the workhouse.

This is a book not only for anyone interested in the history of Rothwell, as a powerful accompaniment to Franklin's Rothwell with Orton: a history of a Midland Market Town (ISBN: 978-1-62620-643-4, 2013), but for anyone interested in the history of philanthropy or in the fast-moving currents and the eddies of post-Reformation history. It is one of the fullest and most vivid accounts we have of an almshouse or home for the deserving poor in turbulent times long before the Welfare State.

JOHN MORRILL FBA
Emeritus Professor of British and Irish History, University of Cambridge Life Fellow of Selwyn College Cambridge

Feast of John the Baptist 2014

Introduction

On the southwestern edge of Rothwell Market Square, next to the churchyard sits Jesus Hospital. From the market square a Tudor gateway leads into the front courtyard of the hospital with its pleasant brown Northamptonshire sand-ironstone buildings and well-kept gardens. A haven of tranquillity away from the hustle-and-bustle of the town. The hospital was founded in 1591, 33 years after the final break with Rome during which time the religious and social landscape of the country had changed.

Rothwell is a small market town in northwest Northamptonshire whose fortunes had wavered in 14th and 15th centuries was for the next one hundred years to become the focus of social and religious changes led by men of greatly differing religious beliefs. In the late 1500's some of the local landowners and people of influence maintained to varying degrees their Catholic faith at the point in time when Catholics were treated with suspicion and persecuted. The most notable of these was Sir Thomas Tresham, famous for his buildings with religious connotations. By the mid 1600's Rothwell was the home of one of the most ardent Protestants, of the time, the lawyer Sir John Lambe, who, after his promotion to Dean of the Arches, by Archbishop Laud in 1633 persecuted and zealously enforced the conformist policies of the Church of England. At the same time Rothwell saw the birth of non-conformity and witnessed the preaching's of some of its leading lights including, John Beverley, Thomas Browning and Richard Davis.

Owen Ragsdale, a schoolmaster who came to Rothwell from Nottinghamshire to teach in the local free grammar school, founded Jesus Hospital and re-founded the free grammar school in the town. The Hospital, adjacent to the church yard of the parish church of the Holy Trinity in Rothwell continues to provide accommodation for the elderly, although today the hospital is run as sheltered housing. The governors of the hospital have deposited in the Northamptonshire county record office a collection of well over two hundred records relating to the bequest of Owen Ragsdale and the running of the Hospital over a four hundred year period. This text primarily uses the Jesus Hospital collection to consider the history of the hospital from its inception in 1591 through to 1900.

Within this collection are some records relating to the free grammar school which Owen Ragsdale re-founded, these will be discussed in the context of Owen Ragsdale's endowment and the property which was used to fund the school only in as much as the trustees of the school were by and large the trustees of the hospital and the records kept by the hospital.

Philanthropy in Elizabethan England

From about the mid 15th century a shift in the pattern of benefaction appeared. The wills of the more prosperous members of society show that endowments to support the local poor were increasing. Prior to this time the majority of

1

benefactions were given to the church to pay for priests to say prayers for the souls of the benefactor and their family. Whilst many 15th and 16th century wills continue to make gifts to the church, an increasing number were giving to the poor, directly through the establishment of almshouse's or similar establishments, or indirectly through the gift of land to the parish to provide money for the use of the poor from rental. With the reformation the practice of gifts to priests to say mass died out and during the reign of queen Elizabeth I and after the number of benefactions to almshouse's increased.

Owen Ragsdale was probably Rothwell's greatest benefactor, he was fortunate in his later life to inherit a fortune from his uncle and coming to the end of his life and having no children of his own gave almost all of his wealth to found Jesus Hospital, and to re-found the free school in Rothwell, in which he had been the schoolmaster prior to its closure by king Edward VI, and to the repair of the parish church. In founding Jesus Hospital he followed a family tradition, his uncle and benefactor having founded a similar establishment in Yorkshire. Within the locality of Rothwell he was in good company, many of the local landowners such as Sir William Laxton (Oundle) and Sir Edward Montagu's (Weekly) founding almshouses in their manors.

Hospital or Alms House

In researching and producing this work it has become very clear that while there are many books on almshouses and similar foundations, they all concentrate on the initial foundation, e.g. date of foundation, by whom etc., and the surviving buildings but give little or no indication of how the foundations were organised, i.e. The number of governors or who they were (e.g. The founder's decedents, the local vicar, the church wardens or other trustees). Jesus Hospital in Rothwell is but one of a large number of similar foundations in Northamptonshire many of which were founded or re-founded during the reign of queen Elizabeth I and thereafter. These include within the surrounding areas, Lord Montague's Hospital at Weekly (1611), The Sawyer Almshouses at Kettering (1683), Nicholas Latham's Hospital, Barnwell (1601) and the Latham Hospital in Oundle (1611) to name but a few.

Before we consider the documentation and history of Owen Ragsdale's foundation it is worth noting that it was called 'Jesus Hospital' although it is not and never has been a hospital in the modern usage of the term. The term hospital originated from the Latin Hospes signifying a stranger or guest. From this came the word Hospitium which came to signify hospitality or the relationship between guest, shelter and a welcome. Documents show that the term hospitalis became increasingly common from c. 1130, used alongside and in lieu of other terminology. By the third quarter of the twelfth century, new houses might be called hospitalis injirmorum (hospital for the sick and injured) or hospitalis pauperum (the hospital of the poor). Later other terms came in to play including 'Almshouse', 'Bede House' and 'Maison Deu'. Rotha Mary Clay writing in 1909[1] wrote that 'hospital', 'almshouse' and 'bede-house' were terms that were used indiscriminately in the late medieval and early post medieval period to describe the same thing, an institution which we would now recognised as an almshouse, the hospitalis pauperum.

During the medieval period hospitals, the hospitalis injirmorum or those institutions caring for the sick only really existed within the monastic precincts, known as 'infirmaries', they provided for the benefit of sick and infirm monks and lay brethren. The only other institutions caring for the sick were those known as 'Lazar Houses', which were provided for the care of those with leprosy (although non-lepers could be placed there). In the post medieval period there were very few 'hospitals' in England caring for the sick until the 18th century.

By the early 13th century hospitals had three constitutive ingredients, a site with a building, a regular income and a designated use for that income (that is, specified alms). The founder or almsgiver in making their endowment procured the site, established a system of support and designated its use. Throughout the medieval period and into the reign of queen Elizabeth I we can see many such establishments (Hospitals and Almshouses), which have these ingredients. In addition, it was usually the case that the benefactor did not fully relinquish the source of those alms: the regular payments or material provision reiterated both the gift and the dependency of the house, in origin, form and provision, on the founder's generosity and intent. The alms of a hospital founder were given in the form regular provision of food, firewood or customary payments. Its repetitive, customary and public performance acting as both a reiteration of this constitution and the means of ensuring constitutional stability.

The term 'almshouse' to describe a residential establishment for the poor, sick and aged as opposed to the use of the term 'hospital' appears for the first time in 1453 when a licence was granted to four men to found a hospital at Dartford in Kent, which was to be known as 'Trinity Alms House'[2]. The term Alms meaning money or services donated to support the poor.

Most medieval 'hospitals' and 'almshouses' were founded by the nobility, clergy, gilds or other wealthy individuals who were committed to providing shelter for the elderly and infirm who are often referred to as 'the deserving poor' and it has been estimated that by the 1520s there were as many hospitals in England as there were monasteries .

During the reformation brought about by king Henry VIII a number of hospitals closed with the monasteries[3]. During the reign of king Edward VI more hospitals and almshouses were closed with the suppression of the gilds. Religious gilds had been major benefactors, particularly of small almshouses in the later medieval period. The reign of queen Mary saw a short lived revival of the catholic church in England, but because of uncertainties about the future and the general instability of the country endowments for the foundation of new hospitals and almshouses were almost non-existent. This remained largely the case until about 1570 by which time there was an increase in confidence for the future and a greater degree of stability in the government of the country.

In this mid Elizabethan period the principal benefactors were mostly wealthy individuals or town and city corporations. One of the first of these new establishments was that founded by the queens favourite, Robert Dudley, Earl of Leicester, in 1571, known as Lord Leicester's Hospital at Warwick. Pious philanthropist such as Dudley, Ragsdale and Burghley brought up in pre reformation Catholic England continued to derive comfort in giving money to the poor albeit in a controlled way. Such piety born out of the teachings of the church and biblical passages such as Matthew 25:

> *'For I was hungry, and you gave me meat: I was thirsty, and you gave me drink: I was a stranger and you took me in: Naked, and you clothed me: I was sick, and you visited me: I was in prison, and you came unto me'.*

No wealthy pious individual wished to be the rich man in the story of Lazarus, Luke 16, 19-23[4], sent to hell because he left the poor man Lazarus wanting at his gate, for in 16th century England it was universally belied that failure to be charitable to the needy would result in either vicious torment in purgatory or damnation in hell. As a result the Tudor period saw a new age of Alms House foundation or re-foundation and other benefactions such as doles to be handed out to the poor. Similarly the universal expectation was that those on receipt of alms would pray for the soul of the benefactor and his family.

This may be seen in part from the rising numbers of poor in almost every community. When Elizabeth came to the throne England in 1558, the country was at war with both France and Scotland. Begging, especially by wounded and disabled solders was commonplace. Recognising the issue and fearful of an uprising by the dispossessed poor a Poor Rate was introduced in 1572, but this did little to help as it was not universally adopted and grain prices were rising. Between 1594 and 1597 the price of grain doubled and many of the poorest died. Accordingly statutes of 1597 and 1691 established a system of parish poor relief that would remain in place until 1834.

Foundations created or re-created during the reign of queen Elizabeth I attest to the continued need to do good works and assist the poor, which was born out of the medieval terror of retribution after death. The statutes of such foundations usually included an obligation on the part of the residents to pray for the souls of the founder and their family, a medieval tradition that continued until at least the civil war. Such obligations including that of daily prayer were usually written into the founding charter or statutes as was the case of Jesus Hospital, Rothwell. These can be seen as deeply catholic beliefs and ones that spurred many older and wealthy people who had been brought up in that faith, or who were members of recusant families to make bequests to found hospitals and alms houses in the century or so following the dissolution of the monasteries and the suppression of the religious gilds which had previously operated many of the charitable foundations for the poor and sick.

Medieval hospitals and almshouses usually had a chapel and a resident chaplain to ensure daily prayers were delivered to God. The Bede House at Higham Ferrers is a good example of this. It comprises of a large open hall with a chapel at one end. The hall would have originally been partitioned into cubicles for the residents. Half way along one side of the hall is a fireplace, which, was used for both cooking and the only source of heat. The un-partitioned area around the fireplace acting as a food preparation area, a place to eat and a general circulation area. A chaplain from the vicarage house next door said Mass twice daily for the soul of the founder / benefactor in the chapel at the east end, the residents even if bed ridden being required to participate. At Higham Ferrers the Bede House was founded to provide a dwelling place for 12 men over 50 years old to live in 'close company' with one woman to look after them. The size of the building meant that within the partitions there was little space for more than a bed and the whole arrangement ensured that the men were always in close company with one another and privacy was seriously lacking. A feature that was to change by the end of the last Tudor monarch.

Many such hospitals were run by gilds and as a result such institutions came under scrutiny during the reformation, many were dissolved with the smaller religious houses, and more with the dissolution of the remaining monasteries in 1539, and their lands and other possessions sold off by the crown. During the reign of king Edward VI all chantries and gilds were required to be surveyed and valued from 1547. There then followed the dissolution of the gilds and chantries and with them further closures of the almshouses, hospitals and schools that they ran. Rothwell Free Grammar School was one such establishment that was closed at this time, only to be re-founded by Owen Ragsdale in 1591.

Building Design

Whilst often called 'hospital', these hospitals were in practice almshouses and the design of the buildings far removed from either of the two principal medieval designs, the hall, chapel and yard (e.g. Higham Ferrers & the Hospital of St John, Northampton) or the monastic style buildings set around a cloister or courtyard (e.g. Brown's Hospital, Stamford). The new buildings created between the reign of queen Elizabeth I and the civil war ranged from those that resembled small manor houses to the slightly bizarre, such as the circular Beamsley Hospital in Yorkshire. Many were built as single storey terraced rows, such as the Sawyer Almshouses in Kettering, some had an upper floor. Those built during the reign of queen Elizabeth I had small rooms, yet compared with their medieval predecessors offered privacy and a greater degree of warmth.

Owen Ragsdale's foundation, Jesus Hospital, resembles a small manor house in outward appearance but was much less comfortable inside. It provided each resident with an individual private bed chamber, albeit without a fireplace. The fireplace for warmth and cooking was to be found in the communal halls. Like a small Elizabethan manor house it was built with a long gallery on the top floor where residents could circulate, sit, converse and exercise during inclement weather. A similar design to that of the common halls at Jesus Hospital is to be found Frieston Hospital, Kirksthorpe, West Yorkshire. Built on a smaller scale in 1595 it has individual bed-chambers off of common halls, with the only fireplaces being in those halls. At Latham's Hospital, Oundle the only fire was in the hall and residents were required by the regulations of the hospital to take it in turn to warm themselves[5].

The post reformation hospitals or almshouses unlike their medieval counterparts rarely had chapels within the premises. They were frequently built as at Rothwell and Barnwell next to the parish church and the act of the master and poor men or women in their uniforms parading into church was a reminder to the whole community of the gifts of the benefactor. In such institutions prayers were still said at the beginning and end of the day, but no longer in a purpose built chapel, but in an ordinary room, usually a communal hall. Medieval hospitals and almshouses usually had a priest or chaplain who led prayers. In the new hospitals and almshouses it was the master or warden, chosen because he could read, write and was a Godly man. What ever the buildings design the general tenet was the same. A building was provided for the use of a set number of old people, usually men who might be infirm and who without the almshouse would unable to survive without support from the parish poor rate.

Gardens

Throughout the medieval period gardens and orchards close to the hospital or almshouse were usually provided to produce food for the community. From the 15th century gardens surrounding the establishment became more common and became the responsibility of the residents. After the reformation the vagrancy acts of king Henry VIII's reign these took of greater significance as sources of employment and daily toil, ensuring that the residents were not idle.

An ordered life

The lives of the residents were ruled by statutes or ordinances. Rules by which they were required to live. These rules in Elizabethan England included the waking day, the times of prayers, the clothes they wore and various criteria relating to their residential eligibility. It was common for benefactors to required that the residents wore a uniform which was provided for them. For example the men of the Hospital of St Cross in Winchester were required to wear a black hat, a black cloak and distinctive badge of the Cross of Jerusalem which identified them as the almsmen as Brothers of St Cross Hospital. In a similar vein the women of the almshouses at Castle Rising in Norfolk were required to wear gowns and a tall hat, which resembles a traditional Welsh woman's hat.

The differentiation between male and female roles was greater in Elizabethan England and men would not be expected to wash clothes and accordingly Jesus Hospital like most early post medieval almshouses employed a woman to wash and carry out cleaning and related chores. In almost all of these foundations the benefactor ensured that the verses of Matthew 25 were followed, food was provided to ensure that the residents did not go hungry, although in some cases the diet might be wanting from a health point of view, and whilst not naked the residents were provided with clothing, usually a uniform which set them out from the people of the town but which also gave out a clear message that here was one who was so poor that they relied upon the charity of the benefactor and his successors, and when unwell an apothecary or physician was called.

As we shall see, Jesus Hospital like many later medieval and early post medieval hospitals was placed on a very public site in an important and politically symbolic town, affording a more open and public display of charitable lordship. However the expectation on those resident was less charitable for while the founder usually endowed the establishment with land, the rental of which paid for food and clothing the residents and provided them with a small stipend or wage, the residents were expected to work, idleness was not a choice that any resident could make. Everyone was expected to undertake some kind of work dependent upon their ability and this is reinforced in Rule 16 of the Statutes of the hospital (see Appendix 1).

Such establishments usually provided for persons who had been resident in the town, village or on the estate of the founding family. In this respect Jesus Hospital is quite different. From a very early period poor men could be nominated for admission from the three hundreds of Rothwell, Orlingbury and Corby, which in total comprised of 75 towns, villages and hamlets.

The Governing Body

It was quite usual for such foundations to be run by feoffees, trustees or governors in a similar way to that of modern charities. In most establishments these feoffees, trustees or governors were usually the town leaders, the yeomen who served as churchwardens or on the vestry, or the overseers. A good example of this is that of Lord Burghley's hospital, in which successive lords of Burghley took an interest. They funded the hospital which provided for 13 men including the warden, but left the nomination of people from within the parish or those parishes covered by the estate and other decisions regarding the running of the hospital to the Ordinaries, who also ran a Sunday School from the premises. In this respect Jesus Hospital has been through much of its history quite unique, for its governors have from the very beginning been members of the ruling elite, Earls, Baronets, Members of Parliament and Manorial Lords. As we shall see later there can be few such foundations that have as impressive a list of Governors and Assistant Governors as Jesus Hospital. Another key difference and probably the reason for such an impressive group of gentry, is that on foundation a society, known as the Society and Fellowship of Jesus Hospital, was created. This society appears to have carried considerable philanthropic weight amongst the landed gentry and ensured continuity of Governors and Assistants from 1591 to 1900.

As the documentary evidence will show the statutes of the hospital which every resident had to have read to them twice per year made great play on the fact that this was a society and fellowship of which they had been admitted as members.

Additionally, every poor man admitted into the hospital and thereby the society and fellowship paid on admission four pence, in the same way as one might pay a one off membership fee.

Dedication

Throughout the medieval and immediate post medieval period hospitals were usually dedicated in the same manner as churches. Typical dedications include The Holy Trinity, St Cross, Corpus Christi or the name of a particular saint. The dedication of hospitals to Jesus Christ, as 'Jesus Hospital' is not seen in pre-reformations establishments. This is probably a post reformation shift in naming of such establishments and probably represents the post medieval equivalent of the medieval dedication of 'Christ's Hospital'. Jesus Hospital appears as a dedication after about 1590 and became a popular dedication in the 17th century. Nationally examples include:

Jesus Hospital, Rothwell	1591
Jesus Hospital, Canterbury (also known as Boys' Hospital)	1595
Jesus Hospital, Lyddington (known locally as the Bede House)	1600
Jesus Hospital, Bray, Berks	1609
Blessed Jesus Hospital, East Carlton	1668
Jesus Hospital, Barnet	1679
Holy Jesus Hospital, Newcastle upon Tyne	1684

Hospitals whose dedication includes the name of Jesus

Notes

[1] Clay, Rotha Mary (1966) The Medieval Hospitals of England, Frank Cass & Co Ltd, London.
[2] Bailey, B. (1988) Almshouses. Robert Hale Ltd, London. p. 65.
[3] Jordan, W.K. (1959) Philanthropy in England: 1480 – 1660. George Allen and Unwin Ltd. London
[4] Luke 19, 19 – 23. *There was a rich man who was dressed in purple and fine linen and lived in luxury every day. At his gate was laid a beggar named Lazarus, covered with sores and longing to eat what fell from the rich man's table. Even the dogs came and licked his sores. The time came when the beggar died and the angels carried him to Abraham's side. The rich man also died and was buried. In Hades, where he was in torment, he looked up and saw Abraham far away, with Lazarus by his side.*
[5] Melville, Lord (1899) 'Lathom Hospital'. Journal of the British Archaeological Association. Second series, 5: pp. 29 – 34.

Owen Ragsdale and his Feoffees

We would know little of Owen Ragsdale (also spelled Raggesdale and Raggesdall) but for the efforts of two persons. The first Ferdinand Pulton, sometimes spelled Poulton, friend of Owen Ragsdale and the second, the Reverend J. Cattell, vicar of Rothwell from 1704 – 1719. Ferdinand Pulton wrote a short text in Latin on the life of Owen Ragsdale, probably shortly after Owen's death in 1591. That original document which no longer survives was translated and transcribed by the Reverend Cattell in 1797. The transcribed document does survive and is in the Jesus Hospital collection at Northamptonshire Record Office.

In addition to Pulton's text on the life of Owen Ragsdale there are other documents, which allow us to build a picture of the life of the man who founded Jesus Hospital. Amongst these are Owen Ragsdale's will and the will of Owen Ragsdale's father, 'Henry Ragysdaile of Kneeton, discovered by the Northamptonshire historian F.W. Bull, at York, when researching Owen Ragsdale in 1929[1].

According to Pulton, Owen Ragsdale was the son of Henry of "Knyton" in the County of Nottingham, gentleman, and of Elizabeth, his wife. Henry and Elizabeth had eight children, three boys and five girls. At least one brother and four sisters survived into adulthood. In 1591, one brother, Robert and two sisters, Elizabeth and Katherine, were still alive and they and their children were to receive bequests from Owens will. Bequests were also made to the children of a further two sisters, Mary and Dorothy both of whom were deceased.

Pulton informs us that Owen Ragsdale as a youth was "a very good genius" and was chosen to be a scholar of Magdalen College in Oxford. According to Foster's Alumni Oxonienses,[2] Owen Ragsdale was a chorister of Magdalen College in 1551, a demy scholar 1555-60, taking and being awarded a Batchelor of Arts degree in 1560.

Owen Oglethorpe, the brother of Owen Ragsdale's mother, was President of Magdalen (1535 to 1552) during the time when Owen Ragsdale was a student and no doubt had some considerable influence in his being admitted to the college. Oglethorpe was a catholic recusant and his beliefs led to his resignation from Magdalen in 1552. Queen Mary on her accession in 1553 rewarded him for his faith and made him Dean of Windsor then, in 1557 she made him Bishop of Carlisle. He was one of the few bishops that supported the accession of Queen Elizabeth I and was present at her coronation in 1559, but despite this she subsequently deprived him of his see and thereafter he is said to have regretted his part in the coronation.

Owen Oglethorpe died on 31st December 1559, the year in which Owen Ragdale took up the position of Schoolmaster at the Grammar School in Rothwell, where we are informed, " he instructed the youth in learning and good manners", presumably also teaching them English, Mathematics and Latin. After he had spent some years in teaching at the school Owen Ragsdale returned to Oxford, "for the improvement of his own learning" This time he studied Civil Law at Lincoln College.

During the course of this period of study in Oxford, Owen Ragsdale learned that he had inherited an estate in Yorkshire from an uncle, Andrew Oglethorpe. This estate, the Manor of Headley, known as Headley Hall, Tadcaster, Yorkshire, included Headley Hall, 8 messuages, 4 cottages, and a windmill with lands in Bramham, Tradcaster, Stutton, Clyfforde, and Beall, sometimes called Beghall. Andrew Ogilthorpe, a wealthy recusant had been killed sometime before 10th May1570, in the Northern Revolt.[3]

Ragsdale married Mary, daughter of Edward Osborne of Kelmarsh Esquire, and widow of Richard Hampden. Pulton describes her as being, "a vertuous and frugal woman", and appears to have initially gone to Yorkshire to take possession of the estate, which he and Mary then sold to John and Henry Saville, gentlemen in 1584.[4] The Savilles were probably property speculators, for in 1587 they sold it on to a William Hewytt, whose son became 1st Baronet Headley.

Following the sale the Ragsdale's returned to the Rothwell area where they purchased property, including the manor of Old, a village about 7 miles from the town of Rothwell. Although now wealthy Owen Ragsdale was not idle, Pulton noting that he was "constantly employed in managing and making up matters of weight and moment", earning "the love and commendation of all ranks and sons of men", but retaining "an humble and a grateful mind towards god.

With his new wealth Owen Ragsdale was also granted Arms by the queen in 1578. The record of the award by Clarenceux reads:

"I Clarenceux the King of Arms have signed these presents with my hand and set hereunto the seal of my office, the 13th May in the year of Our Lord 1578 and in the twentieth year of the reign of our Sovereign Lady Elizabeth, by the grace of God Queen of England, Scotland and Ireland. Defender of the Faith. Signed Robert Cooke alias Clarenceux.[5]"

The Ragsdale Pelican and fleur de lise on a cartouche above the central passage at Jesus Hospital

The Ragsdale Pelican is found above the central passage on the main hospital building (Right), while the full Arms appear on Owen Ragsdale's tomb comprise of a shield quartered. In the top left and bottom right is Ragsdale's pelican with fleur de lise and in the top right and bottom left are the Arms of Oglethorpe, the family of which he was heir. The Oglethorpe arms being a silver cross quartered by ermine with four boar heads holding in their mouths a slip of oak with leaves and acorns. Above the shield is a helmet with a wreath of gold and Jules (Red) and an arm holding strips of palm.

From both the will of Owen's father Henry, and his own will it is clear that the family were devout Catholics. Owen himself appears to have kept to his faith up to his death, although unlike many of his friends he did not suffer financially or go to prison for his faith. His will of 1591 (Appendix 1) gives a clue as to why for it reads; *first I protest from my heart that renouncing all sects, scismes & there lyes, I doe firmly and without all doubt hold and believe ye Christian faith & every part and point thereof as our mother the holy catholicque church instructed by ye promised spirit of truth hath taught and declared: Yet being now right sory that I have not continued a faithfull and fruitfull member of ye same ever since my baptisme"*. This suggests that Ragsdale had probably gone along with the changes made during the reformation but under the surface remained a Catholic, unlike his friend local land owner Sir Thomas Tresham of Rushton, from whom Ragsdale was renting the manor house of Rothwell. Sir Thomas was unwavering in his faith, suffering huge fines for his recusancy and taunting his neighbours and the government through his buildings with their complex religious symbols.

From his marriage to Mary, widow of Richard Hampden, Owen Ragsdale had no children. At the time of their marriage he was in his fourties and probably of a similar age. She had three children from her first marriage, a daughter Ann and two sons, Thomas and Edward. The Hampden children were probably well catered for from their fathers estate but despite this Owen Ragsdale made bequests to them all but reserved the majority of his estate to the founding of Jesus Hospital and the continuation of the free grammar school in Rothwell where he had taught and later refounded.

Rothwell Market House

Before considering Owen Ragsdale's will and his endowment of Jesus Hospital it is worth noting that in the short account of Owen Ragsdale's life by Ferdinand Pulton, Pulton states that *"He restored yᵉ Markett to ROWEL wch: had failed and was lost, & there built a Markett-House at his own proper Charges"*. The Market House in Rothwell was built in 1578 by William Grumbold to the designs of Sir Thomas Tresham of Rushton. It has always been assumed that this was Tresham's first religiously symbolic building built and that Tresham paid for it himself. However, Pulton's account of Ragdale's life suggests that Owen Ragsdale provided the money. The Latin inscription around the building says that Tresham had it built, *"As a tribute to [his] sweet fatherland and County of Northampton, but chiefly to this town [his] near neighbour; Nothing but common weal did he seek; Nothing but perpetual honour of [his] friends"*.

11

From the instructions to William Grumbold we know that Tresham was to provide the materials and from a letter to Sir Christopher Hatton of Kirby that Hatton gave stone from Weldon to complete the work. Pulton appears to suggest that Tresham designed and commissioned the building, but that it was paid for by Owen Ragsdale. No documents survive relating to any such gift, however it has been noted that Owen Ragsdale's arms appear not with those of the local gentry but in a prominent position on the right hand side of the central arch on the south front and those of Ferdinand Pulton on the left side of the same arch which has at its top the Tresham with Throckmorton arms.[6] As noted by Gotch 'The panels over the arches were meant for inscriptions, which they never received, so that Sir Thomas might have meant to acknowledge Ragsdale's help more directly".[7]

Owen Ragsdale's Will

A copy of Owen Ragsdale's will is housed in the National Archives.[8] A copy of the original was made in the 19th century and kept with the other hospital records, now in the Northamptonshire Record Office (see Appendix 1.).[9]

Owen's will was to be buried in the chancel of Rothwell parish church, and as we shall see, whilst everything else in his will was carried out his burial place was not. Owen's tomb chest is in the Saunders Chapel, a portion of the south aisle which had been made in to a chantry chapel by Edward Saunders whose memorial brass lays on the floor. There is no evidence to suggest that the tomb chest has been placed anywhere other than its present location and unless Owen's body is buried elsewhere other than under the tomb chest we must assume this part of the will was not adhered to. The monument is a relatively plain tomb chest bearing Owen Ragsdale's arms, the pelican preening herself, argent between three fleur de lys. On the top of the tomb is a brass inscription which reads:

> *Hic jacet ille vir probus & pius Owinus Ragsdale qui hospitium posuit Jesu. Iste accipiens bendictionem a Domino eam retribuit pauperibus suis. Obiit primo Decembri anno 1591.*

Translated,

> Here lies that good and pious man, Owen Ragsdale, who founded Jesus Hospital. He receiving a blessing from the Lord paid it back to his poor. He died on the first of December in the year 1591.

Detached and now on top of the tomb is a brass plate, now framed with an image of Owen Ragsdale in a gown, kneeling, his hands clasped in prayer. Behind him is a coat of arms with the motto, *"Fecit mihi magna, qui potens est"*. Translated this reads "He that is mighty has done for me great things", which appears to have been Owen Ragsdale's favourite phrase or motto. Above Owen is an inscription which reads, *"Domini ego inutilis servus tuus et omnia opera mea vilescunt coram te, ideo in misericorda tua sola salus et spes mea"*.

Rubbing of Owen Ragsdale's Brass on his tomb in Rothwell Parish Church. He is shown kneeling in prayer, His full coat of arms lye behind him, above which is his motto.

Translated this is, "O Lord I am Thy useless servant and all my works become vile before thee, therefore in thy mercy is my sole salvation and hope".

Recusant Beginnings

The years preceding Owen Ragsdale's death in 1591 and the years that followed were particularly difficult for followers of the Catholic faith and any person suspected of practicing that faith was considered at the very least with suspicion. From 1571 when queen Elizabeth I ratified the articles of doctrine it became treason to reconcile any person into the catholic church or give absolution as a priest. Harbouring catholic priests such as one of the small number of Jesuits that went from house to house of the wealthy catholic families was a serious offence which at the very least resulted in serious fines and often imprisonment, and for the priest if caught, certain death. Similarly any foundation or works created by known Catholics were treated similarly and it is therefore surprising that Royal assent was given to the foundation of the hospital when so many of the feoffees were either practicing Catholics or from know catholic families. Most like Owen Ragsdale would have been a church papist, that is, they attended the parish church and outwardly conformed, but were at heart still catholic.

As we have seen from Owen Ragsdale's will and the statement, "*I protest from my heart that renouncing all sects, scismes & there lyes, I doe firmly and without all doubt hold and believe ye Christian faith & every part and point thereof as our mother the holy catholicque church instructed by ye promised spirit of truth*

13

hath taught and declared: Yet being now right sory that I have not continued a faithfull and fruitfull member of ye same ever since my baptisme; And in that faith I most hopefully and joyfully surrender my soule into the mercifull hands of my Almighty Creator trusting assuredly by ye infinite merits of his dear son Jesus Christ our only redeemer and saviour, and by his most precious blood so abundantly shed for me to be made a partaker of his everlasting kingdoome which that I may obtain I most humbly pray and beseech the blessed Virgin Mary (Mother of God) with all ye blessed company of Heaven and my dear mother ye catholicque church always to be intercessor for me ", Owen was still clearly a catholic although not one who practiced his faith openly. He would have attended church services at Holy Trinity church but kept his catholic faith and beliefs to himself, thus avoiding the financial penalties and imprisonment that beset the Tresham's of Rushton. Something he clearly regretted. Owen's benefactor, his uncle was a catholic Bishop who fell out of favour with Queen Elizabeth I because of his beliefs.

It is clear from surviving records etc. that at least some of Owen Ragsdale's feoffees were recusants these will now be considered. A fuller account of the lives of these feoffees is to be found later (see Governors).

Ferdinand Pulton

In his will Owen Ragsdale requests that Ferdinand Pulton be his executor and if Ferdinand was to decline then he requests Walter Hastings of Ashby (de la Zouch) to undertake the role. Ferdinand Pulton was a known catholic and because of his faith and the suspicions aroused, barred from practising law. He had been born in Desborough, where his family were lords of the manor, and subsequently qualified as a lawyer. By his second marriage Ferdinand had 5 sons and four daughters. The children were clearly schooled in the catholic faith and one daughter, Eugenia went to the Netherlands to become a Benedictine nun and later abbess of a new convent in Ghent (Belgium), and two of his sons became ordained Jesuit priests. The eldest son and heir married into another Northamptonshire catholic family and resided at Irthlingborough where in 1612/13 he and his wife are recorded as recusants.[10]

Walter Hastings of Ashby

Walter Hastings of Ashby, Leicestershire, did not need to accept the position of executor as Owen's first choice Ferdinand Pulton accepted the role. However, it is worth noting that although he therefore played no part in executing the will or founding the hospital (that we know of) he was clearly from a catholic family and that his godfather was Cardinal Reginald Pole who fell out with Henry VIII and refused to return to England when summoned by the king for writing in opposition to the kings divorce.

Thomas Tresham of Newton

Thomas Tresham of Newton was a cousin of the more famous Sir Thomas Tresham, knight of Rushton and less is known about him. The Tresham's were a well-known catholic family and as a result of their faith almost all members of the family, from either branch were treated with suspicion.

Thomas Morgan of Heyford

It is unclear whether Thomas Morgan was a recusant, however his father was Francis Morgan, judge of the King's Bench in Queen Mary's reign and therefore of a catholic family. He was also related to the Saunders family who immediately prior to the reformation had established a chantry at Rothwell.

Oliver Farren of Molesworth

Oliver Farren was lord of the Manor of Molesworth and impropriate rector of that parish having inherited it from his father William. How he came to know Owen Ragsdale is not known. He was not an Oxford scholar and little is known about his life.

George Gascoyne of London

As with Oliver Farren, little is known about George Gascoigne and it is impossible to say whether they were recusants or 'church papists'.

Catholic Associations

There were numerous catholic genry in Northamptonshire at the time of the foundation of Jesus Hospital, including, as we have seen, Owen Ragsdale. Ragsdale was not uncommon in attending services in the parish church and obeying the state, while practicing his Catholic beliefs in private. Few people outwardly manifest their beliefs in defiance of the crown and state as Sir Thomas Tresham. Tresham's punishment of imprisonment and heavy fines was probably a lesson to his Catholic friends in how to behave and not receive the same fate.

Sir Thomas Tresham, his cousin Sir Thomas Tresham of Newton and Ferdinand Pulton were all recusants and yet despite the suspicions that they must have aroused, the foundation of Jesus Hospital as set out in Owen Ragsdale's will was approved by queen Elizabeth I. Catholicism survived in the Rothwell area, probably influenced and shielded by the catholic gentry. Suspicions regarding the hospital foundation and its tolerance of recusants continued through to at least 1613, when, in that year orders were issued to disarm recusants and 'The Hospitall of Rowell" appears in a list of "houses and persons that we think fitte from whome the armes shalbe taken".[11] The list also includes the houses of the Ferdinando Bawde or Baud (Thorpe Underwood and Walgrave) who was an Assistant Governor of Jesus Hospital from September 1600, and the Kinsman (Loddington) and Syers (Isham) families known recusants. Robert Syers the father of John

15

Syers, a Governor of the hospital in the mid 1600's who was fined £20 under Act of 29 October 1586 for not attending church within a month from 1 January 1606; & £60 for 3 months absence from 9 July 1607 on which day he was convicted.[12]

Recusancy charges were not only laid at the Governors of the hospital. A visit to the hospital by the Vicar General and staunch supporter of Anglican orders, Sir Nathaniel Brent in 1635, records that a poor man resident at the hospital was a recusant:

> *There is an hospital in Rowell which I visited, ……There are Twelve poor men, of which one hath been a recusant papist this twenty-six years. My opinion is that his place is void, but I gave order that nothing should be done against him until another hearing.*[13]

Notes

[1]   Bull, F. W. (1924) Jesus Hospital, and its founder, Owen Ragsdale, Northamptonshire Architectural Society.

[2]   Wood, A. (1721) Athena Oxonienses, Vol. 1. p. 694.

[3]   Calendar of the Cecil Papers in Hatfield House; Volume 1, 1306-1571. pp.460-474

[4]   Feet of Fines of the Tudor Period (Yorks): Part 3, 1583-1594. pp.14-31

[5]   Warner, A. R. (1952) The Records and Collections of the College of Arms.

[6]   Isham, G. (1962) Two Local Biographies: Owen Ragsdale and Sir John Robinson. Northamptonshire Past and Present. Vol.III. p.83.

[7]   Gotch, J.A. (1883A complete account, illustrated by measured drawings, of the buildings erected by Sir Thomas Tresham in Northamptonshire, between 1575 and 1605. Taylor & Son Ltd.

[8]   TNA Prob 11/79/26

[9]   NRO JHR 4 – Transcript of the Will of Owen Ragsdale

[10]   Wake, J. & Rev. H. Isham Longden (1935) Montague Musters Book, Northamptonshire Record Society, Vol VII. pp224 – 226

[11]   ibid.

[12]   NRO YO 16 a-b.

[13]   Preface. Calendar of State Papers Domestic: Charles I, 1635 (1865) pp. VII - LII

Ragsdale's Foundation

By November 1591 Owen Ragsdale was probably in poor health and at that time made his will and enfeoffed some of his closest friends to establish Jesus Hospital. They appear to have commenced writing the will on the 10th November 1591, continuing with various additions and amendments on subsequent days. The final will was completed on the 13th November 1591.

The initial feoffment was created on 10th November 1591[1] in which Ragsdale gave power of attorney to Owen Shipley and enfeoffed Thomas Tresham of Newton, knight; George Gascoigne of London, knight; Ferdinand Pulton of Bourton, Buckinghamshire, knight, and Oliver Farren of Molesworth, Huntingdonshire. These feoffees were to use the estate that Ragsdale had purchased in Old, Orton and Rothwell to support Ragsdale's foundation, Jesus Hospital in Rothwell. The following day, 11th November 1591 a set of seven articles was indented to the feoffment[2]. These articles agreed between all parties ensured that:

- Owen Ragsdale could enjoy his premises for the remaining duration of his life, this included the rental income from his premises.
- Owen Ragsdale could alter his wishes during his remaining lifetime.
- On the death of Owen Ragsdale the feoffees were to use the income from his lands as specified to build the hospital to his specifications on the site of his manor of Old and provide for twenty five poor men who were unmarried, aged and pure, that is not lame, impotent, diseased, blind, deaf or an imbecile. These men could remain in the hospital until the end of their lives providing they remained unmarried and did not suffer blindness, deafness, from a contagious disease or were not mentally ill.
- The feoffees should gain royal assent, called the institution Jesus Hospital and appoint one of the twenty-five as master, ruler or governor over the rest of the men.
- The feoffees should make a set of rules, laws, ordinances, constitutions under which the hospital should be run.
- Once the hospital is built the feoffees should elect successors and establish a line of succession.
- The articles could be added to or amended.

It is interesting to note that in 1591 Owen Ragsdale put into his articles a line of succession to ensure the continuation of his foundation. In Elizabethan England this was not always the case and as a result the year after the letters patent granting the foundation were approved a statute was passed to ensure that all new foundations included clear articles of succession [3].

Transcript of the Letters Patent granted by Queen Elizabeth I.

Letters Patent 38 Elizabeth I

29 Jun 1596. Grant (at the petition of Thomas Morgan, Thomas Tresham, George Gascoigne, Ferdinand Pulton and Oliver Farrene, who were enfeoffed of certain lands, rectories and tithes by Owen Raggesdale of Rothewell, Northants, deceased) that there shall be a hospital at Rothewell for the relief of the poor and infirm men of the said town and its neighbourhood according to the good intent of the said Owen Raggesdale, to be called the hospital of Jesus at Rothwell. It is to consist of a principal and 24 paupers. For the better governance of the said hospital, there will be 5 governors, and the aforesaid Thomas Morgan, Thomas Tresham, George Gascoigne, Ferdinand Pulton and Oliver Farrein are appointed as the first 5 modern governors of the goods, possessions and revenues of the said hospital. The five governors shall be a body corporate and are to have a common seal and be capable of possessing property, and of pleading and being impleaded. Licence, in mortmaim, for the governors to hold property up to the clear yearly valueof £200. There shall be 10 associate governors, inhabitants of the county of Northamptonshire, who shall assist the governors, when it seems to good to the governors or the greater part of them. Thomas Pagit of Walgrave, Francis Morgan of Kingesthroppe, George Pulton of Desburrowe, Francis Crispe of Boughton, Francis Tresham of Rushton,William Tate of Dalapre, Edward Furtho of Furtho, William Saunders of Welford, Thomas Mulsho of Thingdon and Robert Spencer of Oldthorpe alias Althrope, are to be the first modern associate governors. Any vacancy among the governors is to be filled by the senior associate governor, while vacancies among the associate governors are to be filled by election by the governors or greater part of them from gentlemen resident in Northamptonshire, being of the age of 25 years or over, seised to their own use of lands there as a clear yearly value of not less than £10, and being neither barons nor knights, or above the rank of esquire. With powers to appoint or remove the principal and 24 paupers of the hospital, and to make statutes for their governance, and for that of the revenues of the hospital, such statutes not being repugnant to the laws of England or previous statutes of the hospital.

Royal Assent

In accordance with Owen Ragsdale's wishes the feoffees sought royal assent for the foundation which was granted by Queen Elizabeth I on 29th June 1596 (overleaf).[4] The office copy of the letters patent [5] is interesting in that the feoffees request was "We seek, in the same vill of Rothwell, a hospital for the good sustenance of paupers and infirm men there and in surrounding parts in the same county", and the letters patent affirms the hospital was *"for the relief of the poor and infirm men of the said town and its neighbourhood"*. Changes made by the Feoffees

The enfeoffment and articles are interesting in that it is very clear that Owen Ragsdale, who owned the manor house and its demesne in Old intended the hospital, be built on that site. What subsequently occurred was that the hospital was built not in Old, but in Rothwell. This point was noted in 1831 by the Charity Commissioners who wrote:[6]

> *The hospital was erected in the town of Rothwell, and not as intended in Olde, as originally designed, and in consequence probably of the revenues being insufficient, or for some other reason unknown.*

Owen Ragsdale's will indicates that on his death the manor house at Rothwell in which he was then leasing from Sir Thomas Tresham of Rushton was to continue be leased for his widow Mary and her two sons, Thomas and Edward Hampden to live in, until the death of Mary. Mary Ragsdale was certainly resident in the manor house at Rothwell when it was sold by Sir Thomas Tresham of Rushton and his son Francis to the feoffees along with tenements adjoining the churchyard for 100 marks in 1592.[7] From a quitclaim of 1526 we can see that the tenement in the leather fair and next to the churchyard had previously been occupied by Richard Wall and then Edward Nyxson. This document is informative as it refers to the manor house, then on the site, as being the Manor Farm of the Duke of Buckingham deceased. [8]

It was probably the intervention of the Tresham's and the cost of this transaction that caused the hospital to be built in Rothwell and not Old and reduced the scheme down from 24 poor men plus a principal to 16 including a principal. It should be noted that although there were 16 chambers associated with the 4 common halls only 12 men along with the nurse and Principal were resident until the mid 1700s, a point that will be discussed later. The change of site from Old to Rothwell did over the long term have at least one benefit, because the hospital was built upon this site and not that at Old, the feoffees were subsequently able to rent out the manor house and demesne at Old, giving the hospital some additional income. However the deal done with Sir Thomas and Francis Tresham, probably largely engineered by their cousin Thomas Tresham of Newton as feoffee, for the site of the manor house at Rothwell was an expense not planned in the scheme of things by Owen Ragsdale.

To put the likely reasons for this deal in context, in 1581 Sir Thomas Tresham was arrested for his Catholic beliefs and from then onwards the Rushton Tresham's were frequently in debt because of recusancy fines and from this we can infer that a deal was engineered with Thomas Tresham of Newton and the other feoffees, most of whom were themselves Catholic recusants, to assist Sir Thomas Tresham of Rushton in paying some of his fines. Despite the recusancy from 1593 Sir Thomas substantially remodelled both his Northamptonshire houses, Rushton and Lyveden and it is probably from sales and such deals as made with the feoffees of Jesus Hospital that this was possible. The deal was complete by the time royal assent was sought for the Letters Patent stature that the hospital was to be built in Rothwell.

The articles and the royal assent show that it was intended that the hospital should provide for twenty-four residents and a warden or principal, however possibly because of the cost of buying the Rothwell site on top of the cost of building, that the scheme was never completed in its entirety. As built the hospital originally had four common halls and four chambers off of each giving a capacity of sixteen residents including the principal and the nurse. However it appears as though two rooms, probably off of the prayer hall were not used as bedchambers and therefore well into the mid 1700's there were only ever twelve residents plus the warden and a nurse.

Transfer of Enfeoffment

The transfer of enfeoffment from the original five feoffees to the new feoffees or governors took place in 1600.[9] Not all of those named in the Letters Patent were named in the transfer. Those to who the estates were transferred included, Edward Griffin, Eusebie Isham, Thomas Mulso of Thingdon (Finedon), Robert Osborn, Thomas Lamden, Edward Bakon, John Pulton and Maurice Tresham of Newton (note: this is Maurice Tresham senior. As we shall see his son, another Maurice was involved in the Hospital in the same century). Initially the surviving feoffees continued as trustees with the new feoffees acting as assistants. Robert Spencer of Althorp is not one of those named in the transfer of feoffment in 1600. However, it is recorded that he became an Assistant, a position he resigned in 1614. Two copies of his resignation letter survive [10] one is dated 1612 and the other is dated and signed for October 1614. The 1612 version is set out Overleaf.

The feoffeees as the first governors appear to have set changed the numbers of governors and assistants. The Letters patent agreed for five governors and ten assistants, but after the transfer of feoffees and the death of the original five feoffees there were always five governors and rarely more than five assistants. The Governors and assistants will be discussed later.

Another change made by the governors about the time of transfer of feoffment was that of the catchment area from which residents could be admitted. As we have seen the Letters Patent afirmed this to be for **poor and infirm men of the**

said town and its neighbourhood, this was subsequently changed to become for, **poor and infirm men of the hundreds of Rothwell, Orlingbury and Corby**, and may have been an appeasement to the governors and assistants in the 1590s most of who were resident in the three hundreds.

Completion of the Hospital

Exactly when the hospital was built and opened is unclear. The undated endorsement of the sale of the hospital site made sometime after 1592 states *"where the hospital is built"* suggesting that once the site had been purchased building work got underway, however there are no surviving documents relating to the building work. If the date stone on the building it to be believed then the shell of the building was completed in 1593. The hospital was certainly open by the time Sir Nathaniel Brent visited in 1635. The quitclaim regarding the Rothwell manor house site by Francis Tresham was not made until 1612.

Funding the Hospital

In the Jesus Hospital collection are a number of records relating to the hospital lands, which relate to the land purchased by Owen Ragsdale. With a couple of exceptions those pre dating Owen Ragsdale's acquisition will not be discussed here. All of Ragesdale's property in the parish of Old, sometimes referred to as Wold, along with property in Rothwell and other villages was by Owen Ragsdale's will endowed for the use of the hospital. That is, the land and property was to be rented out and the resulting income used to provide for the upkeep of the hospital buildings, the employment of staff and food and fuel for the residents.

Owen Ragsdale's largest estate was in the village of Old where he owned the manor. At the time of purchase the manor was already leased to John Lucas of Old, a yeoman farmer.[11] The previous owners Edward Lucas, of London, gentleman and Thomas Lucas of Newington, Buckinghamshire having leased the manor for 60 years at 50 shillings per annum. The lease of 1574 between the Lucas's was for the manorial estate including the Manor House. By 1586 John Lucas was in serious debt and released the mortgage back to John and Edward Lucas for £200.[12] In February 1587 the Edward and Thomas Lucas sold the estate to Hugh Hare esquire, of the Inner Temple, John Cope of London Gent, and William Spencer of Everdon esquire, and it was these gentlemen who sold the estate to Owen Ragsdale on 27th August in that year.[13] Two days after the sale John Lucas assigned the residue of the term of his lease on the manor to Ferdinand Pulton, Thomas Tresham of Newton and George Pulton, two of who were later to become Ragsdale's feoffees and all three Governors of the hospital.[14] The final concord (see glossary) was signed at Michaelmas (29th September) 1587.[15]

The Manor of Old

At the time of its acquisition by Owen Ragsdale the estate in Old included the manor house and four virgate's of land, a windmill, a malt mill and a cottage or tenement plus chief rents amounting to 16s. 6d. John Lucas was the tenant of the windmill and malt mill and John Waman was the tenant of the cottage or tenement. John Waman, described as a labourer, had leased the cottage and some land from Hugh Hare, John Cope and William Spencer on 29 Elizabeth I (1586/87).[16] John's lease gave him full rights over the cottage and land for the lease period, with the exception of Oak, Ash, Elm and any other trees, thus preventing him from cutting down and selling the wood at a profit. The lease, which was for twelve years at 5s. per annum also included a clause requiring him to make all repairs to the cottage and another requiring of him a payment of 8d. per annum for his use of the right of sheep commons. A subsequent deed of recovery and the final concord between Ragsdale, shows that apart from the two mills and John Wamans cottage the estate also included three other cottages, three tofts, a dove house and 20s. of rent in Old and Scaldwell.[17] From a release dated 1st June 1592 we learn that one of the cottages or tenements was known as 'Smetons'.

To ensure its survival it was essential that the hospital kept tight control over its lands and the rental income from those. Regular surveys taken at times when tenants changed and rental agreements and leases, many of which survive give a clear picture of the state of the property endowed to the hospital over time, and from documents of 1592 we can see that of the four yardlands (see Glossary) held by the hospital in Old two yardlands were held by three farmers; John Johnson of Old, husbandman, 1/2 yardland which had formerly belonged with the tenement called 'Smetons', Thomas Warren of Old, Husbandman, held another 1/2 yardland, Henry Petiver of Old, Yeoman, held 1 yardland and one messuage (see Glossary).[18] The other yardland remained with the manor house which had been leased to John Sheppard of Old, by Owen Ragsdale's widow Mary on 19th January 1593 for a period of fifty years. Sheppard had then on 24th January 1593 sub let the house and land to Ann Dalleson of Cransley, in return for Dalleson's being bound for Sheppard to Mary Ragsdale. Mary Ragsdale appears to have acted without reference to the trustees of her husbands will and Oliver Farren had to buy out Ann Dalleson for the sum of £40 and had to agree that she could keep that years crop.

By November 1660 the Old estate was firmly under the control of the Governors of the hospital and in that year they leased the manor house and its land, now known as Spencers Manor, to Richard Tresham for twenty-one years at £30 per annum. Richard Tresham, as part of the lease agreement, was bonded to perform covenants to the hospital trustees. The document informs us that Richard's father William Tresham of Newton had been the previous lessee and that Richard leased the manor house and the lands associated, but not the farm and cottage which were in the occupation of widow Cooper.[19]

A further lease, on the manor house and its demesne lands (see glossary) for 21 years, was agreed between the governors and Richard Tresham on 31st October 1676 at a rent of £30.[20] Richard Tresham did not see out his 21 year lease for on 29th September 1692 he was dead. In that year the governors transferred the lease of the manor house and its land to John Chapman of Old, Richard Tresham's son in law and executor. Although the lease was formally set out in 1692 the accounts show that John Chapman had been in residence since 1689, and that he was paying rent of £7. 10s. 0d. per annum.

As before this lease excluded the cottage and farm formerly in the possession of widow Cooper, now in the possession of John Cooper (In the accounts for c1670 he is referred to as John Coop).[21] John Cooper's lease comprised of the farmhouse with one yardland and a little cottage or tenement formerly known as Lanes Barn, leased for 21 years at £1. 10s. 0d per annum.[22] By 1692 that John Cooper was no longer the tenant and may have been dead as the accounts show *"Received of Thomas Cooper sonn of John Cooper sen of Old".* [23]

From 1689 there is a regular record in the accounts for the rental of a tenement at 10s. per quarter, the location of which is not recorded. The entry follows that of John Chapman's lease of the manor and it is therefore likely that this relates to the hospital's tenement known as Lanes Barn. In 1689 the person renting the tenement is recorded as Erasmus Dexter.

By December 1709 both John Chapman and John Cooper had died. A new lease was made between the Governors and Elizabeth widow of John Chapman (junior) and her son also named John. This new lease included the cottage and Lanes Barn, formerly occupied by John Cooper, a close on the green and one yardland for 21 years at £44 per annum.[24] A dispute over a ley, a piece of pasture, appears to have occurred in 1720 between the hospitals tenants and a neighbour and the hospital Principal, Henry Dormer was sent to measure and view the land.[25]

During this latter John Chapman's lease period we are told that the windmill accidentally burned down and was rebuilt by Chapman. This occurred at sometime after 1692 and the Governors agreed with Chapman to take the new mill in lieu of a fine for the lease, thus the new mill would become the hospitals property at the end of the lease. This new mill along with a ley was subsequently leased to a John Cleaver, of Old, miller, in 1759 for 21 years at 2s. 6d.

By 1767 the fields of the village of Old had been enclosed and Jesus Hospital lands lay in one block together. This is clearly shown on a map of the hospital's land drawn in 1801 (below).[26] An accompanying survey shows that the land at this time comprised of 130 acres, 30 perches of land with a rental income of £211. 11s. 6 3/4d.

From 1794 the hospital's tenant was a Thomas Norton and from the period of his tenure the accounts clearly show how the this income was made up (overleaf).[27] Of the sum of £211. 11s. 6¾d. This was a considerable sum in 1794 and gave the hospital a good income for its needs. Thomas Norton was still the hospital's largest tenant in 1822. After the Napoleonic Wars, prices rose and the state of agricultural income was low. Norton was struggling with repairs to the farms ageing buildings and lower prices when the governors increased his rent. The rent increase was clearly too great and by the end of 1822 he only managed to pay £100 and in the account for 10th August 1823 there is a note stating, *"Mr Norton appearing to owe the sum of £170 to the trustees of this charity it is agreed by him to make him the following abatements bills to be returned him for various repairs amounting to £48. 8s. 3½d."*

In 1826 the state of agriculture locally had improved and a memorandum in the accounts for that year shows that Mr Norton's rent, abaited by £48. 8s.3½d., had increased again. Mr Norton died in 1827/8 and the farm was then let to a Mr John West. West set about rebuilding and repairing the farm, the cost of which was to be met by the governors, and on 30th October 1838 he attended the Governors meeting where he produced his accounts showing that the Governors owed him money, the accounts stating;. *"Mr John West attended & produced his accounts for the repairs of a farm house and premises at Old and other expenses, when there appeared to be a balance due of £452. 17. 7, which the treasurers were ordered to pay".* This payment to Mr West clearly came as a shock to the hospital governors and it prompted them to appoint a land agent, "to take care and superintend the different estates".

John West was subsequently appointed to that role. Up to 1838 the hospital had relied upon the Principal to collect rents and manage their tenants and all other affairs. This assumed the Principal had the necessary skills and was in sufficiently good health to undertake the task. In 1827 the estate at Old was valued prior to being re-let.[28] The valuation notes, *"this farm is in increasingly good state of cultivation and the Trustees should be guarded by such agreement with the incomer that he cannot by bad farming reduce its value".* The valuer recommended the

Plan of Jesus Hospital lands in Old after inclosure. By J. Crutchley 1801
(NRO JHR 170b)

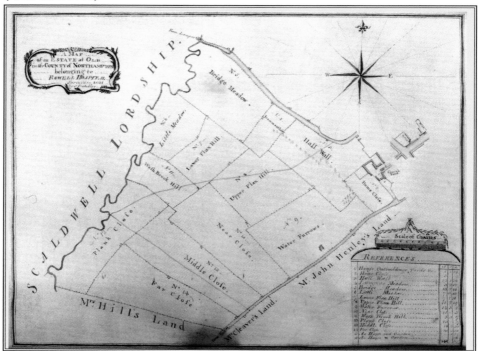

Survey of the hospital estate in Old, 1827

Survey of an Estate at Old in the County of Northampton belonging to the Trustees of Rowell Hospital; in the occupation of Tho[s] Norton	A	R	P	sh	£	s	d
An house with the outbuildings gardens foldyards and stackyards	1	2	19	38	3	1	6
Home Close	3		2	38	5	14	5 1/2
Hall Wall Close	12	1	36	38	23	14	1/2
Lammas Meadow	3	2	12	35	6	5	1 1/2
Bridge Meadow	13	2	16	25	17		
Little Meadow	7	3	16	22	8	3	3/4
Lower Flax Hill	7	1	16	28	10	5	9 1/2
Upper Flax Hill	11	2	19	30	17	8	6 3/4
Water Furrows	14	3	1	30	22	2	8 1/4
Near Close	15		3	30	22	10	6 3/4
Wash Brook Hill	5	3	7	30	8	13	9 3/4
Plank Close	3		7	28	18	5	2 1/2
Middle Close	14	2	30	30	22	0	7 1/2
Far Close	15		30	38	22	17	1 1/2
An house and garden (Jonathan Burgess under tenant)		1	22		3		
An house and garden (Wm Jones under tenant)			26				
Total	**140**		**30**		**211**	**11**	**6¾**

farm be let in two halves and the timber be cut down and sold, being worth about £50. The whole farm being worth £250 exclusive of the timber and land tax.

Jesus Hospital Property in Rothwell

Owen Radesdale gave two endowments of property and tithes in Rothwell. Most of the property was given for the free school, which will be considered later in this chapter. Owen Ragsdale left the income from a moiety (see Glossary) of the vicarial tithes to the hospital along with an orchard detached from the hospital site and at least one copyhold property held of the manor of Rothwell, which like the properties at Old were to be used to provide funds for the hospital. By the early 18th century the Governors were purchasing property and mortgaging the leases. A number of documents survive relating to these properties, which include:

The Five Bells

The Governors acting as mortgage lenders, loaned George Murffin the elder and his wife Anne £500 in 1648 to purchase a property which later became a pub known as the Five Bells. The deeds of the property were held by the Governors and a copy remains in the collection [29] George Murffin the elder and his wife Anne purchased the property from Richard Humfrey, yeoman of Rothwell and from the documentation we are told was a messuage in the common street and that George was a roper. George Murffin was dead by 1681/2 when his wife Anne released the property to her grandson, another George Murffin who continued to pay off the grand parents debt to the Governors. [30.]

In the same year this George Murffin, also described as a roper, married and the marriage settlement agreed by the Governors granted him permission to sell the property if he needed the money and during that year he did just that. The mortgage transferred to John Norman, a yeoman of East Farndon. At the time of transfer to John Norman the property had become an inn called the Five Bells.[31] John Norman was dead by May 1693 when his widow assigned the mortgage to Samuel Ponder of Thorpe Underwood.[32] However it was not until 1704 that Hannah Norman saw any equity from the property. The hospitals documents relating to the property continue with various changes of occupier until 1738, after which the original mortgage had been paid off.

Sun Inn

Amongst the properties mortgaged in the early 18th century was one which was known as the Sun Inn.

Other Property

Another property in Rothwell on which the Governors held a mortgage was that of half of a yardland of agricultural land. According to Henry Dormers Accounts this was in the occupation of Thomas Hayes on 30th April 1707.[33] The mortgage was originally agreed between the Trustees and a widow, Mrs Reynolds of Rothwell. Dormers account shows that she paid 51 shillings interest on the loan of £35. Thomas Hays took up the mortgage and the loan money on repayment was put *"put to interest for the use of Jesus Hospital"*. An abstract of the title deeds of these properties, one of which was the Sun Inn was drawn up in the mid 18th century which is set out overleaf.[34]

On 5th February 1740, a cottage was purchased by the Governors from a Mr York, in 1812 this was, according to the Enclosure Claims, in the occupation of Mr Thomas Cook. [35]

Enclosure by Act of Parliament

In 1812 an Act of Parliament was passed to enclose the open fields of

Rothwell which up to that time had continued to be farmed in the same manner as in the medieval period. All those owning land were required to deliver their claims to the Enclosure Commissioners, who posted notices to that effect on the door of the parish church and in the local newspapers. For reasons unknown, the governors failed to make such a claim and as a result Thomas Marshall, clerk to the Enclosure Commissioners had to write to A.E. Young as Treasurer to the Governors, informing him of a meeting to be held to receive claims to the Commissioners by those who had previously neglected to claim.[36] The Governors subsequently, 15th July 1812, appointed a Mr Hodgson, solicitor, to act on their behalf at the claims meeting and in the enclosure process. The governors do not appear to have met to agree this appointment. Instead Sir John Palmer as the chair of the governors approved the appointment in writing to A. E. Young.[37] Ususally the governors would have employed the services of Mr Marshall, solicitor, for such business, but he was already acting as clerk to the Enclosure Commissioners and was also engaged and acting on behalf of Mrs Medlicot Cockayne in respect of the enclosure.

The costs of enclosure were defrayed by a rate payable by the land owners of the town. The commissioners wrote to the Governors regarding their share of this rate which was £4. 15s. 10d., which the governors were asked to pay by Monday the 19th April 1813. The governors appear to have been uninterested in the enclosure process, and A.E. Young noted his surprise on the letter from the Enclosure commissioners, writing, *"this is for a cottage right?"* At the bottom of the same letter to the governors Thomas Marshall, the clerk to the commissioners wrote: *"N.B. The Governors allotment in lieu of Wool, Lamb and Moduses is set out and fenced off at the expense of the proprietors"*, indicating that the cost of defraying the act was not the only cost they had to bear. From the enclosure the hospital gained a block of land in the north east of the parish which subsequently became known as Hospital Farm.

Hospital Farm Rothwell

After enclosure the hospitals land, which had previously been in small strips scattered throughout the fields of Rothwell was in one block of 42 acres 2 roods 13 perches to the north east of the town close to Abbey Bridge.[38] At that time there was no farmhouse or farm buildings on the land. Records relating to this farm commence in April 1813 when it is recommended that a Mr John Stiles be given the tenancy of the property.[39] John Stiles, who was tenant of the cottage owned by the hospital in the town of Rothwell, had contacted the treasurer, A.E. Young who had then written to Mr John Palmer requesting that he be considered as tenant for the farm. Mr Palmer's son wrote to A. E. Young regarding his father's approval on the 18th April 1813. We learn from a note at the bottom of an account relating to the land in his possession:

John Stiles entered upon the above land in Rothwell at Lady Day
1813 and also upon the house, he paid one year rent for the house,

Abstract of Title Deeds of the Hospital c1724

21 Jan^{ry} 1723	*By Ind^{re} of mortgage between John Hewitt of the one part & James Underhill of the other p^t It is [agreed?] that the said John Hewitt in lous of £40 Did Grant unto the sd James Underhill his heirs [adsignors?] & assigns All that cottage or tenement situate in Rothwele called the Sun and all that one other cottage or tenement in Rothwell afors^d adjoining to the other with their appurts To hold to the said James Underhill his heirs asigners & assignes from the date thereof for the turn of 500 years subject to provises therein named.*
22 Feb 1724	*John Hewitt of Draughton Husbandman By his will did devise all those two houses at Rowell unto his wife Lucy & to his son Samuel Hewitt & made them executors*
19 & 20 March 1727	*By indent of lease & release between Lucy Hewitt widow heir exor & devisee of John Hewitt dec^d & Saml Hewitt one of the son of the said John Hewitt by the s^d Lucy and another exor & devisee & Thos Hewitt son & heir of the said John Hewitt of the one p^t & Joseph Braine of the other p^t. It is so agreed that the sd Lucy, Samuel & Thomas Hewitt for the cons L38 to be paid as therein mentioned Did Grant unto the s^d Joseph Braines, his heirs & assignes To the only proper life & belieef of the said Joseph Braines, his heirs & assignes.*
21 March 1727	*By indent of asignm & quadrn parties Between James Underhill of the first part, Lucy Howlett, Samuel Howlett & Thomas Howlett of the 2^d p^t & Joseph Braines of the 3 part & Thomas Munns of the 4 part Releasing the mortgage to the S^d James Underhill It is so Accepted that the said James Underhill for & in cons of the sum of 42: 6: 8 Did by the residue of his term of 500 years To hold in Trust for the sd Joseph Braine his heirs and asignes to attend the inheritances of the said premises.*
1 Dec^{br} 1736	*By Indent of Mortgage between Joseph Braine one the one p^t & Ann Dyson on the other pt. It is so agreed that the said Joseph Braine for & in cons of 60 to him paid by the s^d Ann Dyson Did Grant unto the s^d Ann Dyson her heir adinors and asignes The said two cottages or tenements with appurts To Hold to the the s^d Ann Dyson her heir adinors and asignes from this date for the term of 500 years subject to the provision or condition there in mentioned wills or indorsements back. X signed by the said Joseph Braine whereby he acknowledges to have received of the said Ann Dyson the sum of 20l and agrees that the said promises within mentioned should stand as a security for the payment of the sd sum of twenty pounds with interest a week as for the Sum of 60l within mentioned.*
07 February 1742	*By Indte of asignm Between Ann Dyson of the one pt Sir Thomas Palmer, Sir John Dolben Bart, John Robinson Bart: Allicocke & Earnly Washbourn Esq the then Governors of Jesus Hospital in Rowell of the other part / reciteing the said mortgage & Indorsement / it is so agreed that the s^d Ann Dyson in cost of the sum of 100l to her paid by the said Governors Did Assign unto the said Governors All those two cottages or tenements & premises and all the right titles & in lease therein to hold to the said Governors there heirs, exors, assignes adinors, sucessors or asigne in as ample a manner as the sd Ann Dyson might or could by corting of the s^d recites indenture or indorsem^t.*

due Lady Day 1814 being £5 and 1/- per year for the land due at Mich 1813 being £48.. 7.. 6 in the year 1814 as will appear in the accounts of the principal Samuel Hafford.[40]

The following year, 1815 it was clear that Mr Stiles was struggling and the middle of that year he was bankrupt. This appears to have been due to a combination of rents and land tax.[41]

The plight of Mr Stiles is best described in a letter to the Governors by the then Principal, Samuel Hafford, who on 19th January 1815 wrote *"This morning I went to Mr Stiles about the rent but he has no money.[42] He told me that he thought about giving an assignment and selling and he hoped he should have enough for everyone. I cannot tell how circumstances are, but there is often people there for money and yesterday there was a distress taken for the levies and taxes. He was at Wellingborough yesterday and the horse he rode on was given up as soon as he came home to a person for a debt, so that he has not a horse left at this time and no live stock neither Cow, Hog or Sheep he has about 8 ton of Clover Hay and some Peas unthrashed in a barn, and a little quantity of Barley that is thrashed and I suppose about 12 or 14 acres of wheat"*.

Another letter, dated 17th January 1815, to the Governors from Samuel Hafford informed them that Mr Stiles was to be *"distressed"* once more as he had failed to pay his poor rate.[43] A Mr Roe was engaged by the hospital solicitors to recover as much of the debt as possible. Mr Roe recovered some of the debt and the solicitors had a notice to quit drawn up. This notice to quit was delivered to Mr Stiles 22nd March 1815 a notice to quit was served on Mr Stiles and his under tenant, Mr Manton and his wife, who were also resident on the farm. At the time of the serving of the notice Mr Stiles owed £201 to the governors.

By October 1815 Mr Stiles had left. The new tenant was Samuel Hafford who was that time the Principal of the Hospital. A letter to the Governors from Mr Hafford to thank them and confirm his acceptance of their terms. The land at that time being valued at 33s. per acre. The farmhouse at this time was the cottage in the town that Mr Stiles and his tenant had occupied. Mr Hafford's acceptance letter to the governors also states *"The house late in the occupation of Mr J Stiles does take in wet very much for want of thatching and the inside is very much broke by taking down furniture &c - I hope you will allow for the necessary repairs that are now wanting then shall expect to keep them so in future"*.[44]

Samuel Hafford ran the farm as tenant whilst also continuing as Principal of the hospital until his death in 1828. He was not resident in the farm house in the town which was occupied by his son Robert. This is unsurprising for as we shall see later, the hospital statutes required the principal to be resident at the hospital. When Samuel died, his son Robert Hafford who was already running the farm applied and was accepted to take on the tenancy of the farm. This was confirmed in the notes of the Governors meeting of 30th October 1828.[45] As was usual, the farm was surveyed at the point of transfer of tenancy (overleaf).

John Stiles Account 1815

	£	s	d		£	s	d
D^{rs} _ Messrs Roe and West as assignees of John Stilles in account with the Governnors of Jesus Hospital at Rowell							
To two years rent of land in Rowell due at Michaelmas 1815	193	10		*By one years property tax from Lady Day 1813 to Lady Day 1814*	7	4	2
To One year & an half rent of house in Rowell due at same time	7	10	0	*By - Do from Lady Day 1814 to Lady Day 1815*	10	8	0
To costs of the distress for the above rents	4	0	0	*By half years Do from Lady Day to Michaelmas 1815*	5	4	0
Balance due to the Asignees and paid by Mr Hodson to W. Roe on 10th June 1818	5	17	5	*By Two years and an half's Land Tax from Lady Day 1813 to Michaelmas 1815*	8	3	1
£	210	17	5	£	216	17	5

Tithes of Rothwell

From about the 9th or 10th century tithes were applied as a direct tax on farming across the country. Originally set up to contribute to the established church they were generally hated by the poor and by the 17th century, those who dissented

Survey of the Hospital Farm, Rothwell 1828

		a	r	p	
First Close	*arable*	4	2		*There are no premises belonging to this land & it is now occupied with other land which is by no means a fair way for either properties.*
Second Do	*Do*	4	2		
Third Do	*Do*	8	2		
Fourth Do	*Do*	18	2		*The farms appear fairly managed*
Meadow Close	*Do*	7	2	24	*and is worth annually 70£.*
House, bakehouse, barn				16	*These premises are occupied by*
Yard & premises					*Robert Hafford and are in tolerable repair. They are worth Annually 5£*

John West

from the established church. Tithes were a tax on gross output and acted as a direct disincentive to efficient farming, for the greater the output the more given to the church. Customarily tithes were one-tenth of the produce of the land and fell into three categories: Predial tithes, payable on the fruits of the earth such as hay, wood, corn, fruit and other crops; Agistment tithes, payable on lambs, wool, calves, milk, eggs and honey; and Personal tithes payable on gains of a man's labour, principally the profits of milling and fishing.

In keeping with most parishes the vicarial tithes of Rothwell and Orton comprised by the early 18th century of a commuted fee for every house, every cow and calf, every seventh pig, every seventh foal, the apple harvest, eggs, hens and cocks. Owen Ragsdale owned and endowed half the tithe of lambs, the whole tithe of wool and half of the fee for the manorial sheep walk to the hospital. Amongst his purchases from the Watson's of Rockingham Castle were these tithes and those of Orton and Thorpe Underwood. The tithes had originally belonged to Cirencester Abbey prior to its dissolution, and as was often the case a wealthy individual such as Sir Edward Watson could buy both the lands and the tithes of former monasteries. In such sales there was frequently an element of speculation, the purchaser selling on for a profit. These tithes comprised the largest part of Owen Ragsdale's benefaction in Rothwell, and are described in detail in the enclosure claim book of 1st August 1812 (below).[46]

Extract from the Enclosure Claims Book August 1812

> *The governors or Trustees of a certain hospital in Rothwell otherwise Rowell aforesaid, called Jesus Hospital , are entitled to a certain ancient yearly modus of five pounds six shillings and eight pence, in lieu of the tithe of wool; and one moiety or equal half part of the tithe of lamb, in, over, and upon a certain antient several sheep walk, in upon and over certain parts of the common fields and other commonable lands in Rothwell otherwise Rowell aforesaid, belonging to the devisees in trust in the will of George Hill, Esquire, deceased; Also, an ancient yearly modus of ten shillings, for the tithe lamb for lambs kept on the hall farm, now vested in the said devisees in trust as aforesaid, when depastured in the fields of Rothwell otherwise Rowell aforesaid. The said Governors or Trustees are entitled to the entirety in kind of the tithe of wool, and one moiety or equal half part of the tithe in kind of lamb, in, over, and upon the residue of the lands and grounds in the said parish. The said Governors or Trustees are also entitled to a cottage common in Rothwell otherwise Rowell aforesaid, belonging to a house in the tenure or occupation of Thomas Cook. The said Governors or Trustees also claim the right of a drift road, or way through the homestead of the Honourable Barbara Cockayne Medlycott, in the tenure of Thomas Perkins, to the orchard belonging to the said hospital.*

As noted previously the payment of Tithes was unpopular and by November 1692 the hospital was experiencing difficulty in collecting the dues. The Lord of the Manor at that time was a Mr Hill and the Governors acted by issuing an order authorising the Principal, Mr. Goode, to sue Mr. Hill and his tenants who fail to pay their tithes. Mr Hill was a lawyer and rather than contesting the case it appears the threat of legal action was enough for him to deal with his tenants. Records relating to tithes of sheep and tithes of wool exist from 1765 to 1783. The following example is found in the accounts for 1765.

As well as having a share of the income from the tithes the Hospital would also have a share of the cost of repairs to the chancel of the parish church, along with the impropriate rector. The hospital clearly paid its share of repairs but the same could not be said of the impropriate rector in the early 17th century. Because of this a letter was drafted to complain that the church was in need of repair and that the parish was not carrying out the necessary repairs but was still charging the Hospital.[47] The surviving undated letter is clearly a draft and it is uncertain if it was ever sent. What is clear is that the chancel deteriorated for at least another century and was not fully restored until the mid 1800's.

Property in Orton

Owen Ragsdale purchased the impropriate rectory and the tithe barn in Orton and Thorpe Underwood from Edward Watson of Rockingham Castle in November 1585. This included all the tithes of corn and wool of both Orton and Thorpe Underwood, the tithes of lambs of both hamlets and the tithes of the mills. Most of this property had previously been in the possession of Cirencester Abbey. The hospital Governors purchased one acre of land in Church Field from Thomas Munn in January 1659/60. Then on 1st May 1667 a John Ellis of Orton and his wife, Elizabeth the widow of Simon Dix of Ratchliffe, Middlesex, sold the hospital one quarter of a yard land in Orton.[48]

In 1600 the rectory was let to John Baud. On 9th September in that year he gave power of attorney to his son Ferdinando to hold the rectory of the hospital for the remainder of the lease.[49] According to the accounts in the 1670s the property in Orton was being rented by a John Ellis of that hamlet at £2. 1s. 4d per annum.[50] It is likely that the remainder, including the tithes were being rented to Mr Gascoigne who was paying a quarterly rent of £16 for some unspecified land. By 1689 William Viall's of Rothwell was occupying some land owned by the hospital for sixteen shillings per year. The account for the quarter ending on Lady Day 1688 states this comprised of "*2 lands a little grass & a woody*" [copse?] in Orton.[51] His descendant Richard Viall's continued to rent this land in the early 1700s.[52] By 1709 the rent paid by the Viall's had increased from 16s. per year to £1 per year.

Mr Gascoigne fell into serious arrears of rent and from December 1689 the hospital's Orton land and the income from the great tithes and the tithe of lambs there was leased to Thomas Ponder for £16. 10s. 0d per quarter. He appears to have run the farm with his daughter who is referred to, but not named, in the Midsummer quarter accounts for 1691. A memorandum in the accounts for 1694 shows that in taking on the Orton estate Thomas Ponder was expected to pay his own rent and the arrears of his predecessor Gascoigne.

By 1692, Thomas Ponder was in arrears. He was to pay the tithes of Orton and then collect the amounts due from the other persons due to pay them and it was as a result of non payment he was in arrears. This non payment caused a legal dispute between Thomas Ponder and Edward Hill, esq., Nathan Hill, gent., William. Stephens, Thomas Shortland, Christopher Mold, all of Rothwell and Thomas Palmer of Orton, over their failure to pay their tithes. The case was taken to the Court of Chancery which ordered an investigation. The court arbitrator interrogated witnesses, the notes of which survive.[53] This arbitrator was Francis Lane esquire of Glendon. He reported back to the Court of Chancery in 1694 which ruled in Thomas Ponders favour, awarding him the 3 years tithes which had been witheld. However, despite the chancery ruling disputes regarding the Orton tithes continued into the mid 1700s.

In 1741 a fresh dispute arose, this time it was caused by the lord of the Manor of Orton, Thomas Peach, who seized the hospitals land and commenced enclosing the parish of Orton. After a year of dispute he finally agreed to pay the hospital £100 per annum in lieu of tithes. This was paid for one year only. At the same time he also agreed to seek an act of parliament for the enclosure of Orton in which he would safeguard the hospital's interests. However, by 1743 no act had been sought and payments in lieu of tithes had ceased. As a result in 1746 the Governors took the case to the Court of Chancery. The Court required Peach and his tenants to appear before them, which they failed to do. As a result the court ordered Thomas Peach to write in response to questions from the Chancery. [54]

Once again the court found in favour of the hospital and on 24th June 1746 the Court of Chancery ordered Thomas Peach to pay the arrears of tithe money's owed to the hospital. Peach responded by saying that he had ordered his tenants to pay the arrears. In the meantime the Governors of Jesus Hospital continued to try and recover their now enclosed lands seized by Peach. Between 1747 and 1755 the case rumbled on in court, then on 26th March 1755 Peach paid the arrears owing to the Hospital[55] and then on 15th October 1755 both parties were summoned to attend a commission, established by the Chancery, for setting out the hospital lands in Orton. Peach and his tenants failed to work with the commissioners, and the situation was inflamed when on 11th May 1758 Peach sent a notice to Daniel Daulby, the hospital's tenants to restore the tithes received and demand no more.

As a result Peach and his tenants were subsequently bonded to attend the Chancery Court to answer a charge of contempt.[56] The letter notice from Thomas Peach was used in evidence in the inquiry and on the back of the paper is a note from the Attorney General stating this to be the case.

The commission completed its work and in 1765 articles and a draft bill were drawn up between the two parties [57] and parliament petitioned as the outcome required a change to the letters patent in respect of the Orton estate.[58] The petition dated 18th February 1765 set out the agreement between both parties. The cost of the enquiry and chancery decision was over £364. The day-by-day account included attendance fee's and meals (including wine and punch) for both the solicitor and his clerk, candles and fuel for the fire and witness attendance fees.

In about 1765 a draft bill was drawn up and subsequently agreed,[59] so that by 1770 the affair appears to have been settled except for the costs and in that year the Governors wrote to Mr J. P. Hungerford of Dingley who had succeeded Thomas Peach as lord of the manor of Orton. The governor's letter does not survive but the reply from Mr Peach Hungerford does. His response to what ever was suggested by the Governors was that he would consult Mr George Hill, before responding either way. George Hill was a sergeant at law and lord of the manor of Rothwell. In understanding what had gone before Mr Robinson (Governor & Treasurer) prepared a statement for his Governor colleagues (below).

Statement of case prepared for the governors

> *Mr Robinson imagine the state of Orton inclosure to be thus. Mr Peach bought the estate of Orton from Mr Geo: Hill, the Great Tythes of which estate & about 3 acres of land, Tythe Barn & house with a right of common over the whole estate belong to the Govenors of Rowell Hospital the will of Mr Ragsdale for the support of a charity at Rowell which Orton is a hamlet. After Mr Peach had purchased the estate about 30 or more years since he had a mind to enclosed the estate & applyd to the then Govenors & offered an agreement to be signed by them & him for £80 a year which was accepted but not signed; as this agreement was in Mr Peaches writing the then Govenors thought it binding (or had forgot it had not been signed). In the meantime Mr Peach enclosed on his own authority, & after it refused to confirm agreement on which the Govenors applyd to Chauncery for redress, but could gain none, as no agreement appeared to the courts satisfaction & the Govenors was left with cost of suit, after this various tryals ensued in some of wich the Govenors gained suit and costs, in others Mr Peach. And to shew the right of the Govenors has cutt gaps in the hedges which Mr Peach suffered you to do unmolested.*
>
> *For some years past there has been a stop to all law suits & agreement have been enter upon but not brought to bear. The tenent of the Govenors has long lost the Tythes & rights to D Daulby of Rowell for £5 a yr, & he has constantly taken the Tythe &c. in kind & enjoyed the commons.*
>
> *Now which suit are allowed to Mr Peaches heirs or with the[e] Govenors Mr Robinson does not know, nor can he specify which suits has been commenced, or which was the issue of which it did. But woud recommend it to the Govenors to take the £105 a year for all your rights in Orton; I have the same confirmed by an Act of Parliament. Mr Hungerford demands large cost, therfore should be glad to know what they are, yet they may be amicably settled & yet it must be so paid, after deducting it where allowed.*
>
> *Mr Oliver, Mr Palmer, Mr Hern has been Solicitors in these suits Mr Hill counsell, these therefore can give better lights into it. In: whether Mr Peach or Tenants has ever been paid rent for the 3 acres of land.*

A meeting between Mr J. P. Hungerford and two of the Govenors, Mr Robinson and Mr Rainsford then took place in October 1722. As a result of the meeting it was agreed between the parties that the dispute should be settled amicably. All costs on either side would be discharged. Mr Hungerford would pay the trustees one hundred guineas per annum and would give one half of the cost of obtaining the Act of Parliament to enclose the parish of Orton. Mr Hungerford followed up this agreement in writing and instructed his solicitor likewise.

From this it appears that although a petition, draft bill and agreement was drawn up not everything was concluded satisfactorily. A footnote in a letter of July 1786 says this was because the rent to Jesus Hospital was supposed to be £80 per annum, not £100 and the Mr Hungerford had realised that the cost of completing the Act of Parliament was likely to cost around £600. George Hill subsequently met with the Governors and wrote to J. P. Hungerford on the 26th October 1773, proposing a solution in which the Trustees made a payment of £50 to Mr Hungerford, on top of their agreeing to pay half of the cost of the act, which at this time had not been completed. Initially Mr Hungerford declined the offer but then reconsidered and accepted, probably fearing increasing fees.

Mr Robinson received Mr Hungerford's letter accepting the offer of £50 to resolve the dispute on the 4th July 1786 and immediately wrote to his fellow governors requesting that if they agree the treasurer should pay Mr Hungerford the money. He also hoped that Mr Hungerford and they could now put the matter behind them. Not all of the Governors agreed with the descision, Mr Dolben of Finedon Hall writing to Mr Robinson to express his concern that an agreement was being made which did not take account of the current value of the tithes. The matter became a regular topic at the govenors meetings and it took almost a year before they all agreed with the proposal. With all parties in agreement the act of Parliament was pursued and concluded by 26th July 1787 when the Governors held a special meeting as set out in a letter, a copy of which was sent to Mr Hungerford.

The final cost of the Act of Parliament to confirm the enclosure that had already taken place and alter the Letters Patent of Queen Elizabeth I cost £364. 12s. 0d., some of which had already been paid, the remainder being split between the hospital and Mr Hungerford, each paying £102. 6s. 0d. The note of the meeting and the authorisation to Mr Robinson, Treasurer to pay the Hospital's half of the amount is recorded in the accounts.[60.] Mr Hungerford's reply has not survived, however he must have accepted as three receipts survive for the Governors half of the amounts due to Mr White, Committee Clerk, (two receipts) and Mr Wartnaby,the Attorney at Law, and thereafter the payments in lieu of tithes are paid regularly without further issue. Tthe Charity Commissioners report of 1831 notes the income as £105 per year as set out by the Act of Parliament.[61]

The Governors Petition to Parliament February 1765

To the Right Honourable the Lords spiritual and temporal in Parliament assembled.

The humble Petition of Sir, Thomas Palmer Baronet, Sir Edmund Isham Baronet, Sir William Dolben Baronet, John Robinson and Charles Allicocke Esquires, The Governors and Trustees of Jesus Hospital in Rowell, in the county Of Northampton, and of Thomas Peach Esquire, Lord of the Manor of Orton in the same county,

Sheweth,

That the said Governors and Trustees are seized in right of the said Hospital of and in several pieces of arable and pasture ground lying dispursed in the lordship of Orton aforesaid with Right of Common in and throughout the greatest part of the said lordship and of and in the tithes of corn, grain and wool, and half the tithe of Lambs, and of and in the Tithe of Hay or a modus in lieu of Tithe Hay in and throughout the said lordship.

That the said Thomas Peach is seized of and in the manor or lordship of Orton aforesaid, and of and in all the messuages, lands, tenements and hereditaments lying within the said manor or lordship, except the said estate belonging to the said Hospital, and one peice of land about three acres lately belonging to Simon Brett deceased.

That several suites and differences have arises and are now depending between the Governors and Trustees of the said hospital and the said Thomas Peach, in relation to the said Tithes and Estate at Orton belonging to the said Hospital; for putting an end to the same, they are desirous, that the said Tithes and Estates, and all other Hereditaments belonging to the said Hospital at Orton aforesaid, shall be vested in the said Thomas Peach and his heirs, freed and absolutely discharged of and from the uses and Trusts to which the same are now liable; and that in lieu thereof one clear yearly Rent Charge should be charged forever upon the said Tithes and Estate of the said Hospital, and upon all the lands and Hereditaments of the said Thomas Peach at Orton aforesaid; which rent shall be paid and payable to the said Governors and Trustees of the said Hospital in lieu of the said Tithes and Estate of the said Hospital, (and shall be subject to the same trusts, uses and charitable purposes to which the said Tithes and Estate of the said Hospital are now liable) by two equal half yearly payments on the 25th day of March and the 29th day of September in every year; and the regular payment of the same secured by such Powers of Distress and Entry as are usually provided for securing the due payment of annual sums charged on lands.

But as by Reason of the several trusts and uses to which the Tithes and Estate of the said Hospital stand limited the same cannot be carried carried into Execution or otherwise than by the aid of Parliament,

Your Petitioners therefore humbly pray your Lordships,

That leave may be given to bring in a bill for vesting the said Tithes and Estates n Orton oforesaid belonging to the said Hospital in the said Thomas Peach and his heirs, discharged from the aforesaid Trusts, and for charging the same together with other lands and hereditaments of the said Thomas Peach in Orton aforesaid, with an annuity Rent

Charge, in the same manner as to your Lordships inquirers great wisdom shall seem meet.

Thomas Peach

Thomas Palmer

E Isham

Property and Tithes in Thorpe Underwood

On 31st January 1844 the Reverend William Smyth of South Elkington, Lincolnshire conveyed to the Governors of the hospital the manor of Thorpe Underwood with its lands in Thorpe Underwood, Harrington and Rothwell, and the right to appoint a vicar every third turn, on condition that it was held in trust for the hospital. [62]

By March 1893 the hospital held a farm in Thorpe Underwood which was then tenanted to Mrs Hall.[63] The land on which the farm stood had beneath the ground a seam of iron stone and in 1913 the Stanton Ironworks Company approached the Governors to lease the land a quarry the iron. The lease was agreed by November 1914 and signed off with Charity Commission approval on 29th September.[64] From the lease it appears the hospital received a surface rent of £5 per acre per year, a minimum mine rent of £75 per annum along with a royalty of $4^{1}/_{2}$d per ton of Ironstone excavated. During the 21 year term of the lease the Stanton Ironworks Company agreed to pay all taxes including land tax due on the Hospital Farm and

Received for a years Tythes of Rothwell & Thorpe Underwood ending at Michaelmas 1765

	£	s	d		£	s	d
Rec[d] for Thorpe Underwood modus	1	0	0	Charges on the said years Tythe for taking a tale of the sheep & lambs	0	3	0
Recd for a parsel of sheep under seven	0	1	10.5				
For 50 sheep of Mr Tongue at a half penny each	0	2	1	Pd for taking the wool	0	3	0
Recd as Tods & a half of wool at £17. 6	24	17	9	Pd for winding the wool	0	3	0
Recd of Jno Bull for two fleeces	0	6	0	Expenses selling, weighing and taking	0	3	0
Recd of George Hill Esq for the Sheep walk & two midle Lays	5	6	8	Money for the wool	0	3	0
				Pd a Constables levy	0	2	9
Recd of Mr Garard Tongue for the whole Flock	0	10	0	Pd a Levey to the poor at 3s 6d each	1	11	6
£	32	4	4.5	£	2	5	0

to save the top soil and restore the land on completion. A further lease for 40 years was agreed in 1926.

The tithes of Thorpe Underwood were leased out to three persons during the 19th century. The rent from which amounted to £1. In 1817 Mrs Langham, Christopher Smith and Mr Higginson each held a third share of the tithes from the hospital. Others, presumably their tenants each paid the Hospital 6s. 8d. for the one-third share.

Other Property

Welford

Within the Jesus Hospital collection are four 17th century documents regarding a ¼ yard land and a cottage in Welford which had previously been the property of the knights of St John of Jerusalem.[65] A further document, an abstract contained in a bundle of 18th century vouchers states that on 2nd October 1668 Robert Morden of Welford, Elizabeth Orpwood and John Orpwood, and John Gilbert a "little" of their cottage and quarter yard land in Welford.[66] The mortgage was for £60. Clearly this was a case of the Governors lending money via mortgages. No mention is made of the property or mortgage after 1668. Within the same abstract is reference to an earlier mortgage. On 13th January 3 James I (1605/6) William Crowe did bargain and sell part of a close in Welford, to John Dunkley. No mention is made of the value.

Little Bowden

Similarly three 17th century documents exist regarding 2 messuage's, 2 gardens, 3 acres land, 1 acre meadow and 4 acres pasture in Little Bowden.[67] The abstract referred to above (JHR80) says that on 25th February 1655 John and Ann Day agreed a 'Bargain and Sale' with John Coles of a cottage in Little Bowden, probably one of the two messuage's referred to above. Money was still being received by the Governors from a Joseph Hall of 'Bowden Parva' in 1727 although this is described as rent money rather than interest.

Great Bowden

One document of 1711 relating to: 1 acre in Great Bowden, being ½ Jenkinsons Close, and the Windmill in South Field.[68]

Bowley

One document of 1697 relates to 2 messuage's, 1 dovehouse, 2 gardens, 1 orchard, 140 acres arable, 40 acres pasture, 12 acres meadow in Bowley, part of Bodenham, Herefordshire.[69] This is noted in the abstract as another mortgage, where it is stated that on 22nd July 1697 William Jenkins conveyed to Matthew Jenkins two messuage's and 192 acres of land in Bowley, in the parish of Bodenham. The mortgage was for £200.[70]

Kettering

Within the collection is one document relating to a moiety of a cottage in Bakehouse Hill, Kettering.[71] This is a bond for Samuel Meadows of Kettering, a butcher, to Anne Brown of Rothwell, widow. Samuel Meadows was to pay Anne Brown £2.15s.0d. per year during her life for the reversion of a moiety of a cottage and appurtenances in Bakehouse Hill, Kettering, of which Samuel Meadows and Anne Brown were the tenants in common.

Free School property

Owen Ragsdale's will states: *"I give all my cottages in Rothwell to certaine feoffees videlic. Sr Thomas Tresham [&] Sr John Spencer knights, George Pulton Esqr. and their heirs to the use of the schole and scolmaster in Rowell…….. I give twenty pounds to the repair of the said scole"*. This was the bulk of his estate in the town and as his will clearly shows it was to provide for the free school which he had re-founded there.

By a decree of the Commissioners of the Commission of Charitable uses in the 36th year of King Charles II (1684/5) it was ordered and decreed that a chapel in Rothwell known as St Mary's chapel be used as a free school, and the yearly rent of £3. 4s. 11d., with which queen Elizabeth I had endowed annually should be used for the use of the school along with the rents and profits from property in the town of Rothwell and Geddington which Owen Ragsdale had endowed. The properties held under endowments mentioned in the decree, comprised of a dwelling house, including a school room, with a small garden adjoining which was the residence of the schoolmaster. This was the original chapel of St Mary into which an upper floor had been inserted to make both a dwelling and school room, four cottages let at £10 per year; a small garden on which a blacksmith's shop had been built, the income from which was £3 per year; an allotment of 1 acre. 2 roods. 11 perches at Rothwell let for £5 per year and an allotment of 2 acres, with a piece of garden ground, formerly the site of a cottage in Geddington let for £8 per year.

Two of the Rothwell premises referred to stood on the main street, on either side of the free school. One by 1690 was leased to Richard Dixon of Rothwell, a fuller. A draft lease survives which unusually states that Richard could not sub-let the property. He was also responsible for all repairs. By the 1830s there was no regular appointment of Trustees to the school, the master receiving the income directly and maintaining the premises, however new schoolmasters were appointed by the Governors of Jesus Hospital.[72] The land occupied by the two cottages remained in the possession of the governors in 1812/3 when parliamentary enclosure took place.[73] The cottages were in poor condition by this time, one, a "house, shop, stable and premises" is recorded as have part of its fabric, "decayed and fallen down". This particular property was in the occupation of John Johnson (previously occupied by Peter Eaton). The other cottage was at the time occupied by Thomas Bull. The cottages had rights of common associated with them and as a result the governors were allotted a small amount of land for each.

The Free grammar School, Rothwell.

Notes

[1]   NRO JHR 1 & 2 - Feoffment, 10th November, 33 Eliz I (1591).
[2]   ibid. JHR 3 - Articles indented to be annexed 1591/2
[3]   38 Elizabeth I, c.5.
[4]   Neil, S.R and Leighton, C. eds. (2007) Calendar of Patent Rolls 38 Elizabeth I (1595-1596). C66/1443-1457. List and Index Society. Vol 317. p.127.
[5]   NRO JHR 5 – 1837 copy of Letters Patent 38 Elizabeth I
[6]   Charity Commission (1831) Reports of the Commissioners. Vol 3. p.186
[7]   NRO JHR 93 - sale of a tenement and croft adjoining the churchyard in Rothwell. 1592
[8]   NRO JHR 100 - quitclaim by Richard Wall of a messuage in the Leather Fair.
[9]   NRO JHR 6 - Feoffment enrolled (transfer to new trustees) 1600.
[10]   NRO JHR 20 - Admissions and resignations of assistants 1612-1749.
[11]   NRO JHR 132 - Mortgage of John Lucas of Old 1586.
[12]   NRO JHR 133 - Release of mortgage 1587.
[13]   NRO JHR 135 - Sale of Manor of Old to Owen Ragsdale.
[14]   NRO JHR 137 - Deed 1587.
[15]   NRO JHR 139 - Final Concord 1587.
[16]   NRO JHR 134 - Lease 1586-87
[17]   NRO JHR 138 - Deed to suffer a recovery 1587.
[18]   NRO JHR 142, 143, 144 - releases relating to properties in Old.
[19]   NRO JHR 146 - Lease of Spencer's Manor in Old to Richard Tresham.

20 NRO JHR 147 - Counter pert of lease with terrier.
21 NRO JHR 29 - Account Book covering the period 1671 - 1748.
22 NRO JHR 164 - Lease, Governors to John Cooper, senior, husbandman.
23 NRO JHR 29
24 NRO JHR 160b - Terrier, lands occupied by James and Elizabeth Cooper.
25 NRO JHR 30 - Account Book covering the period 1702 - 1763.
26 NRO JHR 170b - Map of Hospital Lands in Old
27 NRO JHR 32 - Account Book covering the period 1780 - 1833.
28 NRO JHR 175 - Valuation.
29 NRO JHR 101 - Sale of a property in Rothwell to George Murffin of Rothwell, Roper.
30 NRO JHR 102 - Release - widow of George Murffin to her grandson George a Roper.
31 NRO JHR 103 a & b - Marriage settlement.
32 NRO JHR 106 - Assignment of Mortgage, Hanna Norman of East Farndon to Thomas Ponder.
33 NRO JHR 30 - Account Book.
34 NRO JHR 117 - Abstract of title deeds.
35 NRO JHR 30 - Feb 5th 1740 property *"bought of Mr York by the Governors & now tenanted by Mr Cooke"*.
36 NRO JHR 119. Letter dated 11 July, 1812.
37 NRO JHR 120 - Letter, Sir John Palmer to A.E. Young nominating Mr Hodgson as solicitor to Jesus Hospital. 1812.
38 NRO YZ 8428A – Enclosure Award.
39 NRO JHR 123 - Letter, H. Palmer to A.E. Young recommending John Stiles as a fit person to be a tenant. 1813.
40 NRO JHR 124 - notice of Land Tax charge to John Stiles.
41 ibid.
42 NRO JHR 126– Bundle of Letters regarding the hospital's tenant Mr Stiles.
43 ibid.
44 NRO JHR 125 - Letters, Samuel Hafford to A.E. Young. January & October 1815.
45 NRO JHR 175 - Valuation of estate at Old 1827 and Farm at Rothwell 1828.
46 NRO JHR 121 – Enclosure Claims.
47 NRO JHR 59 - Draft of complaint of Governors regarding repairs to Rothwell parish church.
48 NRO JHR 30 - Feb 5th 1740 property *"bought of Mr York by the Governors & now tenanted by Mr Cooke"*.
49 NRO JHR 59 - Draft of complaint.
50 NRO JHR 29 - Account Book.
51 ibid.
52 NRO JHR 30 - Account Book.
53 NRO JHR 190 - Depositions of witnesses in Chancery case 1693.
54 NRO JHR 195a - Answer of Peach in Chancery case.
55 NRO JHR 200 - Copy of receipt for arrears 1755.
56 NRO JHR 202 - Bond of Peach and his tenants to attend Chancery to answer charge of contempt, 1759.
57 NRO JHR 205 e & f - Draft articles of agreement and draft bill, 1765-87.
58 NRO JHR 205 d - Petition for a Bill, 18th February 1765.
59 NRO JHR 205 f - Draft Bill, n.d.
60 NRO JHR 31 - Account Book, 1763-1823.
61 Charity Commission - Reports of the Commissioners, 1831, Vol 3, p.186.
62 NRO JHR 220 - Conveyance of Manor of Thorpe Underwood.
63 NRO JHR 222 - Letter from Fishers, Land Agents to A.E. Young concerning rents at Thorpe Underwood etc.,1844.
64 NRO JHR 223 - Lease dated 24th November 1914 to Stanton Ironworks Company for 21 years.

65   NRO JHR 228 - 231 - Deeds to miscellaneous properties
66   NRO JHR 80 - Principal's vouchers, 1802 - 1805.
67   NRO JHR 232 - 234 - Deeds to miscellaneous properties
68   NRO JHR 236 - Assignment of Mortgage.
69   NRO JHR 237 - Conveyance relating to property in Bodenham, Herefordshire, 1697.
70   NRO JHR 80 - Principal's vouchers, 1802 - 1805.
71   NRO JHR 238 - Bond, Samuel Meadows of Kettering, Butcher to Anne Brown of Rothwell, 1736.
72   Charity Commission - Reports of the Commissioners, 1831, Vol 3, p.186.
73   NRO JHR 220- Conveyance of Manor of Thorpe Underwood.

Feoffees, Governors and Assistant Governors

As discussed in Chapter 2, a charter was obtained on 29th June 1596 for establishing the hospital and the five feoffees (Trustees) named in the foundation deed were incorporated as Governors. It was also ordained by the charter that there should be ten other discreet and honest men inhabiting the county of Northampton, to be called Associates to the Governors, and these would assist the Governors in all things touching the hospital whenever it should seem expedient to the Governors, or a majority of them, and who, on the death or removal of any of the Governors, should succeed by seniority to the vacant place, without nomination or election. These associates were to be chosen by the Governors, or a majority of them from persons inhabiting the county of Northampton. Over time the number of Governors and Associates, renamed 'Assistants' by the early 1600s, combined was ten. This chapter considers the Feoffees, known Governors and Assistants of the hospital from 1596 to 1900.

Feoffees

Thomas Tresham of Newton (1591 – 1617)

Sir Thomas Tresham of Newton, the son of William Tresham and Katherine daughter of Henry Dymock, and relative of the well known Sir Thomas Tresham of Rushton. There is little known about his early life. He was clearly a friend of Owen Ragsdale but nothing is known about how this relationship developed.

Ferdinand Pulton (1591 – 1600)

Ferdinand Pulton (sometimes written as Ferdinando Poulton), born in Desborough circa 1536, died circa 1618, was friend and biographer, and later executor of Owen Ragsdale's will. He was the son of Giles Pulton of Desborough and lived at Bourton or Boreton a hamlet in the parish of Buckingham. It is probable that Ragsdale and Pulton met when Ragsdale was studying law, for Pulton was a lawyer called to the Bar at Lincoln's Inn. Like Sir Thomas Tresham he was a catholic recusant and therefore unable to practice during the Elizabethan persecution of recusants. He therefore concentrated on writing and in 1609 published '*De pace Regis et regni*' the first attempt made by anyone to complete a comprehensive work on English Law. He also produced two books on English legal statutes, the first in 1577 (*A Collection of Sundrie Statutes 1577*) and the second prior to his death in 1618 (*Abstract of all the penall Statutes 1618*). Ferdinand probably resigned as a Governor by 1600 however Henry Dormer in his list of Governors believed him to still be a Governor in 1612.[1] In his will of 13th November 1613 Ferdinand gave a number of bequests including 20s. to Jesus Hospital, 20s. To the poor women of Christ's hospital Buckingham,10s. to the poor women of Fowlers Hospital Buckingham, £5 to the poor of Buckingham, and 20s. to the poor of Desborough where he was born.[2]

George Gascoigne (1591 – 1600)

George Gascoigne, born circa 1531, died 18th September 1620, was owner of Kirby Hall. He was the son of John Gascoigne of Lasingcroft, Yorkshire and a friend of Owen Ragsdale's. At the time of Owen Ragsdale's enfeoffment of George Gascoigne he is described as being of London, being a lawyer there.

Thomas Morgan (1591 – 1600)

Thomas Morgan, born circa 1536, died circa 1604, was lord of the manor of Heyford. He was the son of Francis Morgan, judge of the King's Bench in Queen Mary's reign, from whom he inherited a moiety of Newbold, and brother of Anthony Morgan of Heyford.[3] He held land in Faxton and during his lifetime he acquired a large estate at Weston-under-Wetherley through his marriage to Mary the daughter of Sir Edward Saunders, Knight, Chief Baron of the Exchequer in Mary Tudor's reign.

Oliver Farran (1591)

Oliver Farren, died circa 1602, held the manor and advowson of Molesworth in Huntingdonshire (now Cambridgeshire). Little is known of his life or friendship with Owen Ragsdale except that he was close enough to become one of the original feoffees.

Governors and Assistants after 1596

Pulton appears faithfully to have discharged his duties as Owen Ragsdale's executor, and in accordance with Ragsdale's wishes obtained Letters Patent from Queen Elizabeth and had drawn up in 1596 the Statutes of the Hospital. The letters patent included that there should be five governors of the hospital along with five assistants and from 1596 onwards these continued to be local gentry through to the late 19th century. The letters patent list the original five feoffees' and the first five governors who were to succeed them.

Overleaf are set out the names of the governors and assistants as derived from the records. I have not reproduced the original entries (as per example above) as not all the Governors and Assistants were identified from these. Alongside each identified governor is included a short note about them and their career and notable events along with their tenure as Assistant or Governor. Most of the Assistants became Governors and so appear in the first section below. Those Assistants who were not subsequently elected as a Governor appear in the second section.

Governors

Sir Edward Griffin (1600)

Sir Edward Griffin of Dingley, died circa 1625, had purchased the priory manor there in 1543 and rebuilt the house between 1558 and 1582. He was attorney general during the reign of Henry VIII, Edward VI and queen Elizabeth I, queen Elizabeth visiting him at Dingley in 1566. He died sometime after 1625, his will being made in that year.[4.] He appears to have been elected as a Governor by 3rd September 1600 but little else is known about his governorship of Jesus Hospital.

Eusebie Isham (1600)

Eusebie Isham, born 26th February 1553, died 11th June 1626, was lord of the manor of Pychley. He was a High Sheriff of Northamptonshire in 1584 and was knighted by king James I on 11th May 1603. He appears to have been elected as a governor by 3rd September 1600.

Thomas Mulso or Mulsho (1600)

Thomas Mulso born circa 1542 and died 12th April 1608 was lord of the manor of Finedon. He had been elected as a Governor by 3rd September 1600.

Sir Robert Osborn (1600)

Little is known about Sir Robert Osborn or Osborne of Kelmarsh. He was married to Margaret Freeman of Great Billing, by whom he had a daughter Katherine in 1584. He was knighted at Whitehall in May 1604 and was lord the manor at Kelmarsh. Sir Robert had to sell his estate in 1618 for reasons unknown at which time it was purchased by John Hanbury, a London merchant. Robert was related to Owen Ragsdale's wife Mary whose first husband had been Edward Osborne, who was probably Sir Robert's grandfather.

Thomas Hampden (1600)

Thomas Hampden of Rothwell was son-in-law of Owen Ragsdale and named in his will, Owen releasing to his son-in-law "all manner of bills & bonds whatever", for him to deal with. It was therefore fitting that Thomas Hampden became one of the first Governors of the hospital in 1600.

Edward Bakon (1600)

Edward Bakon of Cransley was named as Governor in the transfer of enfeoffment. Little is known about Edward.

John Pulton (1600)

John Pulton, died 1641, the son of Ferdinand Pulton's cousin George from Desborough, he was elected as a governor by 3rd September 1600, probably replacing his uncle.

Maurice Tresham (1600)

Maurice Tresham was the nephew of George Tresham of Newton, whose estate he inherited. He was named as one of the six first Governors in the transfer of enfeoffment made in 1600.

Thomas? Tresham (1612)

Henry Dormer, Principal from 1702-28 and other persons researching the governor lineage of the hospital believed that Thomas Tresham was a Governor on 16th September 1612. The recusant Sir Thomas Tresham had died in 1605, his son Thomas was dead by 1574, leaving his son Francis as his heir. Francis Tresham died in December 1605, it is therefore unclear which Tresham was elected as a governor in 1612.

Thomas Pagett (1612)

Listed by Henry Dormer and others as a Governor from September 1612. Thomas purchased the manor of Walgrave in about 1618 which caused a dispute between Robert Lane and Ferdinand Baud, an Assistant Governor of Jesus Hospital, which went to court on 29th October 1618.[5] Thomas Pagett was a lawyer of the Middle Temple.

John Syers of Loddington (1660)

Governor in 1660 not known when elected. The Syers owned lands in Loddington in the 16th and 17th centuries.

Richard Kinsman (1665)

From the admissions proposals we see that Richard Kinsman of Broughton was a Governor in 1665, when he proposed Roger Chapman of Desborough. There is no surviving record of his election and this is the only record of his role as a Governor. Richard was born in 1602 and died in 1666. In his lifetime he went to Sidney College, Cambridge University and appears in the alumni of that college. In the civil war he is described on a certificate signed by General Fairfax as 'Auditor Kynsman'.[6] In other papers he is referred to as 'Richard Kinsman of Broughton in Northamptonshire, Gentleman' (28th November 1649). He was active during the civil war and was in Exeter when it fell to General Fairfax in 1645. As he was resident in the town when it surrendered he petitioned for and was granted an amnesty under the articles of Exeter, however he had to promise never more to bear arms and had to pay at least two years rent of his total estate. Bridges in his history of Northamptonshire records an inscription to Richard Kynnesman 'King's Auditor' in Broughton Church the inscription reads: *RICARDUS KYNNESMAN ARMIGER REGIS AUDITOR OBIIT 27 JUNII ANNO MIRABILI.*[7]

Edward Syer (1665)

Edward Syer of Kettering is another 17th century governor whose name only appears once in any of the surviving records. Like Richard Kinsman he appears in 1665 as a proposer for admission, in this case for a Toby Turner of Rothwell.

Geoffrey Palmer (1665 – 1724)

Geoffrey Palmer appears as a governor from 1665 when he is given as the proposer for the admission of Christopher Taylor of Carlton. However, given that he was admitted as an Assistant in 1665 at which time he would have been only ten years of age (born 1655), he must have been acting on behalf of an absent Governor. He went on to become a Governor alongside his father (see below) on 10th October 1706. After the death of his father he became the 3rd Baronet Palmer of Carlton. From the admission proposals he was a Governor until 1724, the last proposal being made 28th August 1724. He died in 1732.

Sir Lewis Palmer Bart (1670 – 1700)

Elected as Governor on June 10th 1670, Sir Lewis Palmer, (1630 – 1713) was the second baronet Palmer of Carlton. His election as a Governor in 1670 commenced a long association between the Palmer heirs and Jesus Hospital. Sir Lewis remained a Governor until at least December 1710, for on 21st December that year he was the proposing Governor for the admission of William Peake of Middleton to the hospital.

Sir William Montague (1670 – 1700)

Elected as a Governor on 12th September 1670, Sir William Montague of Boughton, died 1706 was the second son of Edward Montagu (1562-1644), first Baron Montague of Boughton, by his second wife Frances, daughter of Thomas Cotton of Connington (Huntingdonshire). He entered the Middle Temple and was appointed Attorney-General to the Queen in 1662. In 1676 he became Lord Chief Baron of the Exchequer but was dismissed in 1686. He remained a Governor of Jesus Hospital until 1700. His last proposal to admit a poor man being that for Richard Storey of Rothwell on 12th December that year.

Sir Roger Norwich Bart. (1671 – 1688)

Elected as Governor on 23rd August 1671, Sir Roger Norwich he held a manor in Rothwell and lands in Oundle and other Northamptonshire towns and villages. Sir Roger, 2nd Baronet of Brampton Ash was born in 1636 and died in 1691 and held a number of offices in his life time including, Captain of the troop voluntary horse, Northants 1660-63, commander for assessment 1661-80, 1689; Verderer, Rockingham forest c1661, Justice of the Peace, 1662-66, 1667-1688, Deputy Lieutenant Colonel of Militia 1662-6, 1667-87, Lieutenant Colonel of the militia 1680-7, Commission of Oyer and Terminer 1682.[8] In 1682 he was also put forward as candidate for mayor of Northampton but the Corporation acted in an underhand manor and elected another.[9] He suffered from poor health but despite this he was largely responsible for re-establishing government control after the dissolution of the Oxford Parliament. His involvement with Jesus Hospital as a Governor certainly lasted through to 1688, for on 7th March in that year he proposed William Knight of Rothwell for admission.

George Tresham

The hospital accounts show that a George Tresham was elected as an assistant in 1671. When he was elected as Governor is unclear, he was certainly Governor and treasurer by 1692 when his signature appears at the bottom of a page of accounts.

Charles Cockayne (1684 – 1686)

Charles Cockayne, 3rd Viscount Cullen was the grandson of the Charles Cockayne who mortgaged Sir Thomas Tresham and as a result acquired Rushton hall. This Charles was born in 1658 and died aged thirty years in 1688. He was a Governor of Jesus Hospital from 1684 to his death in 1686.

Sir Justinian Isham (1685 – 1720)

Sir Justinian Isham 4th Baronet of Lamport, born 1658. He was educated at Christ Church, Oxford but did not take a degree. He was a student of law at Lincoln's Inn when his brother died unexpectedly of small pox and he inherited the estate. He was elected as member of parliament and from 1698 he was head of the Tories in Northamptonshire. He became an Assistant Governor of Jesus Hospital on 5th January 1685 and then a Governor on 20th August 1687, replacing Viscount Cullen who had died. He continued as a Governor up to 1720.

Andrew Lant Esq. (1687 – 1689)

Andrew Lant of Rothwell was elected as an Assistant on 21st December 1687 and subsequently elected as a Governor on 16th January 1688. A memorandum

Memoranda of the election of Andrew Lant as Governor, 1688

> *Memoranda the 16th day of January 1688 Andrew Lant of Thorpe Underwood in ye Countie of Northt was the elected to be one of the Governors of Jesus Hospital in Rowell in ye sayd countie in the room and place of the Right Hon Lord Charles Viscount Cullen late deceased. The said Andrew Lant being elected by Sir Justinian Isham, Sir Roger Norwich*

recording his election as governor was made by the Principal William Goode. Lant appears twice in the records as the proposer, in 1688 and 1689. He made his will in January 1689 and died shortly after.[10]

Sir Erasmus Norwich (1691 – 1719)

Sir Erasmus Norwich, the son of Sir Roger Norwich (above) was born in Brampton Ash on 24th July 1668. He was High Sheriff of Northamptonshire in 1704. He was elected as a governor of Jesus Hospital on 26th September 1691 and continued as such until 1719. He died August 1720.

Francis Lane Esq (1691 – 1697)

Francis Lane Esq. Was the owner of an estate in Glendon, Born about 1650 he was well connected with many wealthy families and his daughter Dorothy became the 4th wife of the Earl of Derby. He died November 1709 and is buried in the church of St. Giles-in-the-Fields, Holborn, Middlesex. He became an Assistant of Jesus Hospital on 26th September 1691 and then Governor on 4th March 1694. His name only appears once in the proposals for admission in February 1697.

Lionel Earl of Dysart (1688 – 1726)

Lionel Tollmache 3rd Earl of Dysart, born 30th January 1649, educated at Queens College Cambridge, was for much of his life a Tory politician, first being returned as MP for Suffolk in a heavily contested election in 1673. In 1675 he was made a freeman of Eye (Suffolk). He served as the member of Parliament for Orford (Suffolk) in 1679 and as a member of the Habeas Corpus Parliament. He was Portman of Orford from 1685 to 1709.[11] In 1689 he was made Earl of Dysart and 1702 made Vice Admiral of Suffolk, a post he held until 1716. In 1703 he was appointed Lord Lieutenant of Suffolk and High Steward of Ipswich and Mayor of Orford in 1704.

As Lord Lieutenant of Suffolk, he purged moderate Churchmen from lieutenancy offices. His support for the "Tack" of the Occasional Conformity Bill led to his removal from his county offices in 1705. Campaigning on the basis of his support for the Tack, he was returned for Suffolk again in 1705. He was a Scottish peer and as such forced to leave the House of Commons by the Acts of Union in 1707. He died on 23rd February 1727.

From 1651 to 1698 he was known as Lord Huntingtower and it is under this name that he first appears on 10th January 1688 when he was elected as an Assistant of Jesus Hospital. He was elected as a Governor on 6th November 1699 when the records show him as Lionel Earl of Dysart and later Earl of Dysart. He continued as Governor up to 1726.

Sir Geoffrey Palmer Esq. (1671 – 1732)

Sir Geoffrey Palmer, the eldest son of Sir Lewis Palmer was born on 12 June 1655. On his fathers death he became 2nd baronet of Carlton. During his fathers lifetime he occupied the other family seat at nearby Carlton Curlieu Hall over the county border in Leicestershire, as life tenant. In 1698 he was invited by 'some friends at Leicester' to stand for the town at the forthcoming election. He was not enthusiastic about entering Parliament but with so many friends urging him to do so gave it due consideration. Rumours prevailed regarding his financial state and he withdrew from the election.[12] His parliamentary ambitions appear to have lain dormant for almost ten years until November 1707 when he stood for knight of the shire on the death of John Verney. Although beaten on this occasion, he topped the poll soon afterwards in the 1708 election, though he subsequently proved an inactive Member. Returned again later that year, he was classed as a Tory in the 'Hanover list' of the new Parliament. At this time Palmer was evidently so beset by financial difficulties that he was compelled to assign parts of the manor of Carlton Curlieu to trustees for a 21-year period towards settling his debts, and in 1711 obtained an Act (supervised for him through the Lower House by Sir George Beaumont, 4th Bt.) to confirm this arrangement. He nominated James Winstanley, Tory Member for Leicester, and Thomas Noble, a future Member, as trustees.[13] He was eventually returned to Parliament in April 1715 and represented Leicestershire until 1722. He died on 29th December 1732. His invovement with Jesus Hospital commenced on 23rd August 1671 when he was elected as an Assistant. He was subsequently elected as a Governor on 10th October 1706 and made presentations for admission up to May 1731.

Sir Gilbert Dolben Bart (1694 – 1722)

Sir Gilbert Dolben was born circa 1658, the first son of John Dolben Archbishop of York (1683-86). He was educated at Westminster in 1671 before going on to Christ Church, Oxford from which he matriculated on 18th July 1674 at the age of 15. He studied at the Inner Temple in 1674 and was called to the Bar in 1681. He took Anglican orders during the interregnum and became dean of Westminster in 1662, which he combined with the bishopric of Rochester from 1666. After an early venture into diplomacy Dolben preferred to follow his uncle Sir William into the legal profession.

He was returned for Ripon in 1685 and was an active Member of James II's Parliament, in which he was appointed to 14 committees. He was appointed to the committees for preventing clandestine marriages, rebuilding St. Paul's, repairing

Bangor Cathedral and naturalizing Protestant refugees, and acted as chairman on the bill to prohibit the import of buttons. He returned negative answers on the repeal of the Test Act and Penal Laws to the lord lieutenant of Northamptonshire, and was dismissed from local office. At the general election of 1689 he was returned for Peterborough, no doubt with the support of the dean and chapter, and continued in Parliament to the end of his life, sitting in the House of Commons even after he had been made an Irish judge.[14] Locally, he bought out his brother and reunited the Dolben's family estate at Finedon.

His relationship with Jesus Hospital commenced on 4th March 1694 when he was elected as an Assistant. He was subsequently elected as a Governor on 12th August 1703, as the following record at the back of an account book shows.[15] He regularly took his turn to propose poor men for admission, the last being on 30th March 1721. He died on 22nd October 1722 whilst still a Governor.

Sir Justinian Isham II (1703 – 1737)

Sir Justinian Isham 5th Baronet of Lamport was the third member of his family to be called Justinian and the second with that name to be associated with Jesus Hospital. Born 20th July 1687, he inherited the Lamport estate on the death of his father in May 1730. On 21st May 1730 he was elected as member of Parliament for Northamptonshire and was a faithful Tory MP for the next four years. He was unopposed in the parliamentary election of 1734 and returned to Parliament. He died suddenly on 5th March 1737. He was elected as an Assistant Governor on 12th August 1703 and subsequently elected as a Governor on 12th October 1720 replacing Sir Erasmus Norwich who had died. He appears amongst those proposing poor men for admission regularly up to 7th March 1735 when he proposed John Bilton of Rothwell.

William Washbourne Esq. (1723 – 1725)

William Washbourne became lord of the manor of Pytchley on his father death in 1702, the family having moved from Herefordshire or Worcestershire in 1685 when they purchased the manor previously owned by the Lanes. William was born in 1668 and became an Assistant Governor for Jesus Hospital on 10th October 1706. He was subsequently elected as a Governor on 6th August 1723. His name only occurs once in 1725 as a Governor proposing the admission of a poor man.

Benjamin Allicocke (1726 – 1749)

The Allicocke's suceeded the Robinson to the manor of Loddington through marriage and by the 1720's were holding the manor there and the manor of Isham. Bridges wrote that the manor was in dispute between the Allicockes, who had a good estate in Isham and the daughters of Lady Robinson.[16] There is no record of Benjamin having been admitted as an Assistant of Jesus Hospital. He was elected and admitted as a Governor on 20th June 1726, in place of William Washbourne.

Benjamin died c1749. His last presentation of a poor man to Jesus Hospital was that of George Baldwin on 16th August 1744.

Sir Thomas Palmer (1722 - c1765)

Sir Thomas Palmer, 4th Baronet, of Carlton was born in 1702, the only surviving son of Robert Palmer of Medbourne Leicestershire. He was educated at Emmanuel college, Cambridge before becoming High Sheriff of Northamptonshire in 1740. In 1754 he entered Parliament as M.P. For Leicestershire as served as an M.P. Until 1765. He succeeded his uncle Sir Geoffrey Palmer as the 4th Baronet of Carlton. He was elected as an Assistant of Jesus Hospital on 25th September 1722. He was subsequently as a Governor of the hospital on 6th October 1733 in place of his uncle Sir Geoffrey Palmer.

John Robinson Esq. (1713 – 1745)

John Robinson, was lord of the manor of Cransley, his family having acquired the manor in 1681. John's father Henry Robinson, was declared a lunatic in 1701 and the following year the estate was put into the care of his wife Susannah. Henry died in 1726 and John Robinson succeeded to the estate. He was elected as an Assistant of Jesus Hospital on 13th December 1713 and subsequently as a governor on 11th March 1726, replacing Lionel, Earl of Dysart. John Robinson died in before May 1745 when there is a note referring to him as the late John Robinson.[17]

Sir John Dolben Bart. (1720 – 1749)

Sir John Dolben, second baronet was born on 12 February 1684 at Bishopthorpe Palace, near York, the only son of Sir Gilbert Dolben. John Dolben was admitted on the foundation of Westminster School in 1700. He matriculated at Oxford University on 11 May 1702, having come into residence as a gentleman commoner at Christ Church on 28 April. Dolben graduated BA on 22 January 1704, graduated MA on 8 July 1707, and accumulated the degrees in divinity on 6 July 1717.

Sir John entered the Inner Temple in 1707 at the request of his father (a bencher), he eventually opted for the church rather than the law, and was ordained deacon in June 1709 and priest in April 1711. He gained swift preferment, first as chaplain to Thomas Sprat, Bishop of Rochester, on 11 April 1711, and then as sub dean of the Chapel Royal on 20th April 1713. Although he was in charge of the thanksgiving service for the accession of George I at St Paul's Cathedral in January 1715 and was in routine control of the chapel, he was dismissed from office on 20th March 1718 together with the dean, John Robinson, bishop of London. The precise reasons for Dolben's dismissal remain obscure. Dolben was compensated for the loss of his Chapel Royal duties by Nathaniel, Lord Crewe, Bishop of Durham, who lived at Steane, near Brackley, Northamptonshire and was admitted by Crewe to the sixth stall at Durham Cathedral on 2nd April 1718.

He exchanged it for the eleventh ('golden') stall on 17th July 1719. He kept regular residence at Durham, but lived mainly as a squire and parish clergyman at Finedon. He was presented to the vicarage of Finedon, Northamptonshire, by his father on 9th August 1714, and instituted on 30 September; he was subsequently presented to the nearby rectory of Burton Latimer on 3rd February 1719 and instituted on 14th March. The following year, 12th October 1720 he was elected as an Assistant at Jesus Hospital. Dolben acted as one of the two proctors in the lower house of convocation for the clergy of the Peterborough diocese from 1714 to 1748.[18] He was elected as a Governor of Jesus Hospital in 1731.

On 22nd October 1722 he succeeded his father as second baronet. He married at Sherborne, on 28 July 1720, Elizabeth, second daughter of William Digby, fifth Baron Digby of Geashill. Lady Dolben died at Aix-en-Provence on 4th November 1730, and was buried on 12th January 1731 at Finedon. The couple had five sons and three daughters. In Aix Cathedral there is a monumental inscription to three of their sons, who, like Lady Dolben, died of smallpox. Dolben's last appointment was to the visitorship of Balliol College, Oxford, on 22nd June 1728. He adjudicated in several disputes, and as the modern historian of Balliol contends, exercised his 'authority with patient and impartial wisdom'.[19] His resignation on 24th March 1755 on health grounds was widely regretted.[20] It was probably the same health grounds that made him resign as a governor of Jesus Hospital on 19th June 1749. Dolben suffered from recurrent ill health for the last thirty years of his life; he died at Finedon on 20th November 1756, and was buried there on 11th December 1756.

Wheeler Brooke Esq. (1728 - 1761)

Wheeler or Wheelows Brookes was the son of Arthur Brookes of Great Oakley. He remained a batchelor dying in 1762. He was elected as an Assistant to Jesus Hospital on 1st November 1728, in place of Richard Kinsman who had died and was subsequently elected as a Governor on 16th September 1743, replacing Ernle Washbourne. He last presented Thomas Smith of Great Oakley to the hospital on 30th June 1761.

Sir Edmund Isham Bart. (1745 – 1772)

Edmund Isham was born on 18th December 1690 to Sir Justinian Isham of Lamport and his wife Elizabeth Turnor. He was educated at Magdelen College Oxford before embarking on a legal career. He became 6th Baronet of Lamport on 5th March 1737 following the death of his older brother Sir Justinian Isham. On 31st March 1730 he was elected to Parliament as M.P. For Northamptonshire, in the seat his brother had previously held. He continued as a Member of Parliament for the county up to his death on 15th December 1772.[21]

There is no record of Sir Edmund being elected as an Assistant to Jesus Hospital. He was elected as a Governor on 5th April 1745. He regularly presented poor men to the hospital, the last being Edmund Smeeton of Desborough on 16th

November 1767. A note in the accounts dated 15th August 1768 records his resignation being accepted and Sir Justinian Raynsford being accepted in his stead.[22]

John Robinson Esq. (1747 - 1791)

John Robinson of Cransley succeeded to the manor of Cransley on the death of his father John in 1746 (see above). He was elected as an Assistant on 29th June 1742, in the place of Sir William Norwich. He was subsequently elected as a Governor, on 4th January 1747, when he replaced Benjamin Allicocke. John Robinson served as a Governor up to his death in 1791, and his name regularly occurs as the nominating governor in the admissions, the last of which was for the admission of William Perkins of Cransley on 5th February 1791.

Ernle Washbourne (1723 - 1743)

According to Sir Justinian Isham *"Ernle Washbourne the sonn of Will Washbourne Borne the 19th of February att 2 of ye Clock one Thursday morning & Baptized ye 22th Anno Domini 1690"*.[23] He was elected Assistant 6th August 1723 and subsequently as a Governor on 25th November 1738 in place of Sir Justinian Isham Deceased.

Ernle's grandfather William inherited the families estate at Pytchley in 1653 and in 1663 the family relocated there from Worcestershire. His son was also called William and he married Hester Ernle and it was from her surname that Washbourne gained his unusual first name. He died unmarried in 1743.

Sir Thomas Palmer Bart

Sir Thomas Palmer was born in 1702, the son of Robert Palmer of Medbourne, Leicestershire. He was educated at Emmanuel College, Cambridge in 1718. He succeeded his father in 1724 and his uncle   Sir Jeffery Palmer, 3rd Baronet of Carlton Curlieu as 4th Baronet on 29 December 1732. He was sheriff of Northamptonshire 1740 - 41 and a Member of Parliament from 1754 until his death.[24] There is no record of his election as an Assistant of Jesus Hospital. He was elected as Governor on 24th June 1764 He died 14 June 1765.

Sir Edmund Isham Bart. (1738 - 1772)

Sir Edmund Isham was born on 18th December 1690, the 4th son of Sir Justinian Isham, 3rd Baronet. He was educated at Rugby (1699 - 1707) and then at Magdalen College Oxford. In 1735 he married Elizabeth daughter of Edward Wood of Littleton in Middlesex. He became a Member of Parliament for Northamptonshire for which he was returned unopposed for the rest of his life, he voted against the Government in every recorded division under Walpole and Pelham, speaking against the Spanish convention in 1739. He opposed the bill for the naturalization of the Jews in May 1753, arguing that the Scriptures and history showed that unconverted Jews could never become true Englishmen. He was also a Judge Advocate at the court of Admiralty from 1731-41.[25]

During his lifetime he was noted as a dandy - at Oxford his laundress had complained that he wore 'four, many times five, shirts a week', and on learning that he had been proposed for election he wrote to his wife,

> *"My Dear - They tell me I must proceed to the election on horseback, and ought to make something of a figure, and should have a scarlet coat, therefore desire you would send to my tailor to order him to make me a scarlet cloth riding coat trimmed black and lined with a black alepine, the sleeves the same as my grey coat, faced with black and scarlet cloth breeches ... You may send it next Thursday by the Northampton coach, or at farthest the Monday after, for I believe the election will be on Thursday se' ennight".[26]*

He became an Assistant of Jesus Hospital on 25th November 1738 in the place of Ernle Washbourne and was subsequently elected as a Governor on 8th May 1745 in the place of John Robinson. He died on 15th December 1772.

Charles Allicocke Esq

Charles Allicocke of Loddington.was initially elected as an Assistant in December 1741 in place of John Bridges the historian who had died. He became a Governor on 14th January 1749, being elected in place of John Dolben who had resigned.

Sir William Dolben Bart.

Sir William was elected as an Assistant on 7th July 1744 in place of Wheeler Brooke and subsequently elected as a Governor on 11th May 1763. He served as a Governor until his death on 11th May 1765 .

Sir John Palmer Bart (1765)

Sir John Palmer 4th Baronet of Carlton, born 1702 was elected 22nd July 1765. In place of Thomas Palmer. He was the only surviving son of Robert Palmer of Medbourne, Leicestershire and educated at Emmanuel College, Cambridge He succeeded his father in 1724, and his uncle, Sir Geoffery Palmer, 3rd Baronet, to become the 4th Baronet in 1732. He was High Sheriff of Northamptonshire in 1740 - 1741 and Member of Parliament for Leicestershire from 1754 - 1765.[27] He died in the year of his election as governor of Jesus Hospital.

Justinian Raynsford (1768 - 1777)

Justinian Raynsford was elected as a Governor on 15th August 1768 Replacing Edmund Isham who had resigned. He died c1777 and prior to his death had been verderer of Rockingham Forest.

George Hill of Rothwell (1777 - 1808)

George Hill was born at Waddington, Lincolnshire, the eldest son of Nathaniel Hill, rector of Waddington and lord of the manor of Rothwell, Northamptonshire. As well as his father, his brother and two uncles were clergymen. Hill's father died in 1732, and George broke with family tradition by pursuing a career in the law. He studied and was matriculated at Clare College, Cambridge, in 1733 and was admitted to the Middle Temple in 1734 and called to the bar in 1741. His practice seems to have been mainly 'chamber practice' of conveyancing and advice. On 6 November 1772, after thirty years of obscurity, Hill was created serjeant and king's serjeant.[28]

Hill married, some time before 1761, Anna Barbara, daughter and heir of Thomas Medlycote of Cottingham, Northamptonshire, and they had two daughters. George Hill of Rothwell was elected as an Assistant on 4th September 1759 in place of Valentine Knightley and subsequently elected as a Governor on 1st July 1777, in place of Justinian Raynsford. He continued as Governor taking an active role in the hospitals affairs and the dispute at Orton, and continued to present poor men to vacancies until August 1796. Hill died at his house in Bedford Square, London, on 21 February 1808, and was buried in the family vault at Rothwell, where there is an epitaph upon him by Bennett, Bishop of Cloyne.

Sir Justinian Isham (1792 - c1842)

Elected as a Governor on 10th Jan 1792, in place of John Robinson Deceased. Sir Justinian continued to present poor men to vacancies un tip April 1842.

Sir William Dolben (1797 - 1814)

Sir William Dolben third baronet (1727–1814), politician and slavery abolitionist, was born and baptized on 12 January 1727 at Finedon, Northamptonshire, the second and only surviving son of Sir John Dolben, rector of Burton Latimer and vicar of Finedon, and his wife, Elizabeth Digby.[29] He was educated at Westminster School and matriculated from Christ Church, Oxford, on 28 May 1744. Sir William was married, at Westminster Abbey on 17 May 1748, to Judith, the only daughter of Somerset English of Eastergate, Sussex, housekeeper of Hampton Court Palace, and his wife, Judith, the daughter and eventual heir of Hugh Pearson of Hampnett, Sussex. At the marriage Judith brought with her a fortune of £30,000. Dolben succeeded his father in the baronetcy on 20 November 1756 and served as high sheriff of Northamptonshire in 1760–61. In 1768 he was elected as a member of Parliament. Judith died aged forty, on 6 January 1771. Sir William then married a second cousin, Charlotte Scotchmer, (née Affleck) on 14 October 1789. She was the widow of John Scotchmer (d. 1786) of Pakenham, Suffolk, a banker. He was appointed a verderer of Rockingham Forest in 1766.

Sir William was dedicated to the Church of England, Oxford University, and the county of Northamptonshire. He gave generously of his time and money to encourage worthy causes, such as the Sunday school movement. He was a member of the Society for the Encouragement of Arts, Manufactures, and Commerce and of the Marine Society, and he was a Radcliffe trustee at Oxford. He is best known for his single-minded dedication to the abolition of slavery. Sir William had been an Assistant from at least c1785 when he was the Treasurer of the Society. He was elected as a Governor on 7th Feb 1797 and continued until his death in 1814.

Allen Edward Young (1807 - 1823)

Allen Edward Young of Orlingbury was elected as an Assistant on 15th October 1771, he was elected as a Governor on 6th October 1807 and resigned in 1823. He was High Sheriff of Northamptonshire in 1796.

Sir John Henry Palmer Bart (1810 - c1859)

Elected as a Governor on 23rd November 1810. He was still a Governor on 24th February 1859 when he nominated William Corby to a vacancy at the Hospital. He was lord of the manor of Carlton, Ashley and Carlton Curlieu, Leicestershire.

John Capel Rose (c1823 - 1884)

In post by 1823 and still in post by 1860.[30] He continued to nominate poor men to vacancies until 26th May 1884. In his life time he was a magistrate and sheriff for Northamptonshire in 1806.[31]

Thomas Philip Maunsell (c1823 - 1865)

T.P. Maunsell was a Governor by 1823. He continued in post through to his death in 1866. He is mentioned in a newspaper obituary of 1860 and last elected a poor man to vacancy on 6th September 1865.[32] During his life he was a local justice of the peace, Sheriff of Northamptonshire in 1821, Member of Parliament for north Northamptonshire from 1835 - 1857, and lord of the manor of Thorpe Malsor.

Sir Arthur de Capel Brooke (c1817 - 1858)

Sir Arthur de Capel Brooke was born in Bolton Street, Mayfair, Westminster, on 22 October 1791. He was educated at Magdalen College, Oxford, where he graduated BA on 20 May 1813 and MA on 5 June 1816. On 27 November 1829 he succeeded his father in the title and estates. He joined the army, rising to the rank of major in 1846. Much of his early life was spent in foreign travel, especially in Scandinavia. In 1823 he published *Travels through Sweden, Norway and Finmark to the North Pole*, which was followed by *A Winter in Lapland and*

Sweden (1827). He was an original member of the Travellers' Club, but in 1827, feeling strongly that many of the newly elected members had little interest in foreign travel, he founded the Raleigh Club, of which he was for many years president. In 1830 some members, with Brooke's apparent approval, set up a Geographical Society, which later became the Royal Geographical Society. In 1854 the Raleigh Club became the Geographical Club which was very closely connected to the Royal Geographical Society. Brooke was thus intimately connected with the establishment and success of the main geographical institutions in the country. He was a fellow of the Royal Geographical Society and of the Royal Society. In his later years he took an active interest in temperance and in various charitable and religious causes. Arthur de Capel Brooke was recorded as a Governor by 1817 and continued in office until his death although in his last two years he was frail and accordingly he last nominated a poor man to a vacancy on 11th May 1856. He died at Oakley Hall, Great Oakley, Northamptonshire, on 6 December 1858.

Sir Geoffrey Palmer Bart (1823 - 1860)

Sir Geoffrey Palmer was in office by 1823 and is recorded in office until 1860. A review of admissions shows his electing poor men until 24th August 1891. He died 12th February 1892 at his home in Carlton Park, Rockingham. According to his obituary he was born in 1809, studied law at Oxford and was called to the Inner in 1835 and was a magistrate for both Northamptonshire and Leicestershire. He was High Sheriff of Northamptonshire in 1871 and was lord of the manor of Carlton, Ashley and Carlton Curlieu. [33]

Allen Allicocke Young (c1835 - 1895)

Born Feb 6th 1806, Allen Allicocke Young was the eldest son of Allen Edward Young of Orlingbury. He inherited his estate in 1835 and about the same time was elected as a Governor of Jesus Hospital. He was an active Governor and a local magistrate from 1829 and a keen member of the Pytchley hunt. He died 21st May 1895 aged 89 years.[34]

Sir William Capel Brooke (c1867 - c1903)

Sir William Capel Brooke is listed as a Governor proposing poor men to vacancies between 1867 and 1903.

Rev. Cecil Henry Maunsell (c1899 - 1911)

The Rev. Cecil Henry Maunsell of Thorpe Malsor was born on 9th January 1847. He was the son of the Rev. George Edmund Maunsell and Theodosia Palmer. He graduated from Oxford University in 1873 and became rector of

Thorpe Malsor. He died a bachelor on 14th October 1911.[35] He is listed as a Governor proposing poor men to vacancies between 1899 and 1911.

Captain Borlase Tibbitts (c1887 - c1903)

Captain J. Borlase Maunsell Tibbitts was the fourth son of Colonel T. P. Maunsell of Thorpe Malsor. He was born at Thorpe Malsor in 1820. He was educated at Eton then entered the Army becoming a Captain in the 12th Lancers. In 1858 married the Lady Mary Isabella, dowager Viscountess Hood, daughter of Richard Tibbitts of Barton Seagrave, and by royal licence changed his surname to Tibbitts (all three husbands of the viscountess changed their name to Tibbitts). He became a Magistrate on May 17th 1862 and was known to be a keen farmer, taking a great interest in his stock.[36] He is listed as a Governor proposing poor men to vacancies between 1887 and 1902 when he died at Rothwell Grange aged 81. He was buried at Thorpe Malsor.

Assistants

Unlike Governors the Assistants are hardly ever mentioned in the records. The exception being those in the role of Treasurer which was frequently undertaken by an Assistant. The earliest recorded assistants were elected at a meeting of Governors held at Lord Cullen's house in Rushton on 23rd August 1671. From the note of the meeting it appears that prior to 1671 there were probably no Assistants. In 1600 the feoffees were still in office alongside the new Governors and so assistants may not have been required at that time. As the memoranda transcribed below shows seven were elected in 1671, all the sons of existing governors. The meeting is noted in the front page of the earliest account book [159] by George Tresham (see overleaf)

In considering the Assistant governors, the following list has been created from those who have been recorded, generally in the form of lists of former Governors and Assistants. Only those who did not subsequently become Governors will be described below as those who were elected as Governor have already been described.

Robert Spencer of Althorp (1596-1613)

Robert Spencer is named in the Letters Patent as an assistant. In 1612 he was given a knighthood and on learning of this he wrote to the Governors to resign, quoting the Letters Patent, which states that assistant governors: " *being neither barons nor knights, or above the rank of esquire*", thus preventing him from continuing in office (for a full transcript of Letters Patent see page 18). A subsequent letter informs us that the first was a draft as he was considering resigning in 1612. This letter also adds further detail regarding Sir Robert's reason for resigning which was the distance from his dwelling (Althorpe) to Rothwell and that he could not deputise or have an assignee to undertake his role. He

JHR 29 Note of the election of seven Assistants 1671 (Transcript below)

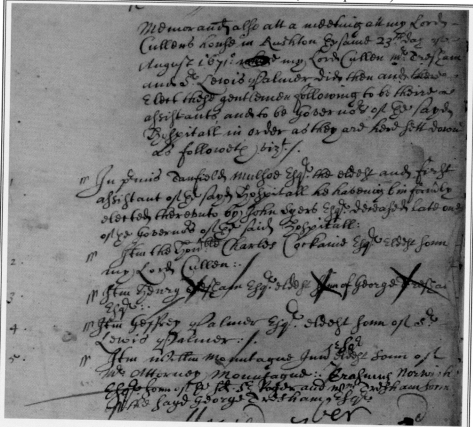

Memoranda allso att a meeting of my Lord Cullens house att Rushton ye 23rd day of August 1671 where my Lord Cullen, Mr Tresham and Sir Lewis Palmer did admit and elect those gentlemen following to be their assistants and to be governors of the sayd hospitall in order as they are here sett down as followeth viz:

Inprimis **Tanfield Mulso Esq** the oldest and first assistant of ye sayd hospitall he having been formally elected thereunto by John Syers esq deceased late one of ye Governors of ye said Hospitall:

Itm: the **hon Charles Cockayne Esq.** eldest sonn my Lord Cullen:

Itm: **Henry Tresham Esq.** eldest sonn of George Tresham Esq:

Itm: **Geoffrey Palmer Esq.** Eldest sonn of Sir Lewis Palmer:

Itm: **William Montague Jun** oldest sonn of Mr Attorney Montague: **Erasmus Norwich** the eldest sonn of the sd Sir Roger Norwich and Mr M Tresham sonn of the sayd George Tresham Esq.

therefore nominated two local persons, one of whom, Arthur Brookes was a kinsman of his. The other being Godfrey Chibnall of Orlingbury. Sir Robert Spencer as a Calvanist would have held religious views at the opposite end of the spectrum from the Catholic Treshams and Pultons, although he is known to have broadly aligned himself with the godly of whatever persuasion, as his interventions in county elections demonstrates.

Tanfield Mulso of Finedon (1671 – 1677/8)

Tanfield Mulso was the son of Robert Mulso, of Finedon and a daughter of Robert Tanfield. His date of birth is not known. He died before 1678 when a Bill (Mulso's Bill) was put before Parliament by his Trustees, *"for Payment of his Debts, and making Provision for his Children".*[37] His children being his daughters Anne and Elizabeth who married two brothers Gilbert and John Dolben, the sons of the Archbishop of York. Anne and Gilbert bought Elizabeth's share of the estate and created the long association of Dolben's as Lords of the Manor of Finedon .[38] As noted above he was elected as an Assistant in 1671 and was probably still an Assistant at the time of his death in 1677/8. According to the note by George Tresham (above) he was the first and eldest assistant to be elected.

Maurice Tresham

Born in 1618, the son of Maurice Tresham of Geddington and Muriel. He was elected as Assistant in 1671, the year of his death. Prior to his election he had been the Principal, being recorded as such in 1669 (see Principal's).

Henry Tresham

Henry Tresham was the eldest son of Sir Thomas Tresham of Newton, one of the original Feoffees of the hospital. Born c1618 he was elected as an Assistant in 1671.

William Montague junior

William was the son of Sir William Montague of Boughton, (d.1706) who was already a Governor having been elected in 1670. William Montugue junior was elected as an Assistant in 1671.

John Allicocke of Loddington

Elected on 25th January 1688, in the place of Andrew Lant.

Moses Bathurst of Hothorp in Rothwell Hundred (1691 - ?)

Elected as an Assistant 28th September 1691, in the place of William Montague.

Richard Kinsman of Broughton (1726 - 1728)

Elected as an Assistant 11th July 1726, he had died by 1728.

John Bridges (1733 – 1741) of Barton Seagrave

John Bridges was baptized at Binfield, Berkshire, on 24 June 1666. He was the eldest of the twelve children of John Bridges (1642–1712), lord of the manor of Barton Seagrave. His father was largely responsible for rebuilding Barton Seagrave Hall. He was educated at Oxford where after two years at Trinity College, Oxford (1683–4), he left without taking a degree, he was admitted to the Middle Temple on 23 April 1684 and subsequently called to the bar on 22 May 1691. On 8 August 1695 Bridges was appointed agent and solicitor to the customs.

From 11 January 1712 he was a commissioner of customs and from 24 November 1714 to 24 November 1715 receiver-general of excise. He inherited his fathers Barton Seagrave estate in 1713 and had houses in both London and Northamptonshire. The Barton estate brought in £460 per annum, enough to make him financially independent and able to resign from a position which his surviving letters to his uncle show he was finding increasingly onerous. From 1718 until his death on 16 March 1742 he was an ardent collector of materials for the history of his native county, not only himself taking notes throughout the county but also employing agents to do the same and to make copies from original records and manuscript collections lent by friends.[39] He was a fellow of the Royal Society and his collected papers on the history of the county were subsequently published in two volumes (The History and Antiquities of Northamptonshire) by the Reverend Peter Whalley.

John Bridges died, on 16 March 1724 at Lincoln's Inn. His health had been poor and his correspondence is full of references to colds, the ague, the colic, and gout, but Hearne's *Diary* shows that the real cause of Bridges' death was syphilis. He was buried at Barton Seagrave on 25 March.

He was appointed as an Assistant at Jesus Hospital in 1733. The record of his appointment as an Assistant also has a footnote stating *"Esqr Bridges gave ye old principal half a guinea for ye entrance".* [40]

Valentine Knightley of Pytchley

Elected as an Assistant on 9th November 1749, in the place of Charles Allicocke who was made Governor in that year.

John Fleming

Elected as an Assistant on 15th August 1768.

William Somerset Dolben (1806 -)

Elected as an Assistant on 6th October 1806. He was still in post in 1814.

Election of Governors and Assistants

Record keeping within the establishment was poor prior to 1702 when Henry Dormer was appointed as principal. He appears to have been a meticulous record keeper and had an interest in the history of the hospital which he referred to as *"ye society and fellowship of Jesus Hospitall"* and shortly after his taking up post produced from the then extant records a list of Governors and Assistants [164] which he maintained throughout his tenure as principal. A successor in 1778 (probably the Reverend Anthony Birkett) made an attempt to identify the governors *"as far as could be made out from the Old Books and Papers of the said Hospital"*.[41] However this list which covers the period from 1612 to 1749 appears to have been largely based upon Henry Dormers original list updated to 1749.

The hospital charity was known in the 18th century as the Society of Jesus Hospital, Rothwell, and as with other societies a membership or joining fee was taken when an Assistant, Governor, Principal or Poor man accepted their place. The record of John Bridges acceptance and entry (above) shows this clearly.

Although styled as a Society, the governors acted in a manner similar to the trustees of any modern charity. They met at regular intervals, usually once a year and prior to the construction of the Principals house in 1778, meeting took place at the house of one of their number, for example on 12th September 1670 a meeting to elect new Governors took place at Richard Kinsman's house whereas the next meeting to elect a new member took place on 23rd August 1671 at Viscount Cullen's house in Rushton. After 1778 meetings took place in the principals house. These meetings were either not recorded in the early years, or the minute books are lost and therefore the frequency of meetings and the items discussed and agreements reached are unknown for all but the (annual) General meeting and specific meetings called for the election of new governors, assistants and principals. Most often we know only that a meeting was called because the accounts show that paid messengers were sent out to the houses of the Assistants and Governors, to 'summon' them to a meeting.

The general running of the hospital was in the hands of the Principal. Where decisions which required Governor approval between meetings needed to be made, the Principal would visit the senior governor and discuss the matter and between them a decision made or a special meeting called. The role of the governors as trustees was to oversee the running of the charity and its estate and ensure financial probity. In addition they elected replacement Governors from among the assistants should one of their number resign or die, appoint and remove the principal if found to be unsuitable and remove any resident who broke the rules of the hospital. From the surviving papers it is apparent that from an early period they took it in turn amongst themselves to nominate to vacancies or potential vacancies. A number of letters / notes of introduction have survived from which it is apparent that a poor person has been given a note and sent to visit the principal of the hospital to request admission to the hospital whenever the next vacancy should occur. Henry Dormer, Principal (1702-28), brought much order to the hospital,

Henry Dormers standardised format for the admission of Governor's and Assistants

The form of admitting a Governor

Sr

We greet you well & for as much as there is a want of a feoffee of Jesus Hospital in Rothwell in the room & place of
lately deceased; we therefore the governors & feoffes of the said hospital do hereby elect you to be our associate in the government of the said hospital according to the orders of the said house made by the donor thereof, desiring that you will declare yourself under your hand whether you will be pleased to accept the same; And we take leave & remain

Your most humble & faithful servants & c.

The form of admitting an Assistant.

Sr

We greet you well & for as much as there is a wanting a Assistant of Jesus Hospital in Rothwell in the room & place of   lately deceased (or elected Governor); we therefore the governors & feoffes of the said hospital do hereby elect you to be one of our Assistants in the government of the said hospital according to the orders of the said house made by ye donor thereof, desiring that you will declare yourself under your hand whether you will be pleased to accept the same; And we take leave & remain

Your most humble & faithful servants & c.

Henry Dormers standardised format to be used by those accepting the office of Assistant

My Lord & Gentlemen

I hereby thankfully accept the place of one of your assistants in the government of Jesus Hospital in Rothwell, to which ye have been pleas'd to elect me in the room of   And I hereby promise to use my best endeavours in promoting the good government & welfare of the said hospital.

I am yr most humble [servant]"

Northampton Mercury - Friday 7th June 1895

> *By the death of Mr A. A. Young, J.P., a vacancy occurs upon the governing body*
> *of Jesus Hospital, Rothwell, and the opportunity therefore presents itself for the*
> *election of a local governor, who has long been needed. Hitherto people out of the*
> *district have had sole control of the hospital, and it will be interesting to see if the*
> *present Governors will comply with local feeling and elect one from the town.*

including the meetings of the governors and setting out standard forms for the admission of both governors and assistants (see page 64). Also set out in the same page is the form of acceptance to be given on acceptance by an assistant.

Local Dissatisfaction with the Governors

By the time of the death of Allen Allicocke Young in 1895 there was considerable local dissatisfaction with how Governors were elected. For 300 years, the majority of the Governors had been the great and the good from places other than Rothwell. The exception to this was George Hill (1777 - 1808). Following the death of A. E. Young a number of newspaper items appeared regarding this dissatisfaction (see page 65 for example newspaper report).

Governors Meetings

Only a few records survive of the meetings of Governors and assistants before 1828, and from those that do it is clear that a 'General Meeting', occurred at least annually in the presence of at least three of the five governors. Specific dates were not set for any of the Governors meetings until 26th November 1825 when it is recorded in the accounts that, *"the last day of October for the meeting of Governors of the Hospital at Rowell for each year in future.* When a meeting was called it was usually called by the senior Governor who then required the principal to inform the other Governors by summons. Up to the time of Henry Dormer, the Principal often undertook to deliver at least some of the summons himself, but by the 1720s these were undertaken by paid messengers sent out from the Hospital, for example in August 1721 a series of summons were sent to governors to attend what was probably an extra ordinary meeting.

Prior to 1825, while some meetings may have taken place at the hospital, they were generally held in the house of one of the governors, for example in August 1671 the meeting took place at Lord Cullen's house in Rushton.

It is clear from the correspondence with William Dolben in the late 18th century and Mr Affleck a few years later that meetings of the Governors were often difficult to arrange as many held high ranking positions in society, Members of Parliament, Justices of the Peace, Sheriff etc. Additionally some like Dolben and Affleck had houses far away from Rothwell for example William Dolben was living in Marlebone, London whilst treasurer and Mr Affleck was resident in Bristol.

In some instances meetings were held solely to elect a Governor and Assistant to fill vacancies, for example, 24ᵗʰ December 1683 and 20ᵗʰ August 1687. At least once in the year accounts were signed off. Prior to 1800 meetings sometimes dealt with the failure of the residents to follow the rules and statutes of the hospital. Such was the case in 1685, 1703, 1705 and 1709. A record of a meeting held on 16ᵗʰ August 1709 to investigate a breach of the statutes by five residents survives and is set out (overleaf).

As the hospital increased its portfolio of properties and problems arose at Orton, the management of property and rent arrears became a frequent topic of discussion at governors meetings. Special meetings were called when the need arose, for example, if a Principal died, or to receive a report, as was the case during the Orton Tithe dispute, where an extra-ordinary meeting was convened on 26ᵗʰ July 1787 when they met to receive the report on the Act of Parliament regarding the Orton tithes.

Records of the governors meetings are from October 1828 sometimes found at the bottom of some of the accounts pages, rather than in a dedicated minute book, suggesting that the treasurer acted as note taker on this occassion. One such note records the death of Samuel Hafford who was both Principal of the hospital and tenant of their Rothwell farm. In this instance it is clear that the treasurer acted as note taker in the absence of a Principal who usually acted as secretary to the meetings. From October 1829 the notes of the Governors meetings change from being notes at the bottom of the accounts to becoming fuller notes of who attended and the decisions made.

When the Governors met they had to travel and probably ate together, irrespective of where they met. There are no records to confirm this, however one record does exist of the drink they had at a meeting in August 1709, when the consumed, " *4 flasks of Florrenes Wine; & messenger, 16s. 6d., 4 Bottles of Sider, 3s. 4d.* and *8 Bottles of Ale, 2s. 10d.* The cost, £1. 1s. 20d., was paid from the hospital funds.

Notes

1   NRO JHR 30
2   Browne, Willis (1755) The History and Antiquities of the Town, Hundred, and Deanery of Buckingham. TNA PROB 11/360/127.
3   VCH A History of the County of Northampton: Volume 4 (1937), pp. 167-172.
4   TNA PROB 11/147/369
5   TNA C78/253
6   The Record Society (1896) Royalist Composition Papers, Vol 35 (2S), No 757.
7   Whalley, Rev. Peter (1791)'The history and antiquities of Northamptonshire: Compiled from the manuscript collections of the late learned antiquary John Bridges, Esq'. Vol ii, P. 87
8   TNA SP29/26/75, BL Add. 34222 f.4, Blackburne, D.F.H. ed.(1932) Calendar of State Papers Domestic, Charles II. 1667, P. 167, 1682, P.78.
9   Blackburne, D.F.H. ed.(1932) Calendar of State Papers Domestic, Charles II. 421, *No.* 106.
10   TNA PROB 11/443/214
11   Wedgwood, J. C. (2002) The House of Commons 1690 – 1715 Cambridge University

Press.

[12] Rutland mss at Belvoir Castle, Palmer to Rutland, 28 May, Verney to same, 28 May 1698.

[13] BL, Verney mss mic. 636/53, Cave to Ld. Fermanagh. 10 Nov. 1707; Nichols, ii. 540.

[14] Henning, B. D. Ed, (1983) The History of Parliament: the House of Commons 1660-1690, Boydell & Brewer.

[15] NRO JHR 29

[16] Whalley, Rev. Peter (1791)'The history and antiquities of Northamptonshire: Compiled from the manuscript collections of the late learned Antiquary John Bridges, Esq'. Vol ii, p. 107.

[17] NRO JHR 30

[18] Aston, N. (2004) 'Dolben, Sir John, second baronet (1684–1756)', Oxford Dictionary of National Biography, Oxford University.

[19] Jones, J. (1988) 'Balliol College: a history, 1263–1939'. Oxford University Press. p.160.

[20] Aston, N. (2004) 'Dolben, Sir John, second baronet (1684–1756)', Oxford Dictionary of National Biography, Oxford University.

[21] Hayton, D., Cruickshanks, E. and Handley, S. (2002), The History of Parliament: the House of Commons 1690-1715, Cambridge University Press, Cambridge.

[22] NRO JHR 31

[23] Isham, J. Parish Register extracts, Being Extracts from the Lost Registers of Barby, Maidwell, Pytchley and Rothwell in Northamptonshire and from the Register of Stonely in Warwickshire.

[24] Namier, L. & Brooke, J. eds. (1964) The History of Parliament: the House of Commons 1754-1790.

[25] Sedgwick, R. Ed. (1970) The History of Parliament: The House of Commons 1715-1754.

[26] ibid.

[27] Namier, L. & Brooke, J. eds. (1964) The History of Parliament: the House of Commons 1754-1790.

[28] Macnair, M. (2004) 'Hill, George (c.1716–1808)', Oxford Dictionary of National Biography, Oxford University Press.

[29] Aston, N. (2004) 'Sir William, third baronet (1727–1814)'.Oxford Dictionary of National Biography, Oxford University Press.

[30] Stamford Mercury Friday 27th January 1860.

[31] Northampton Mercury, 4th January 1806.

[32] Stamford Mercury Friday 27th January 1860.

[33] Northampton Mercury, 12th February 1892.

[34] Northampton Mercury 31st May 1895.

[35] Montgomery-Massingberd, H. eds. (1976), *Burke's Irish Family Records*. Burkes Peerage Ltd, London, U.K, page 801.

[36] Northampton Mercury, 24th January 1902.

[37] Journal of the House of Lords: volume 13: 1675-1681 (1767-1830), pp. 270-271.

[38] Page, W. (1930) A History of the County of Northampton: Volume 3, pp. 196-203.

[39] Brown, A. E. (2004) 'Bridges, John (*bap.* 1666, *d.* 1724)', *Oxford Dictionary of National Biography*, Oxford University Press.

[40] NRO JHR 30.

[41] NRO JHR 17.

The Principal and Other Officers

The Principal of the hospital, occasionally referred to as the warden was the person on whom the Governors relied for the day to day running of the hospital. The statutes set out the attributes required of a person to be eligible for election into the role. As with the poor men he had to be over forty years of age, unmarried, of good name and credit (not in debt) and not indicted or suspected of treason or criminal behaviour, and of good health. At the time of nomination the principle could not have any estate, freehold or copyhold, with an annual values greater that £4, or an annuity worth more than 20 nobles (1 noble = 6s. 8d.), and no personal property worth more than 100 marks, unless he agreed to surrender one third of the value of the estate to the governors and the society.

What is not stated in the statute are the other qualities required of the man. Firstly, he needed to be able to read and write as part of his role was to take minutes of the Governors meetings, he needed to be numerate and keep account of the income and expenditure of the hospital on a daily basis, reporting the same to the governors for inclusion into the accounts. He needed to work with the hospital tenants to ensure that the paid their rents when due, without which he and the men in his charge would not get paid. Lastly he had to be a leader and communicator, ensuring the residents behaved according to the rules of the hospital and exercised the punishments laid down by the Governors when they did not.

On a daily basis, his hours were long, he had to open the gates at four o'clock in the morning and ensure they were locked at nine o'clock in the evening. He then had to assemble the men and ensure they were suitably attired before leading them into the church for prayers in the morning and the evening. Morning prayers or matins usually commenced at 6 a.m. It is clear from the known Principals that at least two were former teachers and others probably came from a similar back ground. It is not clear who the first Principal was, however it was probably Giles Groocock of Desborough. The preface of the State Papers Domestic 1635 in which a visit to the hospital by Sir Nathaniel Brent states that the master there is "one Mr Bowden".[1]

The original articles of foundation set out between Owen Ragsdale and the feoffees required that the Principal should unmarried at the time of his appointment, that is either single or a widower, and that he remain unmarried for as long as he held the post. It appears however that from the early 1800s this rule was relaxed. This relaxation may have been instituted after 1768 when a separate house was built for the principal. As a result the census records from 1841 show the resident principal living on site with his wife and sometimes children. When a married principal died his wife had to leave the hospital and from 1879 we have as an example, Mary the wife of William Dalby who died in Leicester and who prior to his death had lived in the Principals house. Despite this apparent relaxation newspapers running articles on the town were still stating that the Principal had to be single or a widower as late as 1880.[2]

Giles Groocock of Desborough (1612/13)

In a list created by Henry Dormer of the principals up to his time he has written *"The first Principal, or Warden, in this Hospitall was Giles Groocock, of Desborow, he lived in that year 1612."*.[3] On 23rd March 1612/13 he was granted power of attorney by the Governors to collect the Hospital rents on their behalf.[4] This document however does not name him as Principal or Warden, but as husbandman, although Henry Dormer writing circa 1702 clearly believed him to be the first Principal.

Mr Bowden (1635)

Mr Bowden is the earliest recorded Principal or Warden of the hospital. It is not known when he commenced as Principal or when he left / died. He was certainly in post in May of 1635 when Sir Nathaniel Brent visited Rothwell and reported on his visit and his concerns regarding one resident which is contained in the preface to the State Papers Domestic for May 1635.[5] (below).

Preface to the Calendar of State Papers Domestic 1635

There is an hospital in Rowell which I visited, but the master, one Mr Bowdon, knowing of my coming, went out of town before I came, so that I could not redress many things that were there amiss. I have taken a particular note of them, and have given authority to Sir John Lambe to proceed in the business, because he dwelleth in the same town, if he please to accept of it. There are twelve poor men, of which one hath been and is a recusant papist this twenty-six years. My opinion is that his place is void, but I gave order that nothing should be done against him until another hearing.

Henry Palmer of Carleton (c1650 - 1658)

By 1650 a Mr Henry Palmer was the Principal. Again there is almost no information regarding Henry Palmer other than his name appearing in a list of Principle's towards the back of the earliest surviving account book. The single line states *"In the year 1650 Mr Hen Palmer was Mte (Master)."*[6]

Edmund Bacon of Burton (1659 - 1666)

In the same account book we find an entry stating *"In the year 1659 I find Mr Bacon was Principall of this Hospitall"*. Edmund Bacon's name also appears on a lease of Spencers manor and the lands in the town fields of Old, dated 5th November 1660. Nothing else is known of Mr Bacon.

Mr William Cockman of Wollaston (1666 - 1669)

A document of 1666 states that in that year the hospital income was £97. 9s. 4d. from lands leased by the trustees. The principal at that time was William

Cockman who was paid an allowance of 40s. quarterly along with 30s. annually for wood, and 10s. at Christmas, 5s. at the Transfiguration and 4 nobles once in every two years for a gown.

In that year the document informs us there were twelve residents who received an allowance of 20s quarterly, 5s. at Christmas, 2s. 6d. at the Transfiguration and 1 mark every two years for a gown. The hospital is referred to as 'the Society', which has an allowance of 6s. for firing. A woman attended to wash the mends clothes for which she was paid 12s 6d. per quarter.[7] The account book also states that "*Mr Wm Cockman was principle in ye year 1666*".[8]

Maurice Tresham of Newton (1669 - 1670)

In 1669 a there is a very unusual occurrence, a manorial lord takes up the role of Principal. From 1669 - 1670 Maurice (or Morris) Tresham was elected as Assistant in 1671. It is not clear why or how he became the Principal for between 1666 and 1671 for he appears to have been in possession of the manor of Pilton at that time which would have meant his election was void by reason of the value of his estate.[9] The likely reason is that some deal was done to ensure the post of Principal was covered, and gave him accommodation whilst work was undertaken at his house. His name appears against a note in the accounts regarding the election of Assistants in 1671. Maurice Tresham resigned in 1669/70 and his successor, William Goode, was elected in January 1670 (see below).[10]

Undertaking to Appoint William Goode the Elder on the Resignation of Maurice Tresham (NRO JHR 321|)

> *"We whose names are hereunto subscribed the Governors and ffeoffees of Jesus Hospitall in Rothwell doe hereby elect and [illeg] that Wittm Goode the elder, Gent shall succeed Maurice Tresham gent, in the " " Principalls place of the said hospital To have and enjoy the said Principalls place (next and immediately after the resignation of the said Maurice Tresham or after his decease, wh shall first happen) for the time of his natural life & in the same manner as the former principals were won't to enjoy the same he the said William Goode observing the Orders and Statutes of the said hospital witness our hands and sealed the thirteenth day of January in the xxth year of the reign of our Soverigne Lord King Charles the second Annoq Ind 1670.*

Mr William Goode (13th January 1670 - 26th September 1702)

As noted above the Governors elected Mr William Goode of Kettering to the post of Principal on 13th January 1670.[11] From this it appears that the election took place before Maurice Tresham left either due to resignation or death. It is unclear which occurred. It is possible that he took up post in February 1670, for a note in an account book records,[12] *Md: The twentieth day of February 1670 Wm Goode gentleman was elected principall of Jesus Hospitall in Rowell by the right Hon'ble the Lord Viscount Cullen, The Chief Baron Montague, Sir Roger Norwich Baronet,*

Sir Lewis Palmer Baronet, George Tresham Esq. The only certainty is that he was in post by Michaelmas (29th September) 1671, for at that time he submitted his account *"biginning at Michaelmas 1671 as followeth"*.

In 1691 the poor men of the hospital made a complaint about their money being stopped by William Goode.[13] The letter from John Parker, Edward Dunsmore, William Gunalls, Thomas Guess, Nicholas Ward, Joshua Ave, John Dunsmore, Thomas Newborn and John Roase, stated that not only were there allowances stopped or cut short, but that some were charged for their blue coat, and at times the money for firewood was reduced. It is not clear what the outcome of the complaints was, however William Goode continued in post and was described as frail and ill by his son the Rev. Henry Goode of Weldon on 30th August 1696 at which time he was unable to keep his appointment with Francis Lane and Justinian Isham at Glendon to pass over his quarterly accounts.[14] His son suggested annual account keeping for the duration of his fathers life and offered to collect the accounts and deliver them to the Governors. A letter from Francis Lane to Sir Justinian Isham deferred the meeting accordingly.

Despite his failing health William Goode remained as Principal until his death in September 26th 1702 and from his term in office there survive accounts and a few other documents. On his death the accounts and notes of a Governors meeting show that money was owed to the Governors. This was settled by his son the Rev. Henry Goode, Rector of Weldon.

Henry Dormer of Brampton (22nd October 1702 - 1728)

In considering the post of principal it is worth noting the contribution of Mr Henry Dormer to the role. He is best known for the inscribed plaque above the door passage to the hospital gardens which reads:

> Christ bless our Governors, prolong their days
> who plac'd us here to render Heav'n our praise.
> To live contented, private, and resign'd,
> Free from life's toils and humours of Mankind.
> Pleas'd with wise Agur's Mediocrity,
> Too low for Envy for contempt too high.
> What now have we thankfully possess,
> Till we exchange for greater happiness.

Henry Dormer Principal 1721

Henry was appointed to the role of principal on 22nd October 1702 at the age of 62 years. Born in Brampton in 1620 he appears to have been a learned and meticulous man with an interest in the hospital and its history. He set about re-organising the hospital records and in his account book, split into sections he recorded not only his accounts, the receipt of tithes and other financial matters as required of him but created sections for recording current and past governors, assistants, principals and residents, referred to as inmates, in as far as he could deduce them from the records. Without Henry's record keeping and investigations we would know far less about the history of the hospital.

A census of the residents of the hospital in 1705 written by Henry states: *'The Principall Henry Dormer, at Brampton, Aged 65.* This gives a year of birth for Henry Dormer of 1640, and the location of his birthplace as Brampton (Ash), Northamptonshire.[15]

Little is known about Henry's early career and it must be noted that the profession of 'Architect' had barely emerged as a profession separate from that of surveyor or builder. In the design of a new house the functions we consider to be those of an architect were widely diffused amongst those who undertook the building work. Where we do find Henry Dormer stating his profession it is usually that of surveyor.

The earliest known work of Henry Dormer is from an estimate he provided for some slates at Lamport Hall in 1680, by which time he would have been 40 years of age.[16] In 1684 he was at Balscott in Oxfordshire, where he made a detailed map, which is housed at Trinity College, Oxford.[17] By 1685 he is thought to have been the architect and person overseeing the rebuilding of the upper stages of the church tower at Carlton Curlieu, in Leicestershire. The Victoria County History ascribes this work to 1686.[18] However the work bears the date 1685. This tower bears a striking resemblance to the tower at Weldon raising the question of whether that is also Henry Dormers Work.

In 1686 he was working at Lamport Hall. His work at the hall was probably that of surveyor and supervisor. Documents at Northampton Record Office show that he measured walls and windows at Lamport.[19] In 1687 he was employed by Thomas Maydwell at Geddington to survey the Maydwell lands there, from which he produced a terrier.[20]

He is also believed to have been the architect and supervisor for the work undertaken at the Chapel of St Mary in Arden, Great Bowden, Leicestershire between 1693 - 94. There he built a small chapel over the south aisle of a former church, which had been demolished.

His biggest commission (that we know about) came in 1696 when he acted for the Daniel Finch 2nd Earl of Nottingham, who on acquiring an estate at Burley-on-the-Hill, Rutland set about building a new mansion. Henry Dormer is not thought to have been the architect for the work, but supervised the building work over the winter of 1696 – 7.[21] In April 1697 he was succeeded by John Lumley of Northampton, who remained in charge until the house was completed.

The Burley-on-the-Hill project was a major undertaking. Finch wanted a grand house completed within a year. The footings were to be of stone and the upper courses in brick. Because most of the building work took place over the winter numerous difficulties arose. Added to that, the client, Daniel Finch was himself a meticulous man who was heavily involved in the project and kept very detailed records of the building work and costs.

Election Notice for Henry Dormer (JHR21)

> *Know all men by these presents that wee whose names are hereunto subscribed* **Governours** & **Trustees** *for* **Jesus** *Hospitall in Rothwell alias Rowell in the county of Northampton have nominated, appointed and constituted,* **And** *by these presents do nominate, appoint and constitute Henry Dormer of Middleton in the said county of Northampton, Gent: Master or Warden of the said Hospitall which lately became vacant by the death of William Goode, Gent: deceased. To execute and perform, All the Powers, Authorities & Duties belonging to this said place of Master or Warden of the said Hospitall.* **To Have** *and* **To Hold** *the said place of Master or Warden of the said Hospitall.* **To** *him the said Dormer for and during the Term of his naturall life provided he be subject to and observant of the rules, orders and methods of the said Hospitall. And to Have, receive and tak All profits and perquisites whatsoever belonging to the same or usually heretofor enjoyed by the Masters or Wardens of the Hospitall for the time being. He the said Henry Dormer from time to time doing and performing all such duties and being subject to obedient observing All such Rules, Orders & Methods, in the executing of the said place of Master or [Warden of the said] Hospitall for the time being at any time or times hereafter shall be made and established by the major part or number of the Govern^{rs} or trust[ees] shall find fit for the better government or benefitt, of the said Hospitall, and He the said Henry Dormer from time to time during every yeare giving unto ye Governo^{rs}: or Trustees of the said Hospitall for the time being or some of the time a complete and true accompt of all such monies and profitts whatsoever, As from time to time be had & Received by him or his order as belonging to the said Hospitall, And how the same have been Disposed of.*

Henry Dormer's last commission appears to have been a survey of the Lowick estate of Sir John Germain, commissioned by Mr William Lanes and completed in 1702.[22] At the age of 62, in 1702 he applied for and was elected as Principal of Jesus Hospital, succeeding William Goode who died earlier that year. According to his election notice at the time of his election he was residing at Middleton.[23]

The document was signed by Sir Erasmus Norwich, as the most senior of the Governors in 1702, and bears the signatures and seals of Dysart, Isham, Norwich and Palmer. The document also bears two other witness signatures, one is that of George Burton whereas the other is illegible, but may be that of Henry Dormer.

When Henry Dormer died rather than produce a new notice, this one was re-used, and Henry Dormers name crossed out and that of Thomas Chapman of Cottingham written above. All occurrences of the word 'Master' were also crossed out and the word 'Principal' inserted above. Similarly the date was altered to the 19th day of June, but the year and reference to the monarch left unchanged. The senior Governor at the time of Thomas Chapman's appointment was Sir Lewis Palmer Bart. And the document is witnessed by a Henry Halford and the new Principal Thomas Chapman.

On taking up the role he set about reorganising the records of the hospital. A new accounts book was started. In this book he noted the Governors, Assistants and Principals from the past, and made a list of all the admissions he could work out from the existing records. He also undertook some surveying of hospital lands in Orton.[24]

In 1709 he submitted his model for a steeple at Burton Overy church, Leicestershire.[25] The design was considered appropriate but no commission followed. Had a commission followed he would have had to resign as Principal of Jesus Hospital because of the limits relating to absence imposed on the post holder by the statutes of the hospital. No other proposals are known about and Henry continued as Principal of Jesus Hospital, he did however undertake surveying for the local gentry. One such survey was undertaken for Allen Edward Young of Orlingbury in 1710 for which a terrier survives.[26] Henry Dormer died in May 1727.

According to the rules of the hospital on the death of any resident (Principal, Nurse or Poor Man) their property became the property of Jesus Hospital. Richard Tongue, a butcher in the town was Henry's executor and he along with Thomas Dexter in Middleton had some of Henry's possessions (Below). Following his death an inventory of all Henry's possessions was drawn up by Thomas Mills and George Bauldwin who were presumably acting on behalf of the Governors.[27]

Inventory of Henry Dormers possessions at the time of his death in 1728.

An Inventory of the Goods of Mr Henery Dormer Principal of Rothwell Hospital taken May 12th 1727 by us whose names are subscribed In Northamptonshire	£	s	d
In the Lodging Room			
Beding and bedstead	3	0	0
The furniture in the Long Gallery	1	0	
A table and chair and desk and table seat and the pictures	2	0	0
In the fire room			
A table and chair and books and other things	2	0	0
In the stair case outer and brass and other things	0	10	0
In the Stable			
Board and fire wood and hay and Grindle stone and other things	2	0	0
At Mr Tongues House a bedstead fire sheall and tongues	0	5	0
For purss and apparel	25	7	1
At Middleton at Thomas Dexters			
Bed and beding and books and clock and silver tumbler and garner	11	0	0
Thomas Mills *George Bauldwin*			

Thomas Chapman of Cottingham (1728 - 1742)

The Governors elected Thomas Chapman to be the successor to Henry Dormer in 1717. From the accounts it is apparent that he took up post in 1727, for at the top of a page for that year the handwriting changes and in the new hand is written

"The receipts of Thomas Chapman Principal begin June ye 24. 1727". Nothing is known about Thomas Chapman before his appointment, however it is likely that he was a middle class farmer and therefore a man with at least a basic education and supporting this we find on March 26th 1738 Thomas Chapman being described as a yeoman and trustee for the Governors in a mortgage document relating to the 5 bells in the town.

From taking up his post Thomas Chapman went about some aspects of his job somewhat differently to his predecessor. Henry Dormer usually collected the rents due himself and only sent someone else out to do it when unable, for example we find in his accounts where he employed a man to collect the rent from the Orton tenant because he was lame and unable to go. It is also likely that for most of his time in office Henry also notified the governors of meetings personally and attended meeting in their houses. Thomas Chapman's entries show that from taking up post he immediately employed men to collect rents and notify governors of meetings. There are also no records of him going out to visit hospital lands, disputed or otherwise.

John Whitaker of Lamport (1742 - 1752)

John Whitaker was appointed as Principal on 23rd July 1742. As with his predecessor, nothing is known of John Whitaker prior to his taking up post. John Whitaker was no longer in post by 1752 and it appears from a note regarding the appointment of Robert Dexter that he was removed. The reason for his removal being set out in the accounts. [28]

Note in the accounts regarding John Whitaker's expulsion

"We the governors of Jesus Hospital at a meeting held this day Do record to ye first statute expel John Whitaker as Principal for Robbing Gerard Tongue of this parish, Butcher, that being duly proved before us in witness whereof we have set our hands this twenty third day of March 1752".

Robert Dexter of Rothwell (1752 - 1763)

Robert Dexter of Rothwell was appointed on 1st June 1752, following the expulsion of John Whitaker. The notice of his appointment survives and is written almost word for word the same as that for John Whitaker and will not be repeated here. Although the notice id clearly dated 1752 Robert Dexter was actually carrying out at least some of the Principal's duties from 1750/51 for in the accounts we find his hand writing occurring on a page dated 1751 giving his name and the accounts for the last quarter of 1750/51. Mr Whitaker was clearly still alive for the first entry by Robert Dexter is for two payments to Mr Whitaker. This suggests that Robert Dexter had already been appointed as the successor to John Whitaker, who most likely been arrested for the robbery and the Governors awaiting the outcome of his trial. The last payment in the accounts to John Whitaker was made in July 1751, for his gown. All was clear by 23ʳᵈ March 1752 and subsequently as the next note records: "*On June 1ˢᵗ 1752 Sr Thos Palmer. Sr Edmnd Isham Bart. John Robinson & Chas Allicocke Esqrs did elect Robert Dexter Gent of Rothwell to be Principal instead of ye above John Whitaker removed*" Robert Dexter died in 1763 aged 63 years. [29]

William Moore of Northampton (1764 - 1766)

William Moore was appointed on 1ˢᵗ June 1764 to replace Robert Dexter and his name appears against the midsummer quarters accounts for that year. William Moore was not good at keeping accounts or any other records and as a result of his failure to perform was removed in 1766. A few pages of accounts survive for William Moore's last year in office. At the bottom of the last page of these is a memorandum written by the Governors suspending him from his post.

Note in the account regarding William Moor's suspension (NRO JHR 31)

> "*At a meeting of the Governors this 30ᵗʰ Day of August 1766 complaint was made against Wm Moore, Principal, which being fully proved, upon his not accounting for money &c. for the uses of the Hospital, it was then determined that the said Principal is suspended and excluded from any further execution of his office during pleasure*"

The Governors met again, this time with the Assistants, on the 6ᵗʰ September 1766 specifically to discuss and hear the case brought against William Moore, and finding the allegations to be true they expelled him, recording the same in the accounts.

Note in the accounts of the extra-ordinary meeting of the Governors and Assistants to hear the case of William Moore, and his expulsion.

> *At a meeting of the several Governors and Assistants of Jesus Hospital in Rowell in the county of Northampton whose names are hereunder so written holden this day at the said Hospital by appointment of John Robinson Esqr. Notice thereof previously given at the Governors and Assistants of the said Hospital and also to William More Principal of the said Hospital for examining into a Complaint lately made against the said Principal for clandestinely receiving and not accounting for rents and other sums of money belonging to the Governors and for proceeding (if the said Governors and Assistants should see cause) to the expulsion of the said Principal that the said complaint is true and the Principal not having any proof to the contrary, preferring to tender an account of the moneys secured by him. It is therefore ordered by all the Governors and Assistants present that the said William More be and is hereby expelled from being Principal of the said Hospital. Given by our hands this sixth day of September 1766.*

The expulsion note was signed by E Isham, J Robinson and Charles Allicocke as Governors and A Young and G Hill as Assistants. It is not clear whether criminal proceedings followed.

Thomas Rice of Burton Latimer (1766 - 1772)

Thomas Rice was elected to the post of Principal on 12th October 1766. Prior to taking up post he had been the school master at Burton Latimer. A document survives which binds Thomas Rice to render annual accounts to the Governors. The binding fee was £100. Assurance was given by a William Aldwinckle of Middleton and the bond is also signed by Anne and John Aldwinkle and Thomas Rice who affixed his own seal. Clearly the pocketing of money belonging to the hospital by the previous Principal had a considerable effect on the Governors and Assistants and this bond was their way of ensuring the same did not happen again.

Thomas Rice kept his word and produced good accounts. He continued the account book of his predecessors but used it for income only stating a second account book for outgoings.[30] He also appears to have kept a book of tithes which is frequently referred to in his accounts, only the balances from that book being carried forward into his main accounts. Thomas Rice's accounts continue to 1770 and having separate books the income accounts became much more detailed than previous accounts.

John Whittel of Kettering (1772 - 1776?)

The accounts for 1772/73 show a John Whittel as Principal for this year only. His name also occurs in a letter to the Governors from John Palmer c 1794 who applied for the post of Principal. Nothing else is known about John Whittel.

William Cross (1776 - 1778)

As the length of tenure of John Whittel is unknown it is not possible to say when William Cross took up post as Principal. The earliest account for William Cross occurs for the first quarter of 1776. A letter from the Churchwardens and leaders of the town shows that William Cross had died by 1778.

Revered Anthony Birket (1778 - 1794)

On 14th March 1778 the churchwardens and leading towns folk of Rothwell took the unusual step of writing to the Governors requesting that the Reverend Anthony Birket be elected as Governor. The Governors accepted the Rev. Birket who was subsequently elected as Principal. The governors recording their acceptance of his nomination on the back of the letter from the towns folk.

Letter from the Churchwardens and Townsfolk of Rothwell recommending the Rev Birket for the position of Principal. (NRO JHR 21)

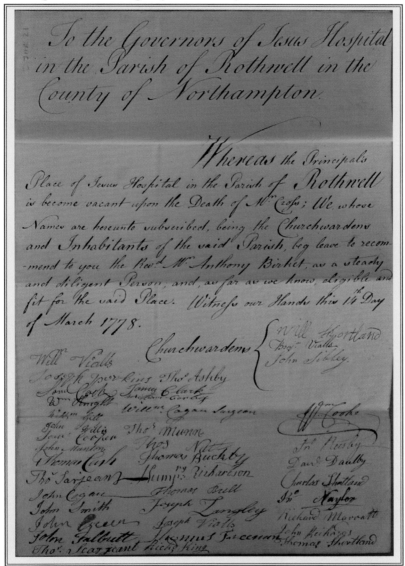

Like his predecessor, Henry Dormer, the Reverend Birket was meticulous in his book keeping and had an interest in the hospital and its history. In June 1789 he set out an account of the hospital's yearly income and outgoings and the property and effects owned by the hospital and himself.[31]

The Reverend Birket resigned the post of Principal in July 1793. His final accounts were signed off on 13th July 1793 and at the meeting of Governors that day the a note was entered into the accounts: *"13 July. On this day the Revᵈ Mr*

Birket resigned the office of Principal of Jesus Hospital. The governors recorded their thanks to him, *"for his just and upright conduct & his constant attention to the good order of the Brethren and Interests of the Hospital"*. They also asked that he accept £10 as a token of their thanks. [32]

It is unclear why the Reverend Anthony Birket resigned. But it is highly likely that he had been considering it for some time as in June 1789 he had made an inventory of the Principals House and other rooms in the Hospital, clearly setting out in each room which were his possessions and which belonged to the Hospital, something no previous or subsequent Principal has done. All of his possessions would upon his death become Hospital possessions and the inventory would suggest he wanted to ensure that if he did resign there should be no dispute over who owned what.

Vacant (1793 - 1795)

From 1793 to at least 1794 the Principals post was vacant. John Palmer, the schoolmaster of Rothwell then wrote to the Governors on 1st January 1795 requesting they appoint him. His letter is interesting in that it tells us that as well as running the free school he had also covered a previous period of absence.

Transcript of John Palmers letter to the governors requesting that he be considered for the post of Principal. (NRO JHR 23)

The Humble Petition of John Palmer who through their favor was appointed Teacher of the school in Novr 1771 and for which your petitioner retains a thankful remembrance. Having through the will of divine providence lost his partner in life, near 6 months elapsed. Your petitioner begs leave Honoured Sirs, with Deference most humbly to solicit your favour and assent to transplace your supplicant into the office of Principal at Jesus Hospital, vacuous by the resignation of Mr A. Burket several months ago. — Your petitioner Honoured Sirs, well knows the duty incumbent in that office, having officially 3 months of a year in 1772 after the Demise of Mr Rice, until Mr Whittel was elected. — If sobriety and punctuality would meet your honours approbation, you supplicant humbly hopes the confidence conferred would not be disappointed. — You Petitioner — honoured sirs, begs leave to promise, he hath seen better days; hath had a suffrage for each county, Northampton & Leicester at the same time, and made use of them, in the good cause You Honours invariably pursue. — Not presuming any claim to your Honours favour on that account; having acted from principle and inclination, — But humbley hope, after a series of more than 23 years in the teaching line (in which, assiduity to his power hath been endeavoured. And thro' the Blessing of God attended with success in many instances of the youth committed to his care.) The school salary Honoured Sirs, being small, barely 10^l p^r Annum at this time, and repairs heavy renders my case very necessitous, and your honours benevolence to the supplication of your Petitioner will be great Charity. —— To the latest period of existence your supplicant, Honoured Sirs, as in Duty bound will be truely thankful.   With humble Deference, your Petitioner Honoured Sirs, is desirous of approving himself your Dutyful, obliged and obedient servant.

Despite his petition John Palmer was not elected to the post, which remained vacant. Samuel Hafford, a local farmer appears to have covered the period of absence and submitted accounts to the Governors, for his name appears in the accounts against the balance for 1794. Samuel applied for the post himself in January 1795, but was not appointed. This may have been because he had a wife and children at home he did not meet the eligibility criteria to be the Principal at this time, although this is uncertain. He did however continue to cover the vacancy until 1796.

John Richards (1795 - 1813)

In 1795 John Richards of Rothwell was appointed as Principal. His name first appears in the accounts for 1796. Nothing is known about him.

Samuel Hafford (1814 - 1828)

As noted previously Samuel Hafford applied to become Principal whilst covering the vacancy between 1793 and 1795. At that time he was forty years of age and married. He reapplied for the post on the death of John Richards (William Daulby also applied at the same time). By this time he was fifty-nine years of age and a widower and accepted by the Governors. His letter requesting the Governors to appoint him, dated 10th April 1813 is interesting in that in the letter he states that "*I have done the business nearly twenty years and I hope to your satisfaction*". Clearly in the period from the vacancy to the end of John Richards tenure Samuel Hafford had been employed by the Governors in some capacity, possibly in keeping the accounts.[33]

He was clearly an able and shrewd man. When the Hospital's tenant became insolvent he proposed to the Governors that he take on the farm as tenant whilst remaining Principal. In practice his son was going to run the farm. He then negotiated for the refurbishment of the property and on his death his son was duly named as tenant. Samuel died September / October 1828.

Rev William Brotherhood (1828 - 1835)

Born c 1765, died 9th February 1835 aged 69.[34] Little is known of his time as Principal of Jesus Hospital. Prior to his election and admission he had served as vicar of Rothwell, although he is also named in the will of Joseph Morris (d. 1816) of Desborough where he is shown as the clerk of Desborough.

According to the Gentleman's Magazine he was educated at Magdalen College, Cambridge where he was awarded a Bachelor of Arts degree in 1793.[35] The magazine also states that he was instituted to the living of Rothwell in 1828, the year in which he also became principal. The ability of an married vicar to live in at the hospital and perform both roles, vicar and principal was probably quite advantageous in the early 1800's for the vicarage which stood on the opposite side of the church yard had been pulled down and the parish renting houses for incumbents. In 1833 whilst Principal he donated money to the funds for the National School Society.[36]

John Adams of Kettering (1835 - 1840)

John Adams was aged 50 years when he took up post as Principal in 1835. A note in an account book tells us that he was from Kettering.[37] He died 12th November 1840 aged 58 years and was buried at Kettering on Thursday 19th November.[38] His obituary in the Northampton Mercury on 12th December 1840 says that he was a Linen and Wool Draper in Kettering before taking up the post of Principal.

William Marriott (1840 - 1842)

Died 8th October 1842, aged 67 years. Buried at Rothwell on 12th October. The 1841 census record him living with his wife Jane at the hospital.

Thomas Davis of Loddington (1842 - 1848)

Thomas Davis from Loddington was appointed on 31st October 1842 when aged 47 years. Prior to taking up post he had been a farmer at Loddington where he lived with two women both name Catherine, one of who was probably his mother, the other aged 35 years was probably his wife who may have been resident with at Jesus Hospital. He died 5th March 1848 aged 54 years and was buried at Loddington. His stipend on taking up post was £35 per annum.

William Daulby of Orton (1848 - 1857)

William Daulby originally applied to become Principal on 19th October 1814 but was passed over in favour of Samuel Hafford. He was eventually appointed to the post on Saturday 28th March 1848 and died on 8th July 1857 aged 69 years.[39] He was buried at Rothwell on 12th July. William commenced on the same stipend as his predecessor. That is, on taking up post he received £35 per annum. The 1851 census records him as being married and records his wife Sarah as being resident with him in the hospital.

John Williams of Cottesbrooke (1857 - 1860)

Following the death of William Daulby several candidates were considered for the post of Principal. At a meeting of the governors held on Saturday 31st October 1857.[40] John Williams was elected. Prior to his election he had been a domestic servant in Sir J. Langham's household.[41] Williams resigned the post in 1859-60, his last accounts being presented for the period October 1859 - January 1860, suggesting that he left by January 1860. It is unclear why he resigned.

William Dalby (1860 - 1875)

Prior to taking up post Mr William Resine Dalby had been a farmer occupying Rushton Lodge Farm.[42] His death in 1875 was both sudden and tragic. He ascended a ladder to work on an apple tree and fell to his death.

An inquest into William Dalby's death was held on 16th September 1875 and a verdict of 'Accidental Death' returned.[43] He was buried in the churchyard of his native village, Rushton. According to the Northampton Mercury a procession was held from the hospital to Rushton.[44] The more infirm residents followed the procession to the town's end, whilst a few of the more able men followed to Rushton to attend his burial. William Dalby was married and during his term as Principal his wife Mary resided with him in the Principals house. On his death she appears to have moved to Leicester where she died. Her death on 10th March 1879 is recorded in an obituary of Friday 21st March 1879, in the Stamford Mercury, where she is described as Martha, relict of Mr William Dalby of Jesus Hospital.

The report of William Daby's death as reported in the Northampton Mercury, 18th September 1875, Page 3

FATAL ACCIDENT - We regret to record the sudden death, under very painful circumstances, of the esteemed president of Jesus Hospital, in this town. On Tuesday Mr Dalby noticing a decayed branch in an Apple Tree in the orchard belonging to the establishment, procured a ladder and saw, climbed into the tree and proceeded to sever the unsightly bough. Owing to some want caution in choosing his position, when the bough fell he fell with it, a hight of 14 feet, and coming into contact with the fallen wood broke his ribs and sustained a fatal injury to his heart. Medical aid was promptly obtained, but was of no avail to save life, the lamented gentleman only survived his fall about a couple of hours. The sad event has cast quite a gloom over Rothwell, where Mr Dalby was universally held in the highest respect, and in his death the inmates of the hospital have sustained an almost unrepairable loss, endeared, as he was, to them by the kindness and condescending urbanity with which he uniformly fulfilled the duties of his onerous and responsible position.

Samuel Jones (1875 - 1889)

Samuel Jones was appointed after the death of William Dalby. He came to Jesus Hospital from Geddington where in 1871 he was the publican of the Royal Oak in Queen Street. The census informs use that he was born in Grafton Underwood in 1819. Living in the Principal's house with him were his wife Sussanah, his daughter Alice and on census day 1881 Caroline Colston, his wife's sister. Samuel died 24th May 1889 aged 70 after a long and lingering illness. According to the Northampton Mercury he was buried in Rothwell churchyard, his coffin being carried by eight of the residents.[45]

Thomas Lovell (1889 - 1904)

Thomas Lovell was appointed after the death of Samuel Jones in May 1889. He was born in Beachampton, Buckinghamshire in 1843 and lived with his wife Fanny in the Principals house. Like his predecessor he was a publican or licenced victualler and prior to taking up the office of Principal he was publican at the Kings Head in Bridge Street, Thrapston. He died on the 18th December 1904.

The Principals Salary

The Principal received a salary rather than a pension. In 1671 this was £20 per year. As with the poor men and the nurse an extra allowance was given for the two feasts, on founders day and on Christmas day. For the principal this amounted to an additional 6s per feast in 1671. This usually rose with the mens salary and whilst no additional amount is stated for the principal in 1724 the Principals salary rose to £25 per year. It remained at £25 per year until 1828 when the Charity Commission recommended an additional £10 per year be given to the Principal.[46] The increase was granted by the Governors in October 1828 bringing the Principals salary to £35 per year.

Clothing

In keeping with the poor men the Principal received a suit of clothing and a gown from the hospital, although as this cost more than that of the poor men it was of a better quality..

Nurses

From the outset the warden or principal was in practice the chief of the poor men, resident and in receipt of a stipend or allowance and not employed as such. Alongside the principal a nurse was resident from the outset. The nurse was a retired woman who like the principal was resident and paid an allowance. According to the hospital returns for 1666 there was a washerwoman who also mended the clothes of the poor men for which she was paid 12s. 6d. Per quarter.[47] As the accounts make no record of any other woman aside from the nurse it must be assumed that the nurse and washerwoman were the same person. In the 18th century the accounts regularly show replacement brushes for the nurse, and from 19th century records the nurse was clearly a housekeeper, who cleaned the shared rooms, washed clothes and undertook other similar tasks such as, in the 19th century, ensuring that when a resident died the room had the required items in it before the new resident moved in.

Most of the early accounts record only 'Nurse' and the amount paid. She appears to have received as a salary the same amount as the men were paid in pension and at the same frequency, for example the account for 1671 records: *"To the twelve poore men and ye woman nurse and my own quaterage"*. Occasionally a name is given and from an account of 1612 we find the earliest recorded nurse, Elizabeth

Watts. Between 1612 and 1703 no other nurses are named in the accounts. From 1703 we find widow Belton and then in 1724 Jane Bilton most likely the same person but spelled differently. She is referred to as *"ye old Nurse"* in the accounts of 1724. In that year we find a memorandum in the accounts stating: *"Nurse had no gown, because she refused a blue one"*.[48] For a short period after 1724 the nurse was given a clothing payment rather than being made to wear the blue cloth uniform of the poor men, but after 1750 the accounts once again show payments for a gown. The Nurses gown was always given at the feast of St Thomas and by 1789 the payment for the gown was one pound. Who made the gown or what colour it was is not stated.

From 1727 to 1731 Anne Black appears in the accounts as the nurse. Anne received £1 per quarter in 1727. The next nurse noted from the accounts or other documents is Hanna Yorke who was in post in 1833 and remained at the hospital until her death in 1838.[49] She appears to have been assisted in her later years by Ann York who was still in post on 28th June 1843.[50]

From 1858 nurses are mentioned more frequently and from the hospital records and the 19th century census's the following list of all the recorded nurses has been produced.

The Nurses Salary

The Nurse was paid a salary or stipend of twenty-one shillings per quarter by 1671.[51] This amount remained constant until 1724 when it was increased in line with the poor men by one shilling per quarter.[52] However by the 1770s the nurse appears to have been receiving five shillings less than the poor men. A further small increase followed in 1796. In 1824 the nurse's salary was £8. 16s. 0d. per year. It remained as £8. 16s. 0d in 1828, at which time the Charity Commission recommended an increase in her salary (their report refers to it as a pension) and it subsequently increased to £12 per annum in October 1828.[53] In addition to her salary the nurse earn extra money for washing the body of a deceased poor man. An example of this is found in the costs of Richard Cook's funeral in May 1770, the full transcript of which is given later (see poor men). In this instance she was paid one shilling and four pence.[54]

Other Staff

Porter of the Gate

An account of 1725 records a payment of 6d per quarter to the 'Porter at the Gate'. Other payments indicate that this was a one off payment each year at the time of Rothwell Feast when a man was employed to watch the gate and prevent unwanted visitors or theft from the hospital property. On June 5th 1721 we find that the person employed to guard the gate was a Thomas Cutbert.[55]

Nurses Identified from the records of the hospital 1612 - 1903

Year(s) in Post	Name	Notes
1612	Elizabeth Watts	
1703 & 1724	Widow Jane Belton or Bilton	In post on 26th June 1703 when paid her quarterage and still in post in 1724 when described as 'ye old nurse'.
1727	Ann Black	
1836	Hanna Yorke	In post in 1836, died 3rd January 1838
1837	Ann York	Still in post 28th June 1843. Recorded on the 1841 census as a nurse at the hospital. Also resident were her husband and two children.
1851, 1858	Sarah Burditt	Recorded on the 1851 census along with Elizabeth Toy as nurses of the hospital, then aged 63 years. Born in Rothwell in 1788.
1851, 1858, 1859	Elizabeth Toy or Tye	Recorded on the 1851 census along with Sara Burditt as nurses of the hospital, then aged 52 years. Born in Eye (near Peterborough) in 1799.
1891	Mary Clark	Recorded as predecessor of Mary Sculthorpe. The 1891 census records her and Ann Shortland as nurses at Jesus Hospital. In that year she was aged 69 (Born 1822)
1891	Ann Shortland	Recorded as predecessor of Jane Bains. The 1891 census records her and Mary Clark as nurses at Jesus Hospital. In that year she was aged 71 (Born 1820)
1892	Mary Sculthorpe	From Middleton, took up post 21st December 1892 at age 46.
1893	Jane Bains	From Malton, took up post 16th September 1893 when age 51
1894	Deborah Tabbern	From Rothwell, took up post 11th June 1894, when age 50
1896	Mary A. Adams	From East Haddon, took up post on 20th December 1896, when she was age 40.
1898	Ann Chapman	Came from Burton Latimer, in post from 9th July 1898 when she was 44 years old.
1899	Ann Rush	In post from 18th August 1899, then aged 58 years. From Burton Latimer.
1899	Ann Haines	In post from 6th November 1899, the aged 52, from Rothwell.
1902	Susan Blake	In post from 6th July 1902, then aged 58, from Desborough
1903	Catherine Cooper	In post from 1st June 1903, then aged 40, came from Isham

Servants

The 1841 census records seven persons on the two pages for Jesus Hospital who were included in the census and therefore resident who were either children employed as servants or relatives of residents. Three are listed as servants, this includes William Fields, aged 15 years, Charles Shortland, aged 25 years who is probably related to a resident, Samuel Shortland and Mary Burbridge, aged 25 years who may also be related to a resident, Richard Burbridge. A further person, Ann Marriott aged 40 years has the same surname (Marriott) as the principal and may be related although this is not stated (his wife, Jane, was resident with him). The other three children are Charlotte (aged 7) and Mary Ann Towell (aged 10) for both of who no occupation is stated, and Amy Saunders aged 3 years who is described as a 'weavers child'. No children or servants in residence are recorded on the 1851 or later census.

Apothecary's and Physician's

Whilst not salaried, Apothecaries and Physician attended the poor men at the Hospital as necessary and were paid for each visit and the medicines or services they provided. Apothecary's bills are regularly recorded in the accounts although rarely named. From 1711 to 1713 Mr Cogan was the apothecary used by the hospital. In 1713 his bill for the preceding two years was 10s. 10d. By the 1720's the apothecary used by the hospital was Mr Baker of Kettering who is named in the accounts having provided *"apothecary stuffe, use by Gam: Gervis when his shoulder broke"*.[56]

Occasionally reference is made to a physician having attended the hospital, for example William Peake attended Jonathan Barker, bled him and the provided medicine in October of 1712.

Notes

1   'Preface', Calendar of State Papers Domestic: Charles I, 1635 (1865), pp. VII-LII.
2   Northampton Mercury 4th December 1880, p.2.
3   NRO JHR 30.
4   NRO JHR 46.
5   'Preface', Calendar of State Papers Domestic: Charles I, 1635 (1865), pp. VII-LII.
6   NRO JHR 29.
7   Bull, F. W. (1924) Jesus Hospital, and its founder, Owen Ragsdale, Northamptonshire Architectural Society.
8   ibid.
9   Page, W. (1930) A History of the County of Northampton: Volume 3, pp. 129-131.
10 NRO JHR 29.
11 NRO JHR 21.
12 NRO JHR 29.
13 NRO JHR 27.
14 NRO JHR 47a.
15 NRO JHR 30.
16 NRO I.L 4127.
17 Lobel, M. D. and Crossley, A. (1969), Victoria County History: A History of the County of Oxford. vol 9. pp. 171 - 188.
18 Lee, J.M. & McKinley, R.M. (1964) Victoria County History: A History of the County of Leicester Vol 5. p.80.

19   NRO I.L 4158, I.l 4136 & 37.
20   NRO BSL 74.
21   Habakkuk, J. (1955) Daniel Finch, 2nd Earl of Nottingham: His House and Estate, p.148.
22   NRO NL115, copy of Book of Survey 1702
23   NRO JHR 21.
24   NRO JHR 212.
25   Lincolnshire Archives, Fac. 9/59.
26   NRO YO 54.
27   NRO Prob 401.
28   NRO JHR 30.
29   NRO JHR 33.
30   NRO JHR 31.
31   NRO JHR 40.
32   NRO JHR 32.
33   NRO JHR 23.
34   NRO JHR 33, Northampton Mercury 21st February 1835. The Mercury records his age as 71 at death whereas JHR 33 records it as 69.
35   Jefferies, F. (1835) The Gentlemans Magazine, Vols 158 – 159, p.440.
36   Northampton Mercury, Saturday 2nd March 1833.
37   NRO JHR 33.
38   ibid.
39   ibid.
40   ibid.
41   Leicestershire Mercury Saturday 07 November 1857
42   Stamford Mecury, Friday 27th June 1860.
43   Leicester Chronicle and Leicester Mercury, September 25th 1875.
44   Northampton Mercury Saturday 25th September 1875.
45   Northampton Mercury 1st June 1889.
46   Charity Commission - Reports of the Commissioners, 1831, Vol 3, p.187.
47   Bull, F. W. (1924) Jesus Hospital, and its founder, Owen Ragsdale, Northamptonshire Architectural Society. p.19.
48   NRO JHR 30.
49   NRO JHR 33.
50   Ibid.
51   NRO JHR 29.
52   NRO JHR 30.
53   Charity Commission - Reports of the Commissioners, 1831, Vol 3, p.187.
54   NRO JHR 40.
55   NRO JHR 30 "*Pd to Thomas Cutbert for garding the gate at Rowell fair*".
56   NRO JHR 20.

The Poor Men

The records within the collection generally refer to those admitted as 'the poor men'. Occasionally they are referred to as 'the men' and some records and much of the 19th century newspaper coverage the term 'inmates' is used. The use of the term 'resident' does not occur until the late 19th century.

Admission Requests

To be admitted to the hospital a poor man had to be nominated by one of the Governors who would then send a letter, often delivered by the prospective resident to the Principal. One hundred and six admission request letters have survived. One of the earliest of these is the request to admit Mr Cave in 1671.

Admission request from Mr Tresham 1671 (NRO JHR 23)

> *To Mr Wm Goode principall of Jesus Hospitall of Rothwell in ye county of Nothampton*
>
> *Wherᵉ as I have formerly granted unto George Cave of Newton in the said county, to come in to the said Hospitall, when my next turne shall be, I therefore desire you to receive him Accordingly, and to let him receive such priveleges As the other poor men usually have.*
> *In willness hereof I have set to my hand*
> *And seal this 30ᵗʰ of October 1671*
>
> *Tresham*

The 17th century requests did not follow a set format, each Governor wrote a short letter in his own hand and manner. That of Sir William Montague being the most official in nature as the request to admit William Alderman of Rothwell illustrates (below).

Admission request from Sir William Montague 1674 (NRO JHR 23)

> *To William Goode Gent ye principal of Jesus Hospitall in Rothwell in the county of Northampton.*
>
> *I William Montague of the Middle Temple London Esq the queenes Matˢ Attorney Generall And one Governors of Jesus Hospitall in Rothwell in the Countie of Northampton being certified from the said principal by his letter dated [illegible] of March last that Christopher Taylor one of the poor men of the said Hospital is dead, And that it is my turn to Present and Nominate a poor man to succeed him. I doe therefor by these presentes & present and nominate William Alderman of Rothwell aforesaid yeoman to be Admitted into the sayd Hospital Accordingly. Witness my hand and seal this second day of April Anno Dm 1674.*
> *W Montague*

Jesus Hospital

From 1702, probably as a result of changes made by Henry Dormer, Principal (1702-28) templates were set out for the appointment of Governors and assistants and probably the admission of poor men. There are clearly laid out templates for Governors and Assistants, and whilst no such template exists for the admission of poor men the letters requesting admission changed to be shorter formal orders to the principal to admit.

Admission request from E Palmer in standardised format. (NRO JHR 23)

> *To the Warden of Jesus Hospitall in Rowell*
>
> *You are hereby ordered to admit Thomas Bosworth of Brampton in Corby hundred into the hospitall at Rowell in the room and place of John Treeves lately deceased. And this shall be your warrent for soe doing, witness my hand the 8th day of*
> *August in the year 1709.*
>
> E Palmer

After 1725 the format of the admission requests changed slightly again as the example of a letter requesting admission for Richard Fisher shows:

Admission request from J Robinson (NRO JHR 23)

> *To Thomas Rice Principal of Jesus Hospital in Rowell in the county of Northampton.*
>
> *Whereas Richard Fisher a poor man of the said hospital is dead, you the said Principal are hereby required to admit Thomas Tomson a poor man of the parish of Cransley in the said county unto the said hospital in the room and place of the said Richard Fisher, It being my turn, as one of the Governors thereof, to appoint a poor man to be placed in the said hospital; and for your so doing this shall be sufficient warrant. Given under my hand this 29th day of July 1770.*
>
> J Robinson

Although it is clear that some form of template existed during the 18th century examples exist which show that the Governors did not always stick to a set format. Admission by warrant in this manner continued through to 1776. Thereafter admission proposal letters cease and it is unclear how the principal was instructed by each Governor in turn.

Alongside the requests to admit by a Governor there survive a few 17th century examples of where the Governor was petitioned to admit a poor man, in two instances, the petitioners commence the letter with their own personal appeal to the Governor whose turn to nominate came next. In both cases the second half of the letter is the petition of the vicar, churchwardens and others. The earliest of these two letters, which is transcribed overleaf, is dated 1679 and the other 1705.

Amongst the signatures supporting the petition in the earlier letter is that of the Principal, William Goode.

Undated 17th century petition of various persons to Sir Justinian Isham, governor, requesting the admission of John Parker senior of Rothwell to the hospital. (NRO JHR 23)

To the Right honble and most honord Sir Justian Isham Baron[tt]:
One of the Governors & trustees (amongst others) of Jesus Hospital in Rothwell als Rowell in the county of Northton.
    The humble petition of John Parker the elder of Rothwell ale Rowell aforesaid

                   Humbly sheweth to yo[r] Honor
That your Honors Petitioner is now because very aged indigent & infirm and not so well able to get his living by his hand labour as formerly And therefour humbly prayes yo[r] honbl favour to give your order to Mr Goode Mr: of the sayd hospitall to admit yo[r] honobl poor petitioner into the sd hospitall to be one of the poor members thereof in the rooms and place of one John Smith who is now newly dead that was one of the poor men of the sd hospitall, and that he yo[r] honobl Petitioner may have have and enjoy the lile benefitt and fitt in the says hospitall as he yt said John Smith had and as other the poor men of the says hospitall now have and enjoy, And yr honobl Petitioner as in all duty shall be ever obliged to pray for ye honoble health & happyness & ever remained yo[r] honobl most humble and obliged serv[t].

                              Parker Sen.

Wee whose names are hereunder written do hereby humbly certifie yo[r] honour that ye honobl Petitioner is a very honest aged indigent poor man and a good church man and in evry way fitly qualified for yo[r] honobl favour towards him in his petition above mentioned by granting ye honoble order to Mr Goode Mr of the sd Hospitall to direct him to admit yor honobl Petitioner into ye sd hospitall in the room and place of John Smith late deceased for whome we also pray yo[r] honoble favour therein & shall remain yo[r] hobnoble most humble & thankful sev[ts].

Andrew Lant
Hen Elkin
Willm Goode Mr of the says Hospital
Tho: Ponder
John Vialls
John Humphrey
James Blockley late vic[r] of Rothwell

The 1705 letter is signed by the vicar and eight of the leading figures of the town including the Lord of the Manor. At the bottom of the letter is a note from Sir William Montague dated June 1705 to the Principal to admit Francis Bennet.

Three other such requests from church wardens and leading towns folk exist, the earliest dates from October 1677 from Desborough parish requesting admission for Thomas Frankling, this was signed by Ferdinand Pulton, Lord of the Manor of Desborough and eleven other leaders of the town (below).

Petition of the people of Desborough to admit Thomas Frankling 1671.
(NRO JHR 23)

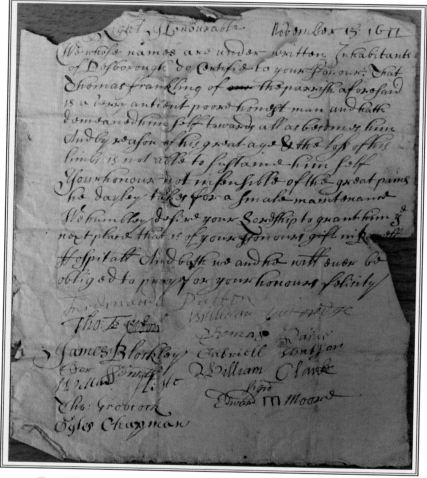

Thomas Frankling (or Franklin) was admitted to the hospital two years later in 1679, by Viscount Cullen of Rushton and although quite disabled remained there until his death in 1684. The other two similar requests all came from the vicar, church wardens and town leaders of Rothwell. In all cases where the parish assisted in a petition the person was very elderly and destitute, and therefore unsuitable for the parish workhouse and therefore likely to be a considerable burden on the parish rate. One of these, a request dated 22nd October 1723 to admit Libbous Driver is signed by 41 of the townsfolk.

Catchment Area

As noted previously the foundation as set out in the Letters Patent was to provide for up to 24 poor men who must have been resident 3 years before their election in Rothwell or one of the three hundreds of Rothwell, Corby and Orlingbury. The map below shows the villages within the three hundreds that made up the hospital's catchment area.

The catchment area of Jesus hospital (green shaded area) within the old county of Northamptonshire.

The men themselves were to be aged 40 years or over, they must have continuously resided in one of the villages in the three hundreds (above) for at least three years prior to admission and be free from infectious diseases etc., and be able to care for themselves and get to church unaided.

Jesus Hospital

In the period from 1665 to 1900 only three men were expelled from the hospital. These were: Edward Dolton from Ashley who was admitted in 1707 and expelled in 1709 because of "*Idiotism*", William Jackson of Dingley, admitted in 1709 who was expelled in 1711 because he became blind and could not guide himself, and William Peak of Middleton who was admitted in 1710 and expelled in 1716 for "*Idiotism*".

'Idiotism' was a term used alongside the term 'Imbecile' in the 17th and 18th centuries to describe a weakness of body and mind. Both of the persons expelled for 'idiotism' were in all likelihood people with an age related mental health problem such as dementia, which meant they could not meet the requirements of the hospital statute.

Most people who were admitted stayed resident until their death and other than those above only one person is known to have resigned his place. This was Thomas Meadows of Carleton, admitted in 1694, who resigned his place in order to enlist as a soldier in about 1702. The date of resignation is not given however, his room was allocated to John Easton of Rothwell in 1702.

Admissions

Admissions were noted in specific admission books from 1835. Prior to that time admissions had been recorded in the principals account book, a practice that appears to have been started by William Goode. Shortly after taking office Henry Dormer gathered together the hospital records and backdated the admissions in his account book. His backdated admissions list commences in 1665. The practice of including admissions in the principals account book was continued by his successors until separate admission books came into use. As a result there is a record of most admissions to Jesus Hospital from 1665 onwards. A list of all the identified admissions from 1665 to 1900 is included as appendix 1.

From when the hospital first opened through to 1768 when a new house was built for the principal the hospital was residence to twelve poor men, the Principal and a nurse. With the building of the new house the number of residents increased to sixteen. In 1833 the two front wings were rebuilt and extended thereafter a second house was built in 1840 for the nurse. These alterations and extensions allowed for an increase in the number of residents to twenty-six.

On admission the poor man paid an admission fee initially this was one penny, but with the addition of further rooms being added in 1768 this rose to four pence.[1] It appears as though this fee acted as an entry fine the entry being into the Society of Jesus Hospital at Rothwell.

Pension

Owen Ragsdale willed that the poor men should receive a pension paid quarterly.[2] By 1671 the men and the nurse were paid twenty one shillings per quarter. This amount remained constant until 1724 when it was increased by one shilling per quarter, with a further smaller increase in 1796.[3] In 1828 the pension of every man was £15. 12s. 0d. per year. In that year the Charity Commission recommended an increase of £2. 8s. 0d. be given to each man, bringing the total pension (the charity commission referred to the pension as 'Alms' in their report) to £18 per year for each man.[4]

In addition to the pension the residents including the nurse received an additional payment on 7th August and at Christmas. In 1828 this stood at 2s. 6d. per man (5s. per year). This additional money may not have been given in cash as various account entries describe it as being for 'their feast', suggesting an organised communal meal on the founders day and at Christmas.

For breaches of the statutes or other misdemeanours the men could have their pension reduced, for example, "*5 shill. is taken of from Braybrook this quarter for a misdemeanour*",[5] and "*Thomas Cox & John Dextyer additional payment of four shillings is to be stop[d] for lying out of the Hospitall & pretending to vote for Members of Parliam[t] for this Conty till our further order to ye contrary*".[6]

These was more extreme than most fines, for example an offence of not attending church or prayers usually resulted in a fine of one penny unless the person was a re-offender in which case he was brought before the governors who then decided his fate. On June 8th 1723 one of the men, James Loveday, who had been resident since June 1716, was brought before Justice Robinson for some misdemeanour. The Principal appears to have taken out a warrant to get him to court.[7] The reason for his court appearance is unknown. James continued to reside at the hospital until his death in 1731. The cost of the warrant and getting him to court was 2s. which was presumably deducted from his pension.

Clothing

From the beginning the residents (Principal, Men and Nurse) were provided with a uniform. In the case of the men this was in the 17th century a cloak, suit and socks, and probably a cap, which is referred to in the original statutes. The cloak and suit[8] was made of a blue cloth which was manufactured elsewhere and made up by local tailors. It is not known where the cloth was manufactured but in the early 1700s Henry Dormer recorded a journey to Market Harborough to collect the cloth and a later accounts record it being collected from Kettering. The cost of a new set of clothes per man was fifteen shillings per person in 1671.

Initially new clothes were given every three years. By 1671 this had changed to become a new set every two years.[9] A new resident entering the hospital in between the period when new uniforms were issued could not expect a new set of clothes. This is clearly set out in a summary of the annual outgoings made in June 1789 which states: *When the Principal dies, or removes, the last new coat and waistcoat are left at the hospital for the next principal; and when any old man die, his last coat, waistcoat and stockings are left for the next that comes in.*[10]

So, on entering his room the new resident inherited the suite of clothes of the former resident until such time as a new suite of clothes was issued, irrespective of fit or condition. This may have caused problems in the early 17th century when the men received a new set of clothes once every three years, or every two years later that century and by the early 18th century this appears to have been recognised for the Governors allowed new clothing annually. A number of vouchers / receipts survive from local tailors making up the clothes.

The socks which appeared in the accounts of the 1670s were not being provided by the early 1700s and had been replaced by stockings in the late 1700's and unusually there is no mention of hats being provided. Most almshouses of Tudor origin which provided a uniform also provided a cloth hat. At Jesus Hospital we find references to "caps" in the early 18th century records.

Bill of Mr Robinson, Tailor, for making 16 suites of clothing for the men and a suite of clothes for the principal, 1772. (NRO JHR 66)

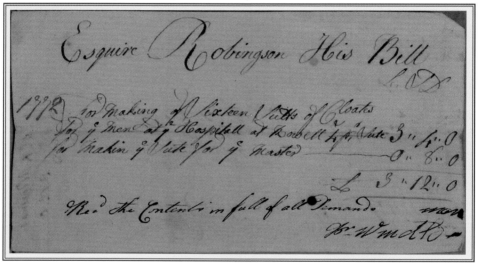

By the late 18th century the uniform issued by the governors changed. The Tudor cloak was replaced by a blue coat and in addition to the shirt each man received a waistcoat and both of these were replaced annually as is shown in the accounts for 7th August 1784, 5th August 1785 and 12th August 1786, when Mr William Alderman, Taylor, of Rothwell billed the hospital for the clothes he had made. In 1787 we find a payment to William Alderman for stockings for the Principal and the men, as well as for the purchase of cloth. From their pension it is likely that the men had to provide the rest of their clothing such as underwear, footwear, trousers and hat. This may explain the variation in dress seen in late Victorian photographs.

From a bill of 1766 we can see that the blue cloth used to make the mens clothes was purchased in 48 yard lengths. Occasionally metal coat buttons were also ordered, 12 dozen in 1764, along with canvas tape and 16 dozen buttons in 1772. In 1764 the cloth cost £7 16s: 0d. By 1766 this had risen to £8: 7s: 9d. In 1772, probably in response to the rising cost of making the suites, the cloth ordered was Grey rather than Blue although there is no formal record of a change being made to the colour in any of the surviving records.

By 1798 Hugh King of Kettering was the tailor employed to make the clothes for the hospital and the price for undertaking the work fixed at four shillings per suite for as long as he held the contract. However, by 1815 the cost of cloth and wages was rising and Hugh King was unable to make the clothes at the fixed price without himself making a loss. He therefore wrote to the Governors requesting an increase in the allowance to make up the men's uniforms (below).[11]

The letter of Hugh King to the Governors 1815. (NRO JHR 53)

> *Gentlemen*
>
> *I humbly request you will take the following circumstance into consideration - having as Taylor made the clothes for the men at Rowell Hospital for the space of about 17 or 18 years - and the allowance per suit being but four shillings and taking into account the great difference in the times since the sum of 4s per suit was first fixed - I confess Gentlemen that I find it quite inadequate at all - and I shall esteem it a great favour if you Gentlemen will candidly consider the case and allow something more per suit. I have I hope I may venture to say done and I am determined ever to do the utmost in my power to give satisfaction to both parties - I must however through myself upon your clemency hoping you will deliberately consider the difficulties of the times and the present high price of journeyman's wages in contrast with the period above alluded to.*
>
> I am Gentlemen
your most obed^t and
Very humble serv^t
Hugh King
>
> *Rowell Augst 29th 1815*

Hugh King's letter failed to move the Governors for the accounts show no increase in payments for the clothing being made by Hugh until 1828 and then an increase of only one shilling per suit. At the same time as Hugh King was providing the suits for the residents the accounts show that John Adams was providing the stockings and other items. In 1822 this amounted to a further twenty-four pounds per year.

In March 1864 the provision of clothes and a variety of other items was put out to tender by the agents acting on behalf of the Governors. The invitation to tender was issued in a range of newspapers across the country, including the Northampton Mercury.[12] From the mid 1700s we start to find entries in the accounts for shoes, for example on 8th November 1777 the accounts show *"Paid Will'm Vialls shoemakers bill"* of £5 and on 31st July 1831 the accounts show that James and William Goode were paid £4. 10s each for shoes.

Fuel and warmth

Whilst the Principal, Nurse and Poor Men all had their own bed chambers, these had no fire place or other source of heating. Only the common halls had fires and these were used both for cooking and warmth.

Letter to the Governors from William Hammond and Richard Greavy agreeing to provide wood as per contract and confirming to types of wood they will provide. (JHR 48)

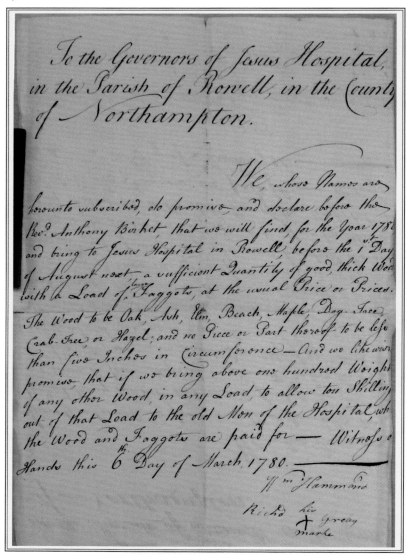

From the earliest accounts it is clear that wood was purchased for each of the halls. Contracts with those providing the wood are clear that the wood had to be hard wood. Coal was not used until 1713 when new grates were made and coal ordered. By the mid 17th century as well as hard wood logs Clots or Clats were also being purchased as fuel. These were the wood by products of the tanning process. In 1773 a bill refers to five loads of 'Billet' wood being delivered (a billet being a term for a chunk of wood). Whilst no document specifying what was to be supplied as part of a contract for wood, a declaration in response to such a specification survives from 1780 and this clearly states the types of wood to be supplied.[13] Wood and coal remained the chief fuel used at the hospital for both cooking and keeping warm (only the shared halls had fires) until 1889 when Gas was installed.

Food and Drink

No records survive which give an indication of the meals eaten by the men living at the hospital. The hospital had its own brew house and was therefore able to produce its own ale for the men to drink. Brewing was still being undertaken in 1784, for on July 26th in that year a new mash vat and tubs were purchased at £. 4s. 6d. The principals accounts only give general expenditure on the hospital property and other items necessary for the functioning of the hospital, e.g. Messengers, it is therefore possible that the men were required to provide for themselves from their pension rather than buying, cooking and eating communally. The likely exceptions to this were on August 7th, Founders Day (also Corpus Christi) and Christmas Day when extra money was provided for 'their feast'. This suggests that on those occasions the men ate communally.

Water was provided from a well until mains water came to the town in the late 19th century. This had a pump which had leather seals and was frequently in need of repair.

Work and Daily Life

The statutes required that *"The Principall, poor and sick men shall every Sunday, Holyday and festival days throughout the year at the beginning of the morning and evening prayer, asemble themselves in the said Hospitall and then go to the church together"* (see Appendix 1.). It is not clear which festival days were observed other than the Founders Day (7th August) and Christmas Day. In the early post medieval period the church still observed most if not all the medieval religious feast days. King Charles I largely supported the existing rituals and festivals and therefore it is likely that the men were required to attend the church for morning and evening prayers at Good Friday, Easter Sunday and Trinity Sunday (the parish church is dedicated to the Holy Trinity) to name but a few. The number of religious observances was probably lessened during the period of the civil war, the long parliament being determined to do away with the echoes of the Catholic past, but most of the feast days returned after the restoration when the decisions of the long parliament were declared null and void.

On Sundays and feast days the men gathered in the courtyard and as the last chimes of the church bell rang out they processed behind the Principal into the church where they had their own pew. The statutes required them to go two by two behind the principal. On such days they were required to attend church for both morning and evening prayers. At certain times in the year the men were required to clean the South aisle and the founders tomb, polishing the brass

99

inscription plates and praying for his soul. As noted previously failure to attend prayers or church resulted in a fine.

On the days when the men were not required to attend the parish church, thy were required to attend prayers in the hospital prayer hall when the bell was rung. We are not told when this occurred but it is likely that it was early in the day. A prayer or poem of religious nature survives in a bundle of vouchers which may have been used at such prayer sessions.

Prayers in the Prayer Hall as depicted in The Graphic Magazine 1888

The fine of 1d for neglect of prayers appears to have been a universal one in the 18th century. For the same fine was levied in a number of the almshouses noted whilst undertaking research. In 1711 John Fisher failed to wear the blue uniform as provided and may have been fined. He was taken before the Governors and on the threat of expulsion made the following promise:

John Fisher's Promise (JHR 28)

I hereby faithfully promise to conform in all things to the rules and orders of the hospital in Rowell, in particular to be compelled in attending prayers in the hospital and at church, to be resident in the hospital and to wear the blue coat allowed and appointed. And do all other things required in that station. In willingness whereof I have set my hand hereunto this 2d day of June 1711.

The breaking of any of the statutes resulted in a fine being levied in the first instance. Clearly in some instances a meeting with the Governors and if unrepentant, removal if the resident continued to break the rules.

Founders Day

Owen Ragsdale died on 1st December 1591 and yet the hospital has always celebrated its founders day on 7th August, the religious feast of Corpus Christi. In the 17th century Corpus Christi was often known as 'Jesus Day' and the association between 'Jesus Day' and the dedication of the hospital is the likely reason for this.

Daily Activity

Little is recorded about the daily activities or work undertaken by the men. Where work is recorded it usually relates to maintenance of the property. Examples include that of John Parker in 1691 who undertook three days work, which was recorded as: *"one was for going to the wood, and two was for hedging and faggotting of the wood"*,[14] 20th February 1718 when the accounts record, *"Pd to our men, for making a saw pit. Levelling ye ground where ye trees grew and filling the sawpit in again"*,[15] and on 15th December 1720 *"Pd to our Old men that weed ye quick and repaired the top of ye Pails with thorns, the bottom wth earth"*.

Each resident had a small vegetable garden immediately behind the hospital main building and it is likely that some of the day was taken up by the maintenance of the vegetable patch as well as cooking, making beer and cleaning for themselves. South of the hospital also stood the hospital orchard and in the autumn the men would have picked apples and at other times pruned and generally maintained the orchard. The older men able to do less probably occupied themselves in conversation sitting on seating in the courtyard or in the orchard.

The hospital only had fireplaces in the communal halls and so life for the residents in winter was tough. To add to problems of low temperatures occasionally pests such as Rats and Mice needed dealing with, for example in April 1710 the accounts show a payment of eight pence to a man (unnamed) for killing rats.[16]

Healthcare

As noted in the introduction, while Jesus Hospital is called a hospital it was to all intents and purposes an almshouse or retirement home for the indigent poor and the healthcare that would be expect to be given now in a place called a hospital was almost none existent. Generally medicines were provided for when a person became unwell and accordingly there are references in the accounts to apothecaries providing medicines. Examples include: Oct 18th 1719 *"Pd ye apothecaries bill for ye Hospitalls use 5s. 10."*[17] May 1720 *"Pd to Mr Baker of*

Kettering for Apothecaries stuffe used by Gam: Gervis when his shoulder was broke in a fall 5s.".[18]

Less often noted are references to doctors, often called 'Surgeons' being called to attend to the residents. From the 18th century the following examples are to be found in the accounts, October 1712 *"pd for Jonath: Barker bleeding and for Wm Peakes physick"* bleeding was usually carried out by a doctor, 1722 *"Apr: 10. Paid Will: Belshare Bill of Physick"* and 1723 *"Aug 20 Pd to a Docter that help'd T. Bosworth.* An earlier account, April 1710 records both money paid to an apothecary named Martins and a bone setter.[19]

In an account entry of 6th August 1708 a doctor is named, the entry reads "*Mr Cogan his bill for ye sick man ye Apothic"*. Mr Cogan being a surgeon in Rothwell in the early 18th century.

By the early 1800's a doctor appears to have been engaged to attend the residents as necessary and from 25th March 1823 a surgeons bill survives. In the 18th century a doctor's visit typically cost the hospital 5s. Assuming a similar cost in the early 19th century this suggests about 21 visits over the course on the year.

When someone became gravely ill the Principal paid for watchers to be at the persons bedside day and night and in the day wash the patient. An example of this occurs in the accounts for 26th March 1749, [20] where it is written, *Pd for Fletcher in his illness watchers sitting up & cleaning who was very much out of order.* Fletcher, it is recorded died the following day.

Death and Burial

When a resident died the Hospital ensured that he was buried. A couple of 18th century memoranda in the accounts give an indication of the expenses of a funeral but lack any detail about where a person was buried, for example in the accounts for midsummer quarter 1703 we find the following lines:

July 31	*Paid for Bread & Ale for John Tongue's funeral rites*	*3*	*0*
August 4	*Also paid 3 watchers that waited on him Serverall nights, & and for their Affidavits*	*4*	*2*
August 6	*Paid to ye Parson for his buriall*	*1*	*0*
	And also to the Clerk for his dues	*0*	*8*
Septem 27	*Paid the Duty to ye Queen, for John Tongue*	*4*	*0*
	And also for a shroud to burry him in	*3*	*6*

From a single sheet of paper in a bundle is a more detailed cost of a funeral (see overleaf).[21] Clearly when a man died at least part of the cost of his funeral was taken from any outstanding pension money, with the hospital making up the balance.

Most of the men who entered the hospital probably died a peaceful death however from the Stamford Mercury 20th Jan 1905, we learn of one resident who

Cost of Richard Cook's Funeral May 1770

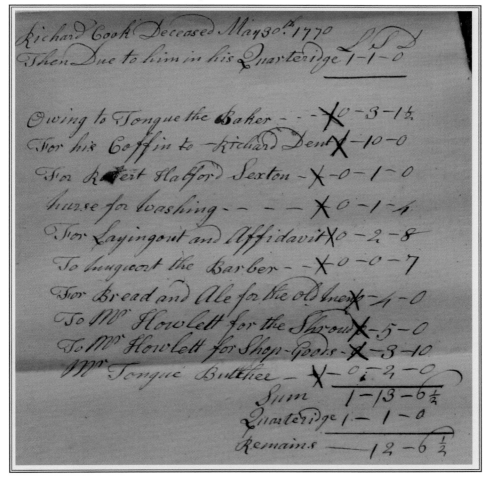

died by less peaceful means. The story highlights the potential problems faced in years past when the only light available was candle light. The resident was a Mr George Chamberlain, who was aged 84. His inquest was told how he woke in the early hours of the morning and in the cold lit a match to see where he was going. He dropped the match into his bed covers which caught light. Another resident heard his cries for help and got him out of the room. The bed clothes were burnt through and the room full of smoke. He died the following day. The coroner concluded that he died from bronchitis from exposure to the cold and the inhalation of smoke.

In its early years the hospital appears to have had its own area for burial of its residents, possibly a section of the churchyard for in the 1700s there are references to "burying place cleaning".[22]

Jesus Hospital

Picture of the residents and staff taken circa 1890. The Principal, probably Thomas Lovell, is seated in the centre, the two nurses are to the right of the picture.

Notes

[1]   NRO JHR 31 note in the accounts of 15th August 1768.
[2]   NRO JHR 29.
[3]   NRO JHR 30.
[4]   Charity Commission - Reports of the Commissioners, 1831, Vol 3, p.187.
[5]   NRO JHR 30 Note in account for the period between the feast of St Thomas to Lady Day 1725.
[6]   NRO JHR 30 Note in the Accounts 1750.
[7]   NRO JHR 35.
[8]   This was not a suite in the modern sense, but a set of clothes to be worn under the cloak.
[9]   NRO JHR 35.
[10] NRO JHR 40.
[11] NRO JHR 53.
[12] Northampton Mercury, Saturday 26th March 1864.
[13] NRO JHR 47.
[14] NRO JHR 27.
[15] NRO JHR 30.
[16] NRO JHR 30 *"Paid a man for killing the Rotts at Hospitall"*
[17] ibid.
[18] ibid.
[19] ibid *"Paid to the Bonn-Setter; & other charges when he put his Legg out coming home"* (the resident is not named).
[20] NRO JHR 31.
[21] NRO JHR 60.
[22] NRO JHR 30.

The Accounts

Hospital accounts in the collection at Northamptonshire Record Office comprise of six account books numerous abstracts a bundles of vouchers, invoices for goods and services from 1671 to 1913. In all of the account books the pages are not numbered and therefore references to the accounts can only be given by book reference and date. For the most part the same is true of other financial items in the Jesus Hospital collection, for example, there are a number of bundles of 'vouchers' (small invoices, receipts and notes) kept by the Principal which were used to prove to the treasurer that the accounts were correct. When the collection was catalogued these individual slips of paper were not individually marked alphabetically or numerically, so again only the bundle reference and a date can be used for reference.

Four of the six account books were those kept by the Principal's and submitted to the treasurer and usually two other Governors. These usually contain the signatures of the governors at the bottom of each quarter years page along with some note indicating the approval and passing of the account. As time went on the accounts became slightly more sophisticated such that by the early 1700s income from rents is set out on the left page and outgoings of the hospital on the right page. In the 1600s these were given on the same page. Two of the books [1] ranging from 1835 to 1913, were the Principal's working copies and list out the payments line by line for the payments to each man and contain other items such as a list of the parishes in the hundreds. Whereas the main account books give one line for pension and stipend payments and set out the income and outgoings (receipts and disbursements) of the Principals.

During the tenure of Henry Dormer as principal we have a period in which two identical accounts appear. On taking up office he continued the account book of his predecessor William Goode. On purchasing a new account book he then re-entered every line of his accounts from the day he took office thus giving a duplicate set of entries. His new account book also contains lists of Governors, Assistants, Principals and Poor Men identified from his own research into the hospital documents in the early 1700s.

It is unclear whether the treasurers ever kept any accounts. If they did they have not survived and the only record we have of any treasurer accounts are contained in two account books where between the accounts of different Principal's there are treasurers entries. These books are JHR30 which contains Treasurers accounts for 1746-1749, along with the accounts of tithes Rothwell and Thorpe Underwood for 1751-1763, and JHR31 which contains Treasurer's accounts for 1766 -1810 and bank statement 1810-14.

The earliest account book [2] covers the period 1671-1702 and has details of allowances and repairs for that period. In The accounts run from the beginning of September in one calendar year to end of August in the following year, and the quarters are referred to as Midsummer (April - June) Michaelmas (July -

September), Michaelmas falls on 29th September, Christmas (October - December) and Lady Day (January - March), Lady Day itself being 25th March. The following year (1672/73) the accounts were signed off at the end of the Michaelmas quarter (27th October 1673) and the balance accepted at that time, i.e. over five quarters rather than the usual four. From then onwards the accounts were signed off at the end of August. The 17th century accounts are usually approved by two or three Governors. However occasionally they are signed off by only one, usually George Tresham of Newton. In response to this Lord Cullen wrote to the Principal, William Goode on 9th November 1681:

> *Mr Goode you may pray Mr Tresham or one of the rest of Governors to pass your account now & at any time hereafter and I will joyne with him on the signing and allowing of them as formerly done & remayned*

> *Rushton Novembr*   *You assured friend*
> *the 9th 1681*   *Cullen*

It is clear that in the 17th century the accounts did not always balance, for example at the end of the Michaelmas quarter for 1680 the three governors (Lord Cullen, Sir Lewis Palmer and George Tresham) appended the following note, "*Examined this account and disbursements this quarter there remains due to the hospital Thirty eight pounds two shillings and tenn pence and allowed by us*". The Governors presumably expecting the principal to recover the missing amount on their behalf. From this point onwards the layout of the accounts change so that receipts and disbursements are on different pages. By 1681 the deficit had increased to £41. 8s. 8d., and a note regarding this is made at the top of the receipts page. From an entry of Midsummer quarter 1689 it appears that at least some of the arrears was Mr Gascoigne's rent and in that quarter a Mr Thew, possibly Gascoigne's tenant, paid £7. 10s. 0d. towards the outstanding arrears. A further note in Michaelmas 1689 states that a further payment on account of arrears was due and that Sir Roger [Norwich] had taken Gascoigne's bond to pay off [the remaining?] part of the arrears in January 1691. In 1689 Gascoigne vacated the property, at which time he still owed £42 in rent to the hospital. The hospital was clearly unable to recover its debt as the debt transferred with the tenancy in that year. The new tenant was Mr Ponder, who took over on 16th December 1689. Mr Ponder took over Gascoigne's debt and paid extra in some quarters to try to clear the debt but despite this he still owed £31. 00s. 11d. on 9th October 1705[3].

In receiving rents and other income on time, and in keeping the accounts balanced the Governors held the principal responsible and possibly due to his increasing frailty, and possibly as a means of recovering outstanding monies, William Goode appears to have not given the men their dues. As a result in 1691 they collectively wrote to complain to the Governors (see page 107).

From the complaint it appears that the Principal with held the first quarter's pension for new entrants, charged the men 8d for their hospital coat, withheld

Complaints of the Poor Men 1691

August ye 3

This is an honest and trues complaint of ye poore Hospitall men

John Parker saith he stopped when he came in the first quarter thirteen shillings
& six pence and he stopped one shilling and four pence for two coates and he
owes me for three days worke one was for gooing to the wood and two was for
hedging and faggoting of the wood

£0 – 16s – 10d

Edward Dunsmore came in ye 30th day January and he gave him nothing the first
quarter and he stopped 8 pence for my coate.

William Gonnalls when he came in the first quarter he stopped ten shillings and six
pence and the next quarter he stopped twoo shillings and six pence and this last
quarter he stopped one shilling and eleven pence for my coat.

£0 – 15s – 11d

Thomas Guess saith when he came he stopped too shillings and six pence for my
coate and he owes me for going to Owld twice and he owes for mowing the orchard
twice one shilling

£0 – 7s – 0d

Nicolis Ward saith he stopped eight pence for his coate

Joshua Are saith he stopped him sixteen shillings when he camin and he stopped one
shilling and eleven pence for my coate Christmas quarter he gave me but sixe
shillings and the Lady Day quarter last past he gave me nothing.
John Dunsmore saith when came in saith he stopped ten shillings

Thomas Newborne saith when he came in he stopped him five shillings and he
stopped for his coate one shilling and four pence

£0 – 6s – 4d

John Roase saith he stopped when he came in fiffteen shillings

£0 – 15s – 0d

In the year 1691

And he stopped one year ten shillings a hall of our wood money which is two pounds

£2 – 0s – 0d

and too years after he stopped every hall 8 pence a year which is

£0 – 5s – 4d

and this year he hath paid us nothing which we should had the first May

£6 – 2s – 8d

What we ought to have a year is	*£54 – 0s – 0d*
and for the woman that looks after us	*£03 – 0s – 0d*
and at St Thomas for the four halls we are to have	*£1 – 10s – 0d*
and Jaysuses Day	*£1 – 4s – 0d*
And a new coate for every man onerlie in too year	*£7 – 0s – 0d*

wages when they were sent out to work, reduced the fuel for the fires in the halls and in other cases reduced the quarterly pensions.

Note in the Accounts witnessed by Henry Goode 1700. (NRO JHR 29)

> *The Acts of Rowel Hospitall were examined and stated June 25. 1700 & then*
> *it appeared to us that there was due from Mr Goode to ye Hospitall at Lady*
> *Day last year the sum of £71: 11s: 11d.*
> *Witness Henry Goode*
>
> *Sworn and allowed by us*
> *J Isham*   *W. Montague*
> *John Allicocke*   *E Norwich*

That William Goode was becoming quite frail is evident from both the accounts and other documents, which by 1690 become increasingly scrappy and from his son's letter to the Governors when he was unable to attend a meeting. The failure of the Principal to keep accounts could result in their expulsion from the hospital and appears likely that in order to avoid this event the Reverend Henry Goode, vicar of Weldon and son of William Goode may have taken on the task of producing the accounts. Changes in the neatness of handwriting and layout of the accounts from 1695 suggest that the Rev. Henry Goode was producing the quarterly accounts for his father from that year. This view is supported by a note made by the examining Governors on June 25th 1700 witnessed by Henry Goode:

When William Goode died in 1702 his accounts remained seventy-two pounds in arrears and from the Michaelmas account page there is a memorandum stating that his son Henry paid this in full (overleaf)

This is the first note of income to the hospital being used to generate money through interest in the accounts. A further note at the bottom of the page states: *"The sums of moneys in Mr Jo: Hortons hands, to put out to Interest is 75 pounds delivered to him the 9th day of October 1705."* This money was used as mortgage loan money for two properties in Rothwell (see property), thirty five pounds being lent to Widow Reynold and subsequently Thomas Hayes and the other forty pounds being lent to Robert Parker. The interest on the loan to Widow Reynold yielding just over 14% interest over the eighteen month period. From an abstract in a bundle of vouchers[4] we can see that the Governors were using spare revenue as loan money from at least 1605.

By 1715 the hospital had three tenants and three others to whom money had been lent .Those renting were Thomas Ponder, renting land in Rothwell and Orton, John Chapman renting the farm and cottages at Old, and Richard Vialls, renting *"2 lands, 2 leys & 2 pastures"* at Orton. Those paying interest on loans to the hospital were Joseph Johnson of Haslebeech who had borrowed £50 at 6% interest,

Note in accounts following William Goode's death

> *Mem^d that the said Mr Henry Goode paid ye said sum of seventy two pounds thirteen shillings & six pence & half penny (mentioned on ye other side) into ye hands of Sir Justinian Isham Bart. one of the Govern^{rs} of Jesus Hospital abt Xmas last & allsoe the further sum of one pound seventeen shillings & two pound half penny for interest of ye same, And the said £2 Justinian Isham did thos ninth day of October Anno Domini One thousand seven hundred and five att a general meeting of the Governors of the said hospital by their appointment pay ye same being in the whole seventy four pounds eighteen shillings & two pounds into ye hands of John Horton of Kettering to plan out with interest for ye benefit of ye said Hospitall.*

John Freenman, who had borrowed £40 at 5% interest and Madd^m (Madam) Allicock of Loddington, which the accounts state *"Rents 20 pounds"*. The interest rate is unspecified.

The above is taken from a single sheet which summarises the income and expenditure in 1715 when Henry Dormer was Principal. When he took up his post as Principal he stated a new account book and on the first page below the receipts for 1703 we find a more detailed section on interest moneys for 1722:

After Robert Parker died the interest on his loan was paid directly to the

Henry Dormers Account Book - Interest Money 1722. (NRO JHR30)

> *Interest Moneys 1722*
> *Belonging to JESUS HOSPITALL*
>
> | | li | |
> |---|---|---|
> | *Joseph Johnson of Hasselbitch rents* | 50: | *at 6 per cent* |
> | *Security from 7 of January* | | *Interest - 3^l* |
> | *John Freeman of Gumbley rents* | 40: | *at 5 per cent* |
> | *Security from 18 of May* | | *Interest - 2^l* |
> | *Thomas Parker of Rowell rents* | 30: | *at 5 per cent* |
> | *Security is from the first of Novem* | | *Interest - 30^s* |
> | *Gilles Chapman of Deasburow* | 20: | *at 5 per cent* |
> | *Security is from 6 of august* | | *Interest - 20s* |
> | *Mr Horton of Kettering has in his hand* | 20: | *at 5 per cent* |
> | *He has paid interest at 9th in ye Co* | | *Interest - 20^s* |

Principal, the amount being £1. 0s. 0d. per half year. The accounts for 1707 also show another person paying interest to the Principal, a Luke Davise was paying interest of £2. 11s. 0d. On a loan of £35. His name only appears the once suggesting that this was a loan over one year. In 1708 another person, Thomas Hayes, was recorded as paying interest half yearly of £1. 0s. 0d. Along with widow Parker.

From the various documents we can see that the Governors provided Mortgages and Loans to at least 29 parties (individuals and couples etc.) between 1605 - 1742. Where the interest charged is stated it is clear that throughout the 18th century the interest rate charged was typically five percent per annum, or as the loan to Joseph Johnson of Haselbeech shows occasionally higher. In the accounts the balance between the income and the disbursements or outgoings is referred to as 'the hospital stock'. In 1705 this stood at £31: 0s: 11d. excluding any money loaned out, this rose to £32: 13s: 1d. by 1706. For some of the loans conditions were probably imposed and while no record of these survive we find the occasional reference in the accounts such as that in Michaelmas 1716 when on top of his interest payment of 11s. He paid an additional 11s. for neglecting the garden. The text reads:

From - Madd: Allicocks ½ years interest and six weeks near,　　　*0 -11 -0*

Should 5 little Ashtrees yt grew in ye Garden　　　*0 -11 -0*

References to Mr John Horton in the accounts suggests that money was given to him (put out to interest) and he either loaned it to someone and they paid the interest directly to the hospital or, he invested it. Occasional references in the accounts alongside interest payments received from him show the amount investested with him, described as 'in his hands', was usually about £20.

A treasurers note of yearly revenue of July 1726 shows that from money out at interest and from rents the hospital income was £210, the majority of which came from interest (overleaf).

Clearly the treasurer was looking at how best to increase the Hospital profits, whether by the purchase of land and subsequent rental, or by continuing to put the money out to interest. Money continued to be put out to interest and an abstract of 1736 [5] shows that in that year the Governors had £272 out at interest and £130 income from rents. By 1789 the amount out at interest had risen substantially such that the hospital had £1200 put out to interest at an average of three percent, yielding £36 per year.

In 1789 a summary of the yearly income and outgoings of the hospital along with an inventory of furniture was made from this we can see the overall income, which amounted to £308. 2s. 8d.[6]

By the early 19th century the Hospital treasurer appears to have started to move the hospital's money away from mortgage investments to Console's. Named after the Consolidation of the Nation Debt in 1743, Console's or Consolidated Annuities became was a form of gilt bond and a major form of Government borrowing after 1751. Organisations such as Jesus Hospital would invest their money with the Government and accordingly paid interest on the amount loaned to them. Clearly

Income from rents and interest 1726. (NRO JHR 36)

The Revenue of Rowel Hospital besides the money yt out at int is	*111:*	*00:*	*0*
The annual charge with ye Addition of 16s per man wch makes 9^l: 12^s p An comes to	*115:*	*03:*	*0*
If we buy Land abt ye value of 7^l p An I will make ye rent	*118:*	*00:*	*0*
But then I hope we shall have a pretty deal of money left			
<div align="center">*Money out at Interest*</div>			
Now waged with A Houghton			
Joseph Johnson of Haslebeech	*50:*	*00:*	*0*
John Freeman of Gumley	*40:*	*00:*	*0*
Joh Parker of Rowel	*30:*	*00:*	*0*
Giles Chapman of Desborough	*20:*	*00:*	*0*
John Langley of Harrowden	*20:*	*00:*	*0*
Jos Hall of Little Bowden	*30:*	*00:*	*0*
Pd by me to Mr Horton to put out	*20:*	*00:*	*0*
Out at June 20th to be put out	*210:*	*00:*	*0*
N.B. July 11th 1726 in Dormans hands when he has Recd all Midsum Qtr	*33:*	*01:*	*3*
N.B. I paid Mr Horton ye aforesd 20l at our meeting at Rowel July 11th 1726.			

a much safer investment than loaning to individuals. From 1757 the rate was reduced to three percent and thereafter often known as reduced annuities. The hospital records show investments in reduced annuities in this period. For example in the account of October 29th 1789 is a note *"Ordered by the Governors that treasurer purchase in the 3% cont £150"* and again on November 20th 1790 and identical note is to be found for another investment of £150. Again the 1st January 1795 the Governors authorised the Treasurer, William Dolben, to purchase a further six hundred and fifty pounds in reduced annuities. On the following page another note states that in the treasurers hands was the sum of £606. 10s. 3d, interest on loans at four percent had yielded £18. 5s. 0d and £1350 was in reduced annuities, the income from which was £40. 10s. 0d.

Further notes indicate that by 5th November 1800 the Hospital had three thousand pounds invested in annuities bringing in £90 in interest per year. Two other sets of reduced annuities, one for three hundred pounds and another for £3000 were by 1802 bringing in £9 and £90 respectively. All of the annuities being held on the governors behalf by Messers Hoare and Company of London.

In 1809/10 the role of treasurer transferred from William Dolben to Allen Edward Young. Young wrote a number of letters regarding the Hospital's investments and issues with property tax which will be discussed later. From a letter dated 6th September 1809, from William Dolben to A. E. Young regarding a meeting of Governors at which Dolben was absent we can see that the hospital stocks at that time were in Dolben's name as treasurer. Every time a Governor changed the new trustees had to complete a power of attorney in the new names and submit it to Messrs Hoare's. For example, on 8th October 1818 Henry Hoare's wrote to A.E. Young enclosing a power of attorney to be signed so that they could act on behalf of the hospital and the £5,987. 12s. 3d in annuities invested at that time.[7]

Because of a lack of treasurers accounts it is not possible to identify the amount of investment in stock made by the Governors between 1818 and 1830. According to a Charity Commission query in 1856 (see Charity Commission p.113) we see that the income from stock was £10,409 in 1830 but had reduced to £1,000 by 1856.

Dispute over Property Tax

On taking up the role of Treasurer, A. E. Young appears to have noted that the hospital had paid too much in property tax which he set about retrieving. In so doing he sought the advice of the Hospital broker, Henry Hoare who in 1810 advised, *"The application for the recovery of the property tax must come from the Trustees or we should have been happy to have what was required on the occasion"*.

Young had first written to the tax office on 26th April 1809 and although a copy of this letter has not survived the reply from the tax office has. The property tax was being charged on the Hospital lands at Old, then in the occupation of Thomas Norton. The letter states that an affidavit had not been received by the tax office and therefore it was not possible to suspend collection of the duty. Property tax was charged of private properties and where rental income was used for charitable purposes it became non taxable.

Letters passed between A. E. Young and the Office of Taxes between 1809 and 1814 when a reply was received indicating following an investigation by a special commission, a refund was not possible. It is clear from the correspondance that then followed, that A. E. Young was not going to accept that the Trustees could not be refunded. Initially he appears to have written to Mr Winter requesting the names of the special commission board members.

This information request was refused and Young accordingly challenged the special commission judgement, which was met by a response from a Mr Watkins who indicated that a refund could not be made after the accounts were closed, on the orders of the Treasury. Young then communicated with the treasury and on 26th November 1816 Young received a letter with attached form inviting him to state the rent charge claim for the years 1809 - 1811, which upon receipt would be duly attended to. The form was obviously completed and returned for on 5th April 1817 a certificate of exemption was received on to which Young wrote to say that £10. 10s. 0d had been received for each of the three years.

Charity Commission

In 1830 the Charity Commission reviewed the charity. In 1833 it asked further questions of the Governors who convened a special meeting in the Principals house on 25th January. Statements of finance and other documents were sent to the commission in response to the letter they had received[8]. It did the same in 1857 when discrepancies were noted between the declarations. The Commission then wrote to the trustees to say that they were to be subject to further scrutiny.

While not all of the correspondence has survived, it is clear that the issue was with the Charity Commission involved property purchases. For a receipt for documents from the Charity Commission dated 21st April 1858 shows that the Trustees forwarded two deeds both dated 31st January 1844, a declaration of interest dated 8th February 1844 and a conveyance dated 11th & 12th July 1837, which seemed to answer the commission questions, and after this reply no further queries were lodged by the Charity Commission and the next items of communication with them in the collection is for 27th July 1897[9] when the Commission gave permission to the Trustees to sell two properties in the High Street for £470 and the balance after sale expenses to be used to purchase 'New Consols'.

Outgoings

The Principal always had money 'in hand' to pay the necessary bills for the hospital. Henry Dormer in producing a summary of the income and expenditure in 1715 described the expenditure succinctly as, "*The annual Disburstm[ts]:(besides constant Repaires & Casua)*".

In the accounts the additional money given to the men for a feast on 'Founders Day' referred to by Henry Dormer is often also referred to as 'Rowell Feast Money' or 'Jesus Day'. The latter indicating that the 7th of August is also the religious feast of Corpus Christi which in post reformation England was often known as Jesus Day.

The outgoings in the accounts show that repairs to the buildings and the orchard were indeed constant and within the items and services purchased a number appear with great regularity. For example the nurse received a new broom at least once a year, the water pump needed fixing almost constantly and the stables constant attention. In this respect the accounts of the outgoings are very informative as they indicate when and what work was undertaken on the hospital buildings, when and where various items such as clothing and fuel came from and in what frequency. However, it suffices to say that the accounts lack detail regarding the poor men or the nurse in residence, for in most cases only a single line stating something like '*paid the mens quarteridge*' is given.

Small items are regularly recorded throughout the accounts to keep the hospital or the garden, and orchard in good order. Such items include new bessoms, garden shears, a wheelbarrow, scythes and sneths and fire place furniture such as coal scuttles, tongs and shovels.

It is clear from a few entries that the Governors expected the Principal to keep every receipt and they would check the receipts against the principal's accounts and where the two did not meet the Principal was held personally responsible either to find the missing receipts or settling the difference. We have already seen that William Goode died in debt to the hospital and in the account for the Lady Day Quarter 1720 we find the following note by William Dolben as treasurer:

How this was resolved is unclear. The ensuing accounts upon examination

Note in the Accounts regarding disparity between outgoings and receipts.
(NRO JHR 30)

> *Memd^{am} 12 Oct 1720*
> *That these accounts were examin'd and allow'd & there is now due to the Governors from the principal ……. And the principal having disbursed four pounds seven shillings two pence more than his receipts for Michaelmas & S. Thomas quarters 1719 & for Lady Day quarter 1720 amounts to [nothing further is written]*

generally state that the "*there is now due to the Governors from the principal*" an amount but most often a subsequent account shows that this was later paid. The most common reason for a disparity being due to a tenant paying their rent late. At the time of Henry Dormers death however there was still money outstanding which had to be settled by his executor, as a note in the accounts states, *& it then appear'd that ye sum of forty six ponds seven shillings & one penny due from ye said Henry Dormer has been fully paid in Discharge of ye said debt by ye said Richd Tongue.*

It is likely that in settling Henry Dormer's debt to the Governors, Richard Tongue had to borrow at least part of the money, for a loan was taken out of the Governors by a Richard Tongue in 1728 for £20, which he finally paid off by 1738. Henry Dormers successor, Thomas Chapman seems to have had a similar issue in his first year. His accounts did not tally and in this instance the Governors deducted the amount from the pension moneys.

Whilst subsequent accounts were signed off it was not until 1731 that Thomas Chapman had his accounts in order, with nothing owed to the Governors, other than those rents due to be received in the quarter of the examination. John Whitaker Principal from 1742 to 1752, whose accounts are very scrappy was in debt to the governors by £136. 8s. 10½d by midsummer 1743. This rose to £171. 10s. 6d by July 1744. In examining the accounts the Governors noted a number of irregularities including recording income twice. By 1745 his debt had again risen, to £175 after taking into account a tenant who was behind with his rent. It appears the treasurer too had things in hand a from the accounts we see alongside Whitakers accounts those in a different hand. This close monitoring of the accounts paid off for on 31st October 1746 the accounts balanced. However, by

1750 the situation had reversed and Whitaker accounts were out of balance by £4. 5s 6d. and eventually removed from office for stealing in 1752.

When Samuel Hafford, Principal died in 1828 his son as executor found himself in the same position as Henry Dormers executive had a hundred years previously in having to make up a shortfall in the accounts. In this instance the sum outstanding was £14, which was settled by William Hafford[10] on 31st October 1828.

From the Governors meeting of October 1828 it was agreed that the premises should be insured in case of fire. The hospital building, the principals house and the adjoining premises were to be insured for £750. The premises at Old were to be insured for £700 and those in Rothwell for £150. This was the first time that insurance had been taken out on any of the Hospital's properties. The first premium was paid in March 1830 and cost £3. 17s. for the year.

In 1831 the Charity Commission reported on the Hospital. There report shows the outgoings of the Hospital in 1828. This is described as ordinary expenditure and as such does not include large building projects such as repairs to the roof etc.

Outgoings of the hospital as reported by the Charity Commission in 1831

	£	s	d
Stipends of the Principal, 18 Almsmen and Nurse	*318:*	*6:*	*0*
Christmas and August Gifts	*4:*	*19:*	*0*
Clothing	*48:*	*2:*	*0*
Medicine and medical Attendance	*6:*	*11:*	*3*
Wood for Fuel	*22:*	*15:*	*0*
Small Household Expenses and Repairs	*14:*	*5:*	*0*
Land – Tax	*3:*	*16:*	*0*
£	*418:*	*14:*	*3*

Notes

[1] NRO JHR 33 & 34
[2] NRO JHR 29
[3] NRO JHR 30
[4] NRO JHR 80
[5] NRO JHR 35
[6] NRO JHR 40
[7] NRO JHR 38
[8] NRO JHR 31
[9] NRO JHR 58
[10] NRO JHR 32

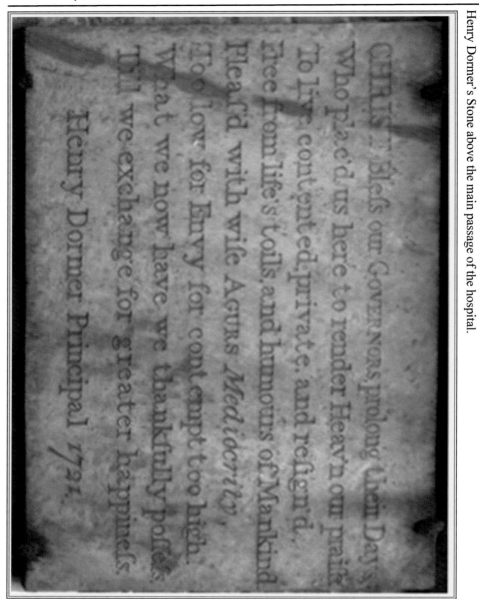

Henry Dormer's Stone above the main passage of the hospital.

CHRIST bless our GOVERNORS, prolong their Days,
Who plac'd us here to render Heav'n our praise:
To live contented, private, and resign'd.
Free from life's toils, and humours of Mankind
Pleas'd with wife Agurs *Mediocrity*,
Too low for Envy for contempt too high.
What we now have we thankfully possess,
Till we exchange for greater happiness.

Henry Dormer Principal 1721.

The Hospital Buildings

The Hospital buildings as they appear today are a somewhat different collection of building to those, which opened as the Hospital in the 1590s. The present buildings comprise of the original building completed in 1593 with two enlarged wings and two houses.

Main Hospital Building

The original building is constructed of coursed ironstone rubble with limestone dressings and stone slate roofs. The wall corners have limestone quoins and the gables at either end of the roof, and the dormer windows set into the roof are all coped. The building is 11 bays wide and has three storeys. The third storey as late as 1831 comprised of one large chamber over most of the length of the building.[1] The was the 'Long Gallery' and shows that the house followed the design of small manorial structures of the Elizabethan era, at which time small manor houses often had a long gallery at the top of the house, with bedrooms below and reception and service rooms on the ground floor. This will be discussed further later in this chapter.

The central attic gable above the north facing side bears the date of completion, 1593. This main building has always had a tiled roof. The accounts show a number of occasions when 'slaters' were employed to repair or fully re-tile the roof. In the winter of 1717/18 a great storm blew off some of the slates from the roof, which then started to leak. The accounts show a payment "*to ye Thacker & for staw, to keep rain out, where the slattes were Blown of with ye great wind*". In the 17th & 18th centuries the slates were probably limestone slates. From an account of June 1707, 6s. 6d. was spent of 1000 slates from Kirby and a further £1. 3s. 6d. paid to the slater to lay them.

Some of the chimneys were rebuilt in 1684, for in that year stone for the chimneys was supplied from the Weldon quarries. The account states "*paid for stone to Tirrell from Weldon for one single tunnel and two double tunnels £1. 2s. 0d.*".[2]

In the centre of the ground floor of the main building is a doorway and passage leading from the north-facing courtyard into the south facing garden. Above this door is a large grey inscribed stone, placed above the arch in 1721 by Henry Dormer, Principal 1701-28. Above this is the crest of Owen Ragsdale showing a Pelican preening herself and three fleur-de-lis. This coat of arms was set in its present position in 1711 and painted, at a cost of two shillings and eight pence. The account entry of 1st January 1711 reads "*Pd for ye setting up the founders coat of arms & for oyle & collour*".[3] There is no record in the accounts of the inscribed stone having been purchased and it is therefore likely that Henry Dormer paid for this himself.

117

As Pevsner noted, the building has some intricacies, there are three gables on the south side of the main wing, whereas on the north side there is one gable and the two wings projecting northwards. Some of the windows are at the heads of the chimneybreasts, whereas those on the south are below the roof line and clustered in pairs.[4]

This main building of 1593 has a main east / west range with two short northern wings projecting northwards from it. Internally before 18th, 19th and 20th century alterations it comprised of four halls or what today might be thought of as communal sitting rooms with four individual bedchambers off each of them. In some of the accounts, bills and receipts etc. the five halls are referred to by name, although the names appear to have changed over time. One of these halls was shared by the Principals and the nurse, until separate buildings were built. The upper floors are accessed by staircases in the corners between the main range and the northern projections, which have entrances from the north facing courtyard. These stairs have stone stair treads with a landing at the top of each and stone newel posts. The landing on the eastern wing is fitted with a cupboard containing a chained bible. According to the listed buildings index the main building has a boarded queen post roof.

As noted above the four halls for the men were all named and the names appear to have changed over time. Generally they appear to have been known by the name of a resident or former resident. In 1699 a lock for the door of Newburns Hall was provided (Tom Newborne died in 1700). In 1770 a wood bill gives the names of the four of the halls as, The Prayer Hall, Aldermans Hall (Samuel Alderman was admitted in 1763), Pellitores Hall (Thomas Pelitor was admitted in 1760), and Mabbutts Hall (Edward Mabbutt was admitted in 1768).[5]

The Prayer Hall was in the early 1700s referred to as the Chapel Hall, suggesting that this was where the men gathered for prayers, the reading of the statutes and general meetings, and given that for the first century and a half the hospital only catered for 12 men, it is likely that the rooms off of this hall were not used as accommodation, but for storage or other purposes associated with the day to day running of the hospital. The prayer Hall was still known as such in 1834 when an inventory shows that within its walls were 9 forms, a pulpit, 2 ladders, 3 pails, 2 slop pails, 2 stools for coffins to stand on and 1 large beam for scales.[6] The inventory completed by William Daulby also states that each hall had an oven and boiler with a large box for coals, and a fender. Other references include one to Braines Hall, Cooks Hall, Fishers Hall and Kings Hall. All of the cooking was undertaken in the communal halls each of which had a fireplace and oven.

The building was designed as a manor house of the Elizabethan era, for as well as the halls and the rooms of the poor men there was the gallery, sometimes referred to as the "Long Gallery", which ran along most of the upper floor with enough space for some seating and a generous walkway. Such 'Long Galleries' are a particular feature of large houses of the period. The furniture and effects of the gallery are described in an inventory of 1789. [7]

Whilst designed like a small Elizabethan manor house, the furnishings of the Long Gallery at the hospital were a long way from those of manor houses, let alone the grand houses of most of the Governors. The Gallery was still known as the Long Gallery in 1834 when an inventory of that year shows the following items present, 1 large chair, 5 small chairs, 1 puss bedstead and one large chest, presumably the same chest noted in the 1789 inventory.[8] This was probably the chest in which all of the hospital's papers, including deeds were kept and which like similar chests in parish churches had a number of locks. In 1703 these locks were repaired and new keys provided, and in the accounts the chest described as *"the evidence chest"*.[9]

Inventory of the Long Gallery 1789

> **In the Hospital Gallery** - *A large chest, an old arm'd chair painted lead colour, an oak table about 38 inches long, and 24 broad, an ink-standish painted red, a sand box, the iron about the fire place, a little pair of Tonges, Poker, Fireshovel, a red stool covered with leather, and marked underneath R.H. And a pair of large scales.*

In August 1710 the accounts show considerable works were undertaken to the fabric of the hospital's main building. This work included re-roofing with slates and re-leading, new laths and re-plastering of some of the walls. Previous repairs had been undertaken to the roof in 1708. From an entry on the same page, dated January 1711, we find that one of the chimneys caught fire. The account entry relates to the one shilling and three pence that was spent on Ale, presumably for those who put the fire out. The accounts show that from at least the early 1700s the chimneys were swept at least once a year including on one occasion being swept by *"a London Chimney Sweeper"*. Continual repairs to the fabric of the main building continued throughout the century. Then in 1767 another major renovation was undertaken. On its completion four men were admitted and the budget increased to allow for additional firewood to be purchased.[10]

Between 1768 and 1833 regular repairs to the fabric were once again carried out. In 1833 at a Governors meeting on the 16th February it is recorded, *"The Governors having taken into consideration the present state of the hospital and finding that considerable repairs are necessary have determined that the whole be well and efficiently repaired as soon as the season will permit and Mr West is hereby instructed to attend to the same forthwith"*. At a subsequent meeting held on 27th May 1833 the Governors, *"Resolved that a plan and estimate produced by W West for enlarging the hospital so as to accommodate 12 more men when requisite be adopted and that the work be immediately commenced and proceeded with as expeditiously as possible.*[11]

Painting of the front of Jesus Hospital showing the original north facing wings c1800 before rebuilding.

The Houses of Offices

To the east of the main range is a single storey L shaped laundry building which matches in style the main range. There is also a small mortuary and until the mid 18th century accompanying these were a thatched stable and the 'houses of offices'.

A number of references in the accounts refer to the buildings known as the 'houses of offices'. These record work done to the houses of which there appear to have been three, for example, we find in 1721 the earthen floor of the houses of the offices were excavated, the soil removed and the houses repaired. In 1723 two new stone steps were provided for the 'house of offices', probably entrance steps.

It is not clear exactly where these houses stood, but it is likely that stood just inside the entrance gate probably to the left of the entrance where the later nurses house now stands. In both 1813 and 1819 there were buildings on either side of the main entrance gate as now. That to the right of the gate was clearly the principals house built in 1778 whilst that to the left was most likely the the houses of offices as the nurses house was not constructed until 1840.

These houses of offices were thatched and the accounts show various payments over time for repairs to the thatch and occasionally full re-thatching. There is no record of their demolition but it is likely that they were demolished when the nurses house was built.

Principal's House

When the hospital opened the principal and the nurse appear to have had bed chambers off one of the common halls, most likely that known as the Prayer Hall. It is possible that the principal's residence may have moved to a building referred to as "*ye howses of offices*" in the early 1700s. In 1778 renovations to the main hospital buildings were agreed and at the same time a new house for the principal was approved. This approval is recorded in the accounts for 1778.

Note in the Accounts Approving the Principals House (NRO JHR 31)

1778
April 18 Ordered
> *That John Robinson Esq Treasurer of the Rothwell Hospital*
> *be impowered to treat for the building of a lodge for the*
> *Principal of the said Hospital; The expense thereof not to*
> *exceed one hundred & eighty pounds*
>> *W Dolben*
>> *John Palmer*
>> *Allen Young*

This new house was built at the northwest corner of the site and comprised of a Kitchen, Parlour and a Brewhouse on the ground floor and a chamber over the Parlour, a first Garret, a Garret over the Parlour, a chamber over the kitchen and a cellar. In 1789 an inventory of the possessions in the house owned by the Governors and the Principal, the Rev Birket was made. This shows that the house comprised of a cellar, a parlour and a kitchen on the ground floor, a chamber (bedroom) over the parlour, a chamber over the kitchen, a garret small bedroom or box room) over the parlour and a brewhouse.

The Nurses House

While in the earliest years of the foundation the nurse probably had a room off of one of the halls, in the early 1800s she had a cottage. A Charity Commission report of 22 January 1824 states, "*a nurse, who occupies a cottage belonging to the charity..*". In the earlier hospital accounts it is recorded as one of the 'houses of offices', but does not get named as the nurse's house in the accounts until 1747 when we are informed, on 23 November straw was purchased for the nurses house, and a thatcher and drawer employed. A further record of 7th January 1750 shows that straw was purchased and a thatcher again employed to work on this roof. The building was still thatched in 1837 and in 1839 when we find payments to the thatcher for work done on the roof of the Nurses house.[12]

In 1840 new house for the nurse was built at the northeast corner of the site. Above the central doorway of this house is a date stone inscribed '1840'. No record

The Principals House (left) and the Nurses House (right) with the hospital gate between them.

regarding the decision to build a house for the nurse exists however, it is likely that this became necessary in 1840 as by that time there were often two nurses employed, and the original Elizabethan house was in all likelihood both too small and in a poor state.

The Stables

As late as 1703 there was a stable block, referred to as "the old stables". The stables, like the houses of offices, were thatched. From the accounts we can see that considerable repairs were undertaken to the stables in 1704. In the winter of that year there was a great storm, which caused damage to the stable after which the stable roof had to be re-thatched again. An identical record of a great wind and the need to re-thatch occurs in the winter of 1711 and again in 1712. The thatch was again repaired with "stubble or straw" in 1715 to the north side of the stables.[13] There is no mention of the stables after 1738, however a large building, possibly the stables is shown on the 1813 map of Rothwell and the 1819 inclosure map.[14] This building is south-west of the main hospital building and up against the west boundary wall. In the earlier years the stables, which may have been a building from the former manorial complex, were important to the hospital and its management of its estates as other than the former monastic tithe barn at Orton the Hospital had nowhere to store its produce. To increase storage space the stable had a new loft constructed in 1707. The new loft was used to store hay and other similar items. The stable was a building that needed constant maintenance, partly

Costs of repairs undertaken in July & August 1704. (NRO JHR 30)

July 10		
For taken of the Thach of ye Old Stable & for taken & throwing down ye old Timber	*1*	*6*
Paid for 2 side pieces, & 42 spares used	*19*	*6*
For Laiths used at ye stables then	*6*	*3*
For a bolt of Iron used at ye stable		*9*
Paid for Laith Nailes, & Nailes for ye Roofe	*2*	*9*
Paid the Carpenter Work, as appears by bart:	*8*	*6*
For 2 loads of Straw from Mr Ponder	*16*	*0*
For one load of Straw from Gd Turner	*4*	*6*
August 5		
Paid ye Thacker & Drawer for ye Stable	*7*	*6*
Paid ye 2 servers of ye Thacker	*3*	*6*

because of its age and partly because it was thatched. In the 18th century a barn was built on the farm at Old at the behest of the Governors because they had so little storage space. Over time this probably rendered the stable redundant and it was demolished. The stable had certainly gone by the 1880s when the first edition Ordnance Survey maps were produced. The first series Ordnance Survey show the present brick built outhouses at the southern end of the garden plots.

Other Buildings

From the documents in the collection there are occasional references to other buildings including the 'Woodhouse' where a doorway was repaired in November 1714.[15] From other references it appears that this was split into a wood storage area for each of the halls, possibly with each having its own door. The hospital also had a laundry in which there was a large sink, usually referred to as the 'Great Sink'. This was occasional cleaned and repaired, presumably when the waste pipe became seriously blocked, for example on November 14th 1720 the accounts show two shillings "*Pd to a Mason & his man for clensing our Great Sink & repairing it & repairing a piece of wall*". A porch is mentioned in the accounts for 1724.[16]

The Gate

Between the two later houses is the original entrance gate. On its external face it has the inscription JESUS HOSPITAL and on its internal face the same coat of arms as found above the central passage, comprising of a pelican and three fleurs-de-lis. This gate way was repaired with stone from Weldon in 1704. An account dated 3rd June in that year shows that the cost of the stone including carriage from Weldon was thirteen shillings and six pence.[17] The masons completed the necessary repair work in August of that year. The work required four men, two masons and two others as the accounts record:

August 15   *Paid the two Masons for repairs of ye Gateway-*   *9 -6*
          Paid the 2 servers of the Mason then-   *4 -6*

The accounts make various references to the 'Gate' and in some instances the term Churchyard Gate is used suggesting that there may originally have been another gate. This would also seem likely as the present gate is a footway gate and not large enough for one associated with a stables and horse traffic. Supporting this is also the reference in the accounts of 1703 to a Carpenter making new gates and a payment to a blacksmith for ironwork. In the same month the accounts also record 2 locks, 3 keys and bolts for these gates.[18] The surviving gate gives access to the courtyard from an almost triangular area at the southern end of Rothwell Market Square and this almost triangular area was into the 19th century known as 'Jesus Green', or 'The Green'.

The Hospital Gate from the Market Place

This gate seems to have been a target for thieves, for in the accounts an entry for 23rd October 1718 reads, *"Our church yard gate was stole & carried away charge to get it again"*. A record in the accounts shows that the key to the hospital gate was stolen and taken to Brigstock and a man had to be sent there to recover it.[19] The thief presumably having been apprehended in that village.

The Curtilage

The land on which the hospital stands originally comprised of two roughly rectangular enclosures running North/South down the hill from the market square (See plan). The hospital buildings all stand within the first of these north / south enclosures, the one nearest the Market Square. The southern enclosure, accessed originally by a track, disputed after enclosure was the hospital orchard. It was not accessible from the southern half of the upper rectangular enclosure because of the steepness of the hillside.

Plan of Jesus Hospital and its surroundings in 1813 (Digitally redrawn from the 1813 map of the town). NRO (M(T)M 390

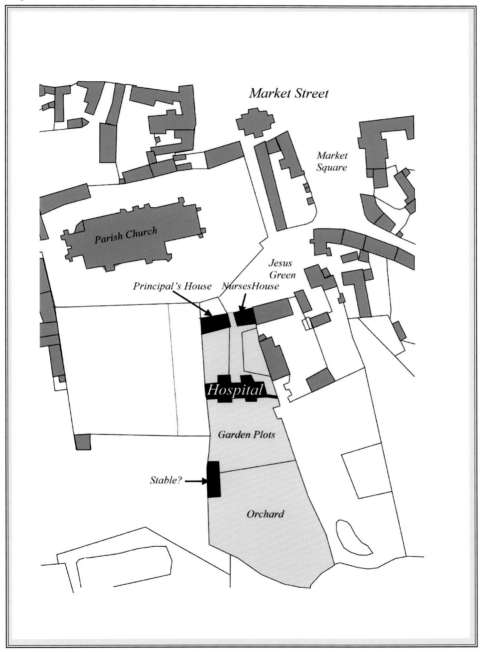

The Pump

Somewhere in the immediate vicinity of the building stood the hospital water supply. A pump, probably drawing water from a well beneath is regularly recorded. A well with oak over the top of it is recorded in 1715, when the oak was replaced. It had a wooden frame and leather seals and on the ground surrounding it black stones. These were probably cobbles painted with pitch. The accounts refer to the painting of the stones in the 18th century. The drain taking away surplus water from the pump is occasionally referred to as the "Watercourse in the Court" when repairs were carried out.

The Clock

Various references in the 18th century refer to the clock or the dial. The word 'clock' is first used in 1705. Probably a sundial that was used as the main timepiece for all but the Principal.

The Garden

In Elizabethan England self-sufficiency was expected. The pension of the men would allow them to buy meat and other necessities, but they were expected to grown at least some of what they ate in the garden. The garden lay on the southern side of the main building in the upper enclosure. This was not a communal garden where the men grew vegetables for one another but a garden in which each man had his plot. Unlike many establishments of the period the statutes do not make any specification regarding the gardens.

The Orchard

The hospital had an Orchard from the outset. The orchard was accessed by a road across some land, which belonged to the manor. After enclosure the use of the road was disputed by Mrs Medlicott who then owned the land it crossed. The Enclosure Commissioners refused to get involved and the outcome of the dispute is unclear. The road is not shown on any maps of the period and from the scant descriptions that exist it appears to have crossed over land to the side of the hospital, but whether east or west is unclear.

Within the accounts there are various records relating to the hedge around the orchard, the purchasing of new fruit trees and other trees. From such records we can see that the orchard contained both apple and pear trees, for example on January 3rd 1704 the account of Henry Dormer shows "*Paid for two Sawers, field ye wood in the Orchard, & cut it to pails*" then on the 18th November 1704 "*Paid for teen Apple trees for ye orchard*" at a cost of 5s. 6d., presumably as replacements for those felled in January. Further trees were then bought on 23rd December 1704 for another line reads "*And for 5 more apple and 2 pear trees 6 - 0*", and in December 1712 we find a record for "*10 young Plumtree's to plant in our Orchard*". The orchard as well as trees was also planted with vines and there are numerous references and payments for pruning these. It also had a pond within its bounds, a wooden gate and at least one seat, and some mounds are referred to in 1706 .

Plan of the hospital buildings before their conversion to sheltered housing in 1957.

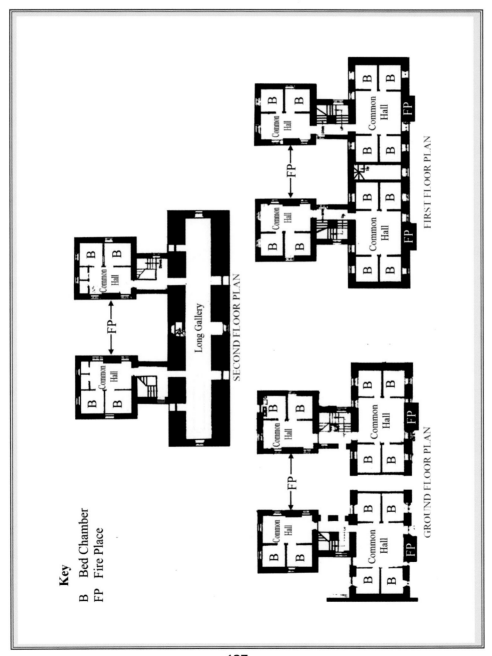

There are a large number of lines in the 18th century accounts relating to the perimeter of the orchard. For example in 1705 the enclosure around the orchard was ditched and part of the hedge reset for a line reads; "December 19th *Paid for Ditchen & quick setting part of the Lower end of the Orchard; & stocking up four Ashtrees there 3 - 6*". That the hospital's accounts show so many lines relating to the hedge around the orchard and pales is clearly because the fruit was a target for theft by some of the (poorer) towns folk and occasionally we find a record relating to such theft. For example in September 1720 a warrant was obtained from Sir John Humble a local magistrate to bring two boys before him on a charge of robbing the hospital orchard. 2s. 8d. was spent on the warrant, which included the cost of 3 men going with the principal to apprehend the boys. Another record in the accounts for August 1713 shows a payment for new pales, nails and work, "*the Orchard being then broak oppen & robbd*". Following this incident the orchard boundary was strengthened in the following March when two labourers were employed to put new hedging on top of the pales. By 1729 the problem was so bad that the Principal employed 2 men to watch the orchard for 3 nights.

As well as theft, moles also seem to have been a particular problem in the 18th century. Mole catchers were regularly employed to eradicate moles from both the hospital grounds and the orchard, for example, on November 24th 1711 a Mr Bosworth was paid "*for taken ye Moles in the gardens & Orchard; then and before*", for which he was paid 1s. 10d. Records of similar payments occur in almost every quarter's accounts.

In 1771 the orchard was rented out. When it first became rented out is unclear, but in that year the tenant Samuel Pendred was given notice to quit. From 1771 it was maintained by the principal and residents, for their own benefit, well into the early 20th century. The only references after 1771 tend to relate to accidents associated with pruning or the theft of fruit by the townsfolk.

Picture of the rear of the hospital in 1888. (Graphic Magazine)

Notes

[1] Charity Commission - Reports of the Commissioners, 1831, Vol 3, p.186.

[2] NRO JHR 35.

[3] NRO JHR 30.

[4] Pevsner, N., Cherry, B. ed. (1995) The Buildings of England, Northamptonshire, Penguin Books. p.393.

[5] NRO JHR 60.

[6] NRO JHR 33.

[7] NRO JHR 40.

[8] NRO JHR 34.

[9] NRO JHR 30 - 12th September 1703 *"Paid for mending the two locks, & for two new keyes for ye evidence chest"*.

[10] NRO JHR 31.

[11] NRO JHR 32.

[12] NRO JHR 33.

[13] NRO JHR 29.

[14] NRO M(T)M 390, NRO Map 2878.

[15] NRO JHR 30 - Accounts November 15th 1714.

[16] ibid - 18th March 1714 *"Pd to a Carpenter for putting up the ceiling in the Porch"*.

[17] ibid.

[18] ibid - March 18th 1703 payment for the new gates, March 21st payment to John Smith a smith for ironwork and on March 24th payment for locks etc.

[19] NRO JHR 29 *"Feb 12 Pd for Key fetching from Bridgstock wch was stole out of ye hospital gate"*

Epilogue

The 20th Century

After the two great wars Britain saw many changes in the lifestyle of its population. While there are poor elderly people the degree of poverty and their expectations of life in their retirement are no longer the same as those for whom the hospital was established. Today people retire and have pensions. From the 1580s through to the late 1800s pensions were a rarity. People from poor families could expect to work until the day they died or for as long as they were able. Therefore the original purpose of the hospital as an almshouse was no longer required and this brought about the most momentous changes in the history of the hospital since its foundation.

In the years between 1900 and 1959 the number of seriously poor people in the three hundreds who may have wished to enter the hospital declined. The number of those resident reduced until there was but one resident in 1961. The buildings, designed for the largely independent poor of the 1590s were no longer fit for the needs of the elderly of the 20th century and for a period the hospital closed.

Before changes could be made to the use of the hospital a change to the original royal warrant was required. Permission was sought of parliament and the changes approved in the Jesus Hospital (Rothwell) Charity Confirmation Act, 1959. Money was identified, planning permission was sought and subsequently approved to upgrade the premises and allow the picturesque Elizabethan and later buildings to provide for 1960s and future generations of elderly persons. Following modernisation the hospital reopened on 24th April 1962. The unveiling carried out by the Countess Spencer. Under the new scheme instead of the 24 elderly persons and a Principal provided for by Owen Ragsdale's endowment, the new scheme provided flats for 6 single men and 4 couples.

Along with the changes in the needs of older persons and the need to make the building suitable for the 20th century, the system of government of the hospital that had served the hospital well since 1593 also needed to change. In the 20th century there was a change in Governors, no longer were the Governors solely from the landed gentry of Northamptonshire, they included at least one local person with an interest in the town and its people. It was decided that whist a governing body would remain, the Governors would work alongside a housing association, which would employ a warden to live in the Principals house and provide assistance to the residents.

The overall aim of the hospital in 2014, despite some changes over time, remains largely as set out by Owen Ragsdale and is now described by the Charity Commission as:

> *"the object of the charity is to provide almshouses for poor men, not less than sixty years of age and of good character who are resident in the county of Northamptonshire and preferably in the urban district of Rothwell, at the time of appointment. A total of ten almshouses are available to meet this object.*

Jesus Hospital and Local Provision for the Poor

In considering Jesus Hospital's history the question arises, how did Jesus Hospital fit in with the parish provision for the poor? Clearly, poverty and vagrancy was an issue of great concern in Tudor England. During the reign of King Henry VIII laws were enacted which banned vagrancy, despite this hospitals/almshouses were allowed to continue proving the residents were engaged in some labour or handy work according to their strength and ability, that is not idle. By the reign of queen Elizabeth I not only were the numbers of poor people rising but also were the fears of those in power that the poor and disaffected might rise up in revolt against them. This was aided by the fear that recusant noblemen might rise up and lead them in revolt. In some ways this was not without foundation for in 1569 catholic revolts had taken place in the north of England.

Between 1594 and 1597 there had been a series of poor harvests across the country, which further increased the number of poor and starving. As a result of the concerns about the rising number of poor people and the possibility of revolt attention was given in 1597 to establishing a poor rate system in England. Some parishes had already established such systems, but this was not universal. The statute of 1597 started the process of parish poor relief and was followed by a further statute, the 'Poor Law' of 1601, which required every parish to establish a poor rate, employ collectors to gather in the rate and overseers to ensure its distribution. Overseeing the whole process was the parish vestry, usually a group of middle class men such as yeomen farmers and businessmen, with the vicar as the chairperson. This 1601 'Poor Law' created a system, which remained in force until the 'New Poor Law' of 1834. In a subsequent amendment attempted to establish a clear public responsibility for care of the poor. Under these laws, the poor were divided into two groups. The "deserving poor" were those deemed unable to work primarily the disabled, blind, and elderly and the "undeserving poor", the able-bodied unemployed. The administration of the poor laws at local level prior to 1834 rested with the parish officers, the churchwardens and the overseers of the poor.

The overseers could give outdoor relief that is help in cash or other forms to the deserving poor living at home. Those who could work were provided with employment, generally within the parish workhouse, this type of relief being known as indoor relief. To keep welfare beneficiaries under the supervision of their providers, the laws also discouraged the migration of the poor among administrative regions, or parishes.

Because of the way that Jesus Hospital had been endowed and it statute formed it served more than one parish, in fact the parishes of the three hundreds of Rothwell, Corby and Orlingbury and had its own governing body quite separate from the parish officers in any of the parishes. It could not therefore be used by the officers of anyone parish as a means of providing for that parish's poor. That however did not stop the parish officers and local town leaders of both Rothwell and Desborough from trying, and in the small number of cases which we know about, their petitions to the Governors for a very elderly deserving poor man, were successful (see admissions).

Usually a poor person moving to another parish required a settlement certificate from their home parish to live in another parish. The certificate guaranteed that if they became a burden on the poor rate that their home parish would reimburse the host parish. There is no evidence that any man moving into Jesus Hospital ever required a settlement certificate. The hospital gave the poor men a pension and if a poor man was removed it was always on condition that he returned to his native parish, thus negating the need for such certificates. In this way the poor mans parish did not lose out; even if the man was removed the parish was saved from giving relief for the duration of the admission. Removal was rare and the founding feoffees appear to have recognised the fear that should any person be expelled they would fall on the mercy of Rothwell parish or one of its neighbours. To ensure that this was not the case the statute required that the Governor proposing or electing a poor man for admission certify in writing that election, on the understanding that should the man be expelled the Governor would then become personally responsible for him. Over time a couple of expulsions did occur but it is unclear whether the electing Governor actually took up the responsibility or whether the poor person once again became the responsibility of a parish.

Once resident at Jesus Hospital each man was included in Rothwell's poor rate, their payment along with that of the Principal and the nurse being provided by the charity and paid when due to the overseers of Rothwell. Therefore in this respect Rothwell parish can be seen as a net benefactor of income towards the poor rate from the residents of Jesus Hospital, some of who were from other parishes, and all of whom if still living in their own homes would have been exempted from paying the poor rate. This poor rate provided work for the idle poor, the income of their labour being used in an attempt to lessen the impact of the poor rate on those in the parish eligible to pay, a workhouse for those who were destitute, an apprenticeship scheme for young persons, often orphaned, and small payments for those poor persons with passes going through the town on route to other places.

The eligibility for admission and the requirement for the person having a good credit history probably excluded most people in receipt of assistance from a parish and so it must be concluded that Jesus Hospital cannot be considered as an integral part of the provision for the poor of Rothwell or any other parish in the three hundreds, it was from the outset an entirely separate entity, unlike many of the almshouses in towns and villages administered by trustees who were the same people who ran the parish vestry.

Summary

The collection of records now in the Northamptonshire Record office were deposited by the Governors in 1967 and have provided the basis for this study of the hospital's history. They show, when compared to other similar establishments that Jesus Hospital is quite unique. It is without parallel in terms of its governing body. No other similar establishment can show a similar august body of wealthy land-owning gentlemen, peers of the real, members of parliament and high sheriffs as that of Jesus Hospital Rothwell and it appears to have been the first (that I have found) bearing the name 'Jesus Hospital'. The collection of records of the hospital are better than for almost any other similar establishment in the county of Northamptonshire and without which this history could not have been written.

In considering the history of the hospital and its present day role it is interesting to observe that the building of the hospital in Rothwell rather than at Old as intended by Owen Ragsdale, and the choice of his feoffees to whom the charity was entrusted is what has ensured its survival to this day. Had the building been built in Old it would probably be a private dwelling rather than a home to the elderly of the community as Ragsdale intended, as is the case of other similar establishments in the county, for example, Montague's Hospital in Weekly.

Ragsdale's choice of feoffees and the way they established succession is clearly another reason for the survival of the hospital. These were gentleman from the wealthiest in society and the positions they held ensured that the money received from the rental land endowed was put to good use for the benefit of the hospital, invested through the use of loans and mortgages in the 17th and early 18th centuries and then put into stock in the later 17th century onwards. The returns from the money paid the bills, the pensions and wages, and when necessary provided for major capital works to ensure that the hospital buildings were kept in good order. On occasions however we see that the choice of Governors did not always work, either because of distance, when they were away from their Northamptonshire estates for long periods or when competing pressures meant that the hospital business took second place.

We have seen from the records that Jesus Hospital was the first establishment to have the dedication to Jesus Christ and has a number of unusual characteristics not seen in other 16th or 17th century establishments in the county and seldom outside the county. Amongst these are:

> **The Building** - At a time when most hospitals and almshouses were being built as terraces of small individual dwellings the hospital was built to resemble a small manor house complete with long gallery. And yet it was unlike its predecessor, the medieval hospital or almshouse in that it contained individual bedchambers rather than partitioned bed spaces in a large hall.

The Catchment area - With the exception of Latham's almshouse in Barnwell, which took in the poor elderly from the two Barnwell villages and Old Weston and Kimbolton (Huntingdonshire), all the other 16th and 17th century foundations in the county accepted people from the local parish or one or two neighbouring parishes. No other hospital/almshouse accepted poor elderly persons from the parishes of three hundred's.

The Feoffees / Trustees / Governors - Once established the trustees of most foundations were the parish officials, such as the vicar, churchwardens and overseers, in whom the benefactor entrusted the on-going maintenance. A few such as Laxton's Hospital in Oundle were entrusted to other organisations, in this instance the Grocers Company of London and fewer still continued to be overseen by the founders heirs. Jesus Hospital was founded with a set of articles which required a line of succession of trustees who were separate from the organisation of the poor law administration / poor relief systems of any one parish. This appears to be without parallel in the county and possible nationally.

Recusancy in Northamptonshire - A Final Note

The collection of records relating to Jesus Hospital gives a good insight into Catholicism in Northamptonshire at the beginning of the 17th century. Because practising in the Catholic faith had been banned and was punishable by fines and imprisonment most Catholics like Owen Ragsdale remained hidden, attending Church of England services while practicing all other aspects of their faith in their own homes. For a number of Ragsdale's friends hiding their faith was not an option to be considered. As we have seen Sir Thomas Tresham, one of the original feoffees was heavily fined and imprisoned for his open and often eccentric displays of his Catholic faith.

Friendships between the wealthy in Northamptonshire and their desire to undertake philanthropic gestures such as governorship of Jesus Hospital appears at the beginning of the 17th century to have ignored any differences in faith between them. This is seen in the appointment of Robert Spencer, Eausabie Isham and Ferdinand Pulton to the governors and assistant roles between 1593 and 1612. Ferdinand Pulton, closest friend of Owen Ragsdale was like Ragsdale a Catholic, conforming to the requirements of the state while practicing as a Catholic in secret. Robert Spencer, was a Calvinist and while not treated with the same suspicion as a catholic was probably considered with some suspicion by all parties. Between these was Eusabie Isham, sheriff of Northamptonshire from 1584. He had been tasked to seek out Catholics in the county, but in 1585 he wrote to Lord Walsingham saying:[1]

I haue travelled unto these places wth certaine justices next adioyninge to have manifested the effect of her ma'ties pleasure but divers of them were not at home nor w'thin the Countie as by examination and searche yt

135

*dothe appeare: .... names knowen unto any w'th whom I have had
conference aboute the same and as we suppose there was not any
suche at any time dwelling in the said countie*

Clearly Isham knew his fellow governors and assistants and must have
either sympathised with them or possibly used his position as a governor
to keep and eye on them. Whichever is correct will probably never be
known, but the early years of foundation of of Jesus Hospital does none
the less give an insight into a group of wealthy Catholic families at the
beginning of the 17th century, only one of whom (Sir Thomas Tresham)
features in most of the studies of recusancy in the midlands in the late
16th and early 17th century.[2]

Notes

[1]   TNA SP 12/183, f.143.
[2]   Most studies focus on the Tresham, Compton, Vaux, Catesby, Throckmorton and
    Arundel families.

Appendix 1.
The Hospital Statutes

A number of copies of the statutes survive including one copy (undated), probably the original (NRO JHR 8), which is bound in part of a 15th century illuminated manuscript. Additional rules were added to the statutes between 1685 and 1705. The statutes as set out in an undated 18th century copy of the original (NRO JHR 11) are transcribed on the following pages.

The statute begins with the purpose of the Statute (below), then sets out each rule one by one (overleaf). Such statutes continue a medieval tradition originally based upon the rule of St Benedict, by which the residents of such hospitals were expected to live.

Statute, Rules and Orders concerning the nomination Government, maintenance, direction, punishment, expulsions and removeing of particular bodyes part of the corporation of or residents in, or resorting unto Jesus Hospital in Rowell in the county of Northton: made and agreed upon by Tho: Tresham, Geo: Gascoigne, Ferdinando Polton, and Oliver Farren esquires being ye now survivers of those in the Letters Patent of our late Sovereign Lady Queen Elizabeth bearing date ye 29th day of June in the 38th year of her reigne be mentioned and appointed to be the first Governours of the goods, possessions and rents of the said Hospitall, and thereby also autherised to make and ordaine Statute, rules and orders for the same.

1

Who shall elect a Principul

First it is agreed, ordained and appointed that the Principall of the said Hospitall for the time being, shall be forever hereafter be elected chosen and nominated by the five Governors or their successors, or by four or three of them at the least and that the said Principall shall at the time of his said election and admission, be a man of forty year of age at least; which before hath lived in good name and creditt, and which hath not been indited araigned vehemently suspected for the comitting of any treason, murder, robery, felony, purjury, adultry, fornication, Drunkenness, Vagerant, or Rogueish life, outragious swearing: often quarelling or ffighting; nor of any other great or greaveous crime; he which hath upon his body and dangerous inffecteous disease, and the said Principall shall at the time of his said election be unmarried; and always after during his continence in that office and place shall remain unmarried; and that any man after shall marry or comitt any of the said offences aforesaid and that by all ye Governors which at the house of the said Hospitall; together with the most part of the then assistant; which at the house of the said hospital, shall examine the cause at some convenient time by any of those Governors appointed, thereafter reasonable notice of that time first given to all the rest of the Governors and Assistants; for the time being shall think him guilty thereof; or that the said Principal shall consume any of the rents or revenues of the said Hospital, or being thereunto required shal not make a just and perfect accompt of his receipts and payments touching the said Hospitall, either unto all the then Governors, without any of the assistants, or those Governors at the said house at some convenient time by any of the Governors appointed, therefore after reasonable notice of that time given to all the rest of the governors and assistants for that time being, shall together with the most part of the then assistants give warrant for or allowe, detain, deduct, or defaulke any of the wages or stipend of the said poor and sick men after he hath received the same; and that it is or shall be due and payable unto them; he so offending in any of the causes aforesaid, shall presently cease to be Principall there, or enjoy that office, and to be expelled from the said Hospitall by the Governors without any of the said assisstants, or by these Governors at the said house at some convenient time by any of the said Governors appointed therfore after reasonable notice of that time given to all the rest of the Governors, and assistants for that time being with the part of the then assistants shall examine the said cause and pronounce him faulty therefor and never after shall be admitted into any society, fellowship, office, or cometh into ye said Hospitall.

2

What hability the Principall man be

No man shall hereafter be admitted into the said office or place of Principall , or after continue in the same which shall have any land, tenements, or other hereditements either copyhold, or freehold, above the clear yearly value of four pounds, or which shall be seised or possed of any annultic, or annuities, rent or rents, lease or leases, for life, lives, or years, above the clear yearly value of twenty nobles, or which shall be owner, or possessor of any money, jewells, plate, household stuffes, goods, chattels, or good debts, above the value of one hundred marks unless the partie so to be admitted shall before his admittance give and assure to the said Governors and their successors; the third part of the value of his then estate absolutely without condition.

3

The Principalls office & duty

The office duty and charge of the said Principall of the said Hospitall, from time to time, shall be to receive, collect, and gather all such rents, revenues, duties & sums of money, as from time to time shall be due and payable to the said Governors of the said Hospitall, and their successors, for and to the said use, of the said hospital; and again to disburse, employ and lay forth the same *money to the said Principall, poor and sick men, for their stipend and wages, and for and towards the repair of the house, edifice, buildings, courts, walls, gardens and other places and parts of the said Hospitall, and to other such uses and in such force as the said five Governors, or four, or three of them by their warrant, in writing assign and appoint, and all of his receipts and payments to*

To receive pay and account

Recording the names of the Officers

To make and give a time and perfect accompt whensoever it shall be demanded or required as aforesaid, and also the office and duty of the said Principall from time to time shall be to write or procure to be well and legibly written in a book for that purpose, provided, the names, surnames, aditions and dwelling dwelling place of every of the Governors, assistants, Principall, poor and sick men, which shall be elected, chosen, come or succeede of, or into the said Hospitall; and the day and time of every of the said elections, or admissions, and the day of their severall deaths, or other displacings, or removings; and who shall be appointed to succeed, be chosen or put into every of their places, and if any should be expelled, or put forth for any cause, to write and set down the cause and time thereof, and also the time of the warning which shall be given of any vacancy to every Governor, which should have notice thereof, whereby the neglect of any new election may the better appear.

4

The Principall shall cause ye poor to perform the statute.

And moreover the office and duty and charge of the said Principall from time to time be vigilant, diligent and careful that such statements, rules & orders as now or hereafter shall be made by the said Governors, or successors, touching the ordering and government of the Principall and poor sick men may be well and faithfully fulfilled and kept; and to make true report from time to time to the said Governors, or assistants, or most of them; which of the said poor or sick men shall be disobedient to the STATUTES, rules and orders, and shall infringe and break the same, or any of them, or how and in what manner, time and place of the said offence shall be comitted to the intent that all the said Governors without any of the assistants or those Governors which with the most part of the said assistants, shall at the same house, at some convenient time by any of the Governors appointed therefore after reasonable notice of that time given to all the rest of the Governors and assistants for that time being, examine the said complaint; may inflict such punishment upon the said offender as they shall think the said several offence shall deserve, and moreover the said Principall shall have special regard that the said Hospitall, and every chamber, court, yard, garden, walke, wall, ffenceway, and other part and place thereof may in convenient time be well and sufficiently repaired and kept wholesome, sweet and clean, wherein he shall and may imply such of the poor and other inferior members of the said Hospitall to work and labour as he shall think mete and to cause all and every of the poor and sick men of the said Hospitall (so far as their health and strength will permit them) to be in person aiding and assisting to the said repair, and also to the avoiding and removing of any Noysome, unseemly, or unwholesome thing, which may tend to the offence of the said poor or sick men, or any other repairing to the said Hospitall, and to that every of them have their own cost and charges, good shift of apparell and linnen, and sufficient bedding for himself not only at his coming in, but also from time to time.

5

The howers to go forth and come in at 4: 5 or 6 as convenient may be offered not before full daylight but upon necessity

And further, the said Principall shall keep the keys of the gates of the said Hospitall, and shall shut the same or cause them to be shut every night at nine of the clock; and open of the same at four of the clock in the morning if it be day and shall not himself go forth nor suffer any of the poor sick men to go forth of the said Hospital before four of the clock in the morning, if it be day-light, or to come in after nine of the clock at night without some reasonable and speciall cause to be signefied and allowed by the said Principall.

6

The Principall shall be resident

The Principall of the said Hosp[itall for the time being shall be resident at the said Hospitall, and shall not be absent from thence above one day in a month, nor shall lye forth of the said Hospitall above one night in a month without special leave and consent from one of the Governors of the said Hospitall first had and obtained in wrighting, nor by any such licence or consent above six days in the month nor above forty days in one year, upon pain of forfeiture of his quarters wages to be due to him at the quarter next ensuing his said offence and further the said Principall shall not be absent from the said Hospitall above fourteen days in one whole year without such licence aforesaid, upon pain of forfeiture of his said office office or place, and

The Principalls Deputy

at the times when the said Principall shall be absent from the said Hospitall above one whole day and a night he and the Governor which doth licence him shall substitute and appoint one of the poor or sick men of the said Hospitall to be his Deputye for the time being shall have all such and the like Authoritye and charge, as the said Principall hath or ought to have.

7

Certifying the Death of the Principall

When the Principal of the said Hospitall shall dye, or depart, from the said Hospitall, or for any cause leave and forfait his said office, or place, or be removed from thence, the he which shall be the most senior anciently elected, or first chosen of the said poor or sickmen shall as convenient speed after as he can, seal and locke up all the money, goods and papers which the said Principall had in custody at the said house, at the time of his death, or with one month before, or advertise, or procure to be advertised thereof to the five governors of the said Hospitall for the time being, or such, or so many of them all then shall be dwelling or remaining in the afiresaid county of Northton, which Governors all five together, or those of them which next after such death shall resort to the house at some convenient time by any of the Governors appointed, therefore after reasonable notice of that time given to all the rest of the Governors and assistants, for the time being, and their with the most part of the then such assistants as at the said house shall then be, shall with such speed go conveniently may be after notice and intelligence thereof as is aforesaid, make election of one other meet and sufficient man for that purpose qualified as is aforesaid to be Principall of the said Hospitall, and by their letter or certificate under their hands shall signifie their said election to the senior, most ancient or first elected of the said poor, or sick men, or to all the said poor, or sick men, which letter or certificate with the date thereof, and the name, surname and late dwelling place of the person so elected and certified to be Principall shall be presently or after written, or cause to be written by the said new elected Principall, into a book for that purpose provided, and also the said letter or certificate shall be preserved and kept amongdt other the evidences of the said Hospitall.

8 *The Government during the Vacation of the Principall* *Deputy Principal*	*Imediately from and after the said office and place of the Principall shall become void by death, departure, deprivation, forfaiture, or by other ways, or means until these shall be so as aforesaid made choice of some other to be Principall of the said Hospitall, and the same shall be certified with his name by writting as is aforesaid, he which for the time being shall be senior, most ancient or first elected of the said poor or sick men shall be Deputy Principall of the said Hospitall and shall have use, occupy and enjoy the office, place, duty and charge of the Principall of the said Hospitall, and look to the safe custodye and well ordering of the said goods and writtings of the former Principall, and also shall receive such benefit and comodity by these Statuts, rules and orders, or by other Statuts rules or oders hereafter to be made be or shall be ordained, asigned and appointed, to and for the Principall of the said Hospitall without any other or further nomination, election or admision except yet shall seem good to all the five Governors which with the most part of the then assistants shall then next repair to the said house together at some convenient time by any of the Governors appointed therefore after reasonable notice of that time given to all the rest of ye Governors and assistants for that time being; and these make choice of some other of the said poor or sickmen to be deputy Principall of the said Hospitall until such time as choice shall be made as is aforesaid of the new Principall and his name certified as is aforesaid, in which Case he is so chosen shall be deputy Principall and none other.*
9 *Who shall elect and admit the poor*	*And it is established, ordained and agreed the every poor of sick men which from time to time shall be elected and admitted into the Society and Fellowship of the said hospitall shall be elected chosen and appointed by such of the Governors and their assistants or their successers as hereafter is mentioned. Viz that to the next place that shall be void, the said Tho Tresham shall nominate whom he shall think good, and to the next after that the said George Gascoigne, and after him the said Ferdinando Pulton, and after him the said Oliver Farren and after every other Governor which now be or hereafter shall be by himself successively to have one turn in such sort and order as they be or shall be named to be Governors every of them in his seniority or anciently in that place as he is or shall be first or formerly chosen thereunto shall have one turn for himself to choose and nominate a poor man eligible and meet to be placed therein, so that he or they within thirty days after notice or warning to him given that his turn is, then to nominate of appoint one poor man to supply the place thats void, do nominate and certifie the same as hereafter is mentioned or otherwise he shall loose his turn, and the next in such order as is aforesaid shall supply the same; within the like term of thirty days after like notice given of the default of the former, and so in order one after another and they all failing to begin at the foremost or eldest in that place again and so to persue their turns in the same order wherein they are to be well advised that the parties they name be very likely to meet and be eligibale and will perform their parts and dutys in and to the same Hospitall and live orderly and quietly with the rest of their company, and that if they shall deserve to be displaced from thence, that they shall not be chargeable to the inhabitants of Rowell aforesaid, or the Hundreths or Towns near thereunto but be returned upon him that did nominate him to that place, all and every which nomination is to be certified in writting under the hand and seal of him that maketh the same and delivered unto the Principall of the said Hospitall for the time being; or the deputy within thirty days next after such notice as aforesaid, and such of them as doth receive the same certificate shall admitt him which shall be so nominated and certified unto*

141

the society and fellowship of the said Hospitall, and shall write or cause to be writ*
surname and late dwelling place, with the day of his admission and by what warra*
letter he is admitted into a book for that purpose provided, taking of the poor man
admitted four pence and no more.

10

*What sort of poor
men are not
eligible*

Every poor and sickman that shall be elected, chosen and admitted into the society
fellowship of the said Hospitall, shall be a man which before hath lived in good na*
creditt, which hath not been indicted, arraigned, or vehemently suspected for the
committing of any treason, murder, robbery, felony, perjury, adultery, fornication,
drunkeness, Rogueish life, crime, nor which shall have upon his body any dangero*
infectious disease as shall be loathsome to others, and shall bring meet bedding an*
and other necessarys for himself and give the same to the corporation.
Outrageous swearing other fighting nor any other great notorious or grievous cri*

11

Who be eligible

No poor or sick man shall be eligible into the said Hospitall, or being elected shall*
continue in the said Hospitall, but such be as which be do and remain unmarried, *
which at his admission, admittance into the said Hospitall, shall be forty years of a
the least, nor any blind person, nor such as be so lame that he cannot go to church
nor any poor lunatic, or party be straught of his witts, and but such as have dwelle
continually remained in the said town of parish of Rowell, or in one of the hundred
Rowell, Orlingburye and Corby, which be the nearest parts of the said county of
Northampton by the space of three years together at the least next before his admis
into the said Hospitall, saving that it shall and may be lawful to and for the said T*
Tresham, George Gasicogne, Ffernando Pulton and Olver Ffarren, or to or any fo*
three of them during their lives in regard of their charges care and pains taken in t*
Building and erection of the said Hospital, to elect and make choice of, to be admi*
into the Hospitall any poor or sickman dwelling before in any parts of this realm, *
as with in some other part as out of the said county of Northampton being otherwis*
their Statutes and orders eligible and saving also that it shall and may be lawful to
said five Governors, and their successors, or to, or any four, or three of them to ele*
cause to be admitted into the said Hospitall, any poor or sickman being otherwise *
order eligible which shall be of the kindred of Owen Ragsdale esq. deceased found*
said Hospitall in what parts of this realm of England soever the said kinsman did b*
dwell.

12

*Election of the
poor*

When any of the poor or sickmen admitted to the said Hospitall shall dye, resign g*
this place or for any offence or lawful and rteasonable cause be removed, then the
Principall of the said Hospitall shall within fourteen days at the furthest of such de*
removing signifie the same to such of the Governors or assistants to whom the elec*
the next doth belong, who shall within thirty days at the furthest next after such not*
elect nominate and appoint one other poor or sick man in place of the other being *
removed and shall by writting under their hand certify the name surname and late
dwelling place of him so elected and nominated to the Principall of the said Hospit*
which Principall shall imediatly upon the receipt of the said warrant or certificate
him so elected and nominated into the society and fellowship of the said Hospitall *
appoint him a chamber, and then shall his name surname and late dwelling place a*
dates of the effect of the letter or warrant of such the said Governor or assistant by*
he was elected and nominated and the day of the said admission into a book for tha*
purpose provided, taking the poor or sickman for his said admission, and the said *
four pence only.

13
The yearly stipend of the Principall and poor men

The Principall of the said Hospitall for the time being shall yearly have his stipend and wage five pounds six shillings and eight pence of lawful English money, a chamber in the said Hospitall to be called and known by the name of the Principalls Chamber, and a piece or part of the garden to be appointed by all the Governors, or those Governors with which the most part of the assistants at some convenient time by any of the Governors appointed therefore after reasonable notice of that time being given to all the rest of the Governors and assistants for that time being, shall so appoint the same or every of the poor or sick man shall have his stipend and wages ffifty three shillings and four pence of like lawful English Money, a chamber in the said Hospitall and a piece or part of the garden to be assigned as is aforesaid, which said stipend and wage of the said Principall and poor men shall be paid unto them at four feast in the year, by equal and even portions, that is to say, at the Feast of St Michasel the Archangell; St Thomas the Apostle; the Annunciation of the Blessed Virgin Mary and the Nativity of St John the Baptist, of the rents and revenues of the said Hospitall, or as soon after every said feast as the said rents and revenues may be received of the farmers or tenants of the lands of the said Hospitall.

14
Repairing to the Church

The Principall, poor and sick men shall every Sunday, Holyday and festival days throughout the year at the beginning of the morning and evening prayer, asemble themselves in the said Hospitall and then go to the church together, the Principall going before, and the poor and sick men following after two and two in a seemly and decent manner and attend in their best apparell and as near as may be in one uniform fassion of <u>Gowns, Cloaks and Caps</u> and in like manner, there sitt as near together as they may quietly and devoutly all the service time, and at the end of service shall return from the church together in order as is aforesaid.

15
Care of the Founders Tombe

The Principall of the Hospitall and every of the poor and sick men shall have special care and regard that the tombe in Rowell church of Owen Ragesdale Esq: deceased founder of the said Hospitall and the epitephes, Inysscriptions, walls, pavements and other things thereto annexed may be kept whole, safe, bright and clean, and if anything therein shall hereafter be decayed, impaired, defaced, or blemished, the Principall shall cause the same presently to be repaired, at the charge of the said Hospitall, and moreover shall cause such of the said poormen as he shall think fit good weekly or more oft (if need be) to sweep, scrub, wash and otherwise keep clean the same.

16
No poor man shall be idle or begg

Every poor and sick man remaining within the said Hospitall shall according to his age, health and strength on the working days do some labour or work for and towards the increase in his liveing and by no means give himself to idleness, drunkenness, vagrant life or begging. Provided that the Trade he giveth himself unto be not Noysome in smells or noice to others, or cumbersome in taking up the room of others and the Principall of the said Hospitall shall make dilligent inquiry when where and in what manner every of the said poor or sick men doth imply himself, and spend his time, and make relation to the Governors or the most part of them which of the poor or sick men being able to be idle and which shall resort to the Ale=house or any other house or place of great disorder, to the intent that the said Governors or those Governors which with the most part of the then assistants shall at the said house at some convenient time by any of the Governors appointed therefore after reasonable notice of that time given to all the rest of Governors and assistants for that time being to examine the cause may instantly inflict such punishment upon the offender by abatement of their wages, expulsion or otherwise as they shall think the offence deserve.

17

*No poor man
shall lye forth
of ye Hospitall*

No poor or sick man admitted to the said Hospitall shall lye any night forth of the same Hospital without licence and consent of one of the Governors of the same Hospitall, or of the Principall or his deputy first had and obtained, nor by any such licence or consent above four days in one month, or twenty days in one whole year, on pain of forfiture on pain of twelve pence to be taken out of that quarters wages, which shall or ought to be due and payable unto him, at the quarter or rent day next after the same offence committed, or any stranger not being of the corporation to be suffered to lodge above one quarter of a year in the said house.

18

*Impairing of ye
Hospitall or
any goods there*

If the Principall or any of the poor or sick men which shall be admitted to the said Hospitall shall break, diminish, loose graye or impair any walk, windowm casement, glass, iron purtition, dore, lock, key, or any other things which is or shall be parcel of the said hospital or by any means annexed to the same or which shall be given, bestowed or provided for or to the use and benefit of the same Hospitall, their shall at his own cost, or charge, or expense and amend the same in as short and convenient time after as he may do it; and in receipt of such repaire or amendment in convenient time it shall and may be lawfull to and for the Governors of the said Hospitall, or any of they, or to or for the said Principall to retaine in his of their hands so much of the offenders wages or stipend which after shall be due and payable unto him, as shall and will be able to repaire, renew and amend the same, and therewith to cause the same default to be repaired, renewed and amended.

19

*The statutes
read twice in
ye year*

And it is established ordained and decreed that these Statutes, rules and orders, and all other statutes, rules and orders hereafter to be made ordained or decreed by the said Governors of the said Hospitall or by any of their successors shall be for ever hereafter openly and distictly read twice every year in the Principalls Chamber of the said Hospitall, by the said Principall, his deputy or assigne in the insents and hearing of all such the said poor and sick men of the said Hospitall as can conveniently be there, that is to say, on the feast day of St Michael the Archangell and the feast day of the Annunciation of the Blessed Virgin Mary at two of the clock in the afternoon of ye same days, to the intent that the said Principall, poor and sick men knowing the substance, intent and true meaning of them, may dilligently and carefully and effectively perform the same, and avoid dangers, gains and penaltys thereof.

20

And it is further established ordained and decreed that every poor weak or sick man which shall be admitted into the society of the said Hospitall shall at the time of his said admission, or admittance, give the whole intrest right and title of all his bedding, naper,y household stuff, and utensiles of house which he shall bring into the said Hospitall, to be by him used or occupyed there, unto the Governors of the same Hospitall and to their successors to the use and benefit of the said Hospitall and the poor people therein placed, reserving to himself only the use and occupation thereof during the naturall life, To be after the death of the poor weak or sick man by the said Governors or any of them or any of their successors, or assignes, or the Principall for the time being distributed amongst and unto such of the poor weak and sick men of the said Hospitall, or otherwise, or to the repaire or other benefitt or pleasure of the said Hospitall, or of the poor men therein being; as to the said Governors, their successors or assignes or any of the shall seem meet and convenient; and at all times after maintain the like and supply the things worn and decayed, and make new gifts of the new things so brought in for supply.

*There is an other order longe since made for the general increase of stipends
and money to be allowed at certain feasts and for fewell and gowns.*

Tresham

Additional Statutes

The following additional statutes appear in an 18th century copy of the statutes.

In the year 1685 *Att a general meeting att Jesus Hospitall at Rowell by
the Governors that were there Viz The Honorable the
Lord Viscount Cullen, Sir Roger Norwich, and Sir
Lewis Palmer Baronts; they did then order and allow
to each of the five halls, thirty five shillings for
fewelling, to buy either coles or wood for the poor mens
use as ye Principall shall find it most convenient for
their advantage*   *The allowance for
wood and cole*

alsoe

In the year 1703 *Att a general meeting att Jesus Hospitall at Rowell by
the Governors that were there Viz Sr Justinian Isham,
- Sir Erasmus Norwich, and Sir Lewis Palmer
Baronets; They did order and allow to the twelve poor
men to have once in two years a Coate or Gown to the
value of fifteen shillings each; The nurse a gown of the
same value; and the Principall a coate to ye value of
thirty shillings.*   *Allowance for
coats or gowns*

In the year 1705 *And it is further established, ordained and decreed by
the same governors above mentioned; that every man
belonging to this society or fellowship (of Jesus
Hospital in Rowell) shall decently and orderly come to
prayers, as soon as the bell has done ringing, to ye
place appointed for divine service; He that does not
repair to prayers and doth wilfully neglect his dutie
herein; he shall forfeit each time one penny, to be
deducted out of his quarteridg except he shews
reasonable cause to be excused, The moneys so
forfeited shall be kept in the Principalls hand until he
thinks fit to dispose of it amongst the rest of the society.*   *Repairing to Prayers*

In addition to the original statutes and those added in the late 17th and early 18th centuries we
find further additions contained in a book of abstract of the late 19th :

JHR 14 - 19th Century Additions to the Statutes

*And it is further established, ordained by the Governors, that every man belonging to this
Society be fined 2s. 6d. each time for getting drunk and 3pence more if he is led home and 6 out
of it to be given to those who lead him. And Neglecting to go to Church on Sunday shall forfeit
1d. if he is well and able to go* (see below). *And also the poor men of the said hospital so far as
they are able to be in person aiding and assisting to the said repairs and also to the mending
and removing of any noissome, unseamly and unwholesome thing. Or any other repairing to the
said hospital.*

22nd June 1870 At a meeting of the Governors at the hospital house.......... it was further established, ordained and decreed that the washing for the future is to be done by the nurses, and not allowed any more to be taken out, excepting those that now take it out. And also to see that a sufficient change be kept up from time to time according to the rules. Namely, two pair sheets, 2 pillow slips, two pair of stockings, three shirts, two towels, one bed bedstead, blankets, counterpane, bolster and pillows, & 1 mattress.

A small piece of paper inserted in the page dated 14th July 1829, also states:

Also to do what he can towards keeping the hospital paths & premises clean & in good order as far as in his power lies.

Another at the back of the book dated 7th June 1829 states:

And it is further established and ordained that any man belonging to this hospital swearing or using bad language shall be fined the sum of 6d. and any man reported to the Principal of using bad language in the street shall be fined a similar sum.

H. G. B.

Appendix 2. - Residents of Jesus Hospital
1665 - 1902

The following pages set out the known admissions and deaths or expulsions of every resident whose name appears in any of the surviving documentation.

Date Admitted	Name of person Elected & Admitted	Place of Residence	Proposing Governor	Year of Death
1665	Roger Chapman	Desborough	Richard Kinsman	
1665	Toby Turner	Rothwell	Edward Syers	
1665	William Coleson	Rothwell	Lord OBrion Cullen	
1665	Christopher Taylor	Carlton	Gefferie Palmer	1674
1667	Nicholas Ward	Cransley	John Syers	
1667	John Mayhew, Gent.	Brampton	George Tresham	1672
1667	William Gilby	Rothwell	Lord OBrian Cullen	1688
1668	John Smith	Carlton	Gefferie Palmer	1689
1668	Richard Scott	Orton	John Syers	1679
12th May 1668	William Coles	Desborough	Lord OBrion Cullen	1676
28th November 1668	John Dimbleby	Brampton	George Tresham	1677
27th September 1669	Richard Turner	Rothwell	Gefferie Palmer	1676
1st July 1670	William Ireland	Rothwell	John Syers	1673
23rd April 1672	Christopher Potts	Rothwell	Lord Viscount Cullen	1677
30th October 1672	George Cave	Newton	George Tresham	1684
3rd July 1673	Thomas West	Wilbarston	Sir Lewis Palmer	1676
20th April 1674	William Allderman	Rothwell	William Montague	1680
26th April 1676	Simon Losbey	Brampton	Sir Roger Norwich	1694
1st May 1676	Stephen Smith	Rothwell	Lord Viscount Cullen	1687
3rd May 1676	William Phillips	Barford	George Tresham	1683
30th April 1677	William Chapman	Carlton	Sir Lewis Palmer	1679
14th July 1677	George Baxter	Old	Lord Chief Baron Montague	1679
5th May 1679	William Teate	Rothwell	Sir Roger Norwich	1689
30th August 1679	Thomas Franklyn	Desborow	Lord Viscount Cullen	1684
29th December 1679	Edward Baker	Rothwell	George Tresham	1685
27th July 1680	Thomas Newbone	Carlton	Sir Lewis Palmer	1700
7th January 1680	Ralph Scott	Rothwell	Lord Chief Baron Montague	1694
24th December 1683	Thomas Norton	Rothwell	Sir Roger Norwich	1684
28th July 1684	Thomas Broadwater	Rushton	Lord Viscount Cullen	1694
26th September 1684	Thomas Hipwell	Rothwell	Hon. Charles Cockain Esq	1694
26th December 1684	William Palmer	Rothwell	Sir Lewis Palmer	1687
12th February 1684	Stephen Robinson	Old	Lord Chief Baron Montague	1685
20th January 1685	Nicholas Ward	Cransley	Sir Roger Norwich	1697
8th March 1685	William Wittering	Rothwell	Lord Viscount Cullen	1686

Date Admitted	Name of person Elected & Admitted	Place of Residence	Proposing Governor	Year of Death
20th June 1686	Thomas Munns Junior	Rothwell	Hon. Charles Cockain Esq	1696
14th July 1687	Thomas Guest	Rothwell	Sir Lewis Palmer	1705
14th March 1687	Thomas Ashby	Rothwell	Lord Chief Baron Montague	1690
7th March 1688	William Knight	Rothwell	Sir Roger Norwich	1691
10th August 1689	John Parker	Rothwell	Sir Justinian Isham	1701
9th January 1689	George Height	Rothwell	Andrew Lant Esq.	1691
14th September 1690	John Rose	Carleton	Sir Lewis Palmer	
1691	Joshua Ave			
1691	William Gunalls			
6th April 1691	John Harison	Rothwell	Hon. Sarjeant Montague	1691
23rd January 1691	William Jennings	Rothwell	Sir Erasmus Norwich	1700
12th June 1693	John Dunsmoor	Rothwell	Sir Justinian Isham	1708
30th June 1694	Joseph Ayres	Rothwell	Andrew Lant Esq.	1709
30th July 1694	Thomas Meadows	Carleton	Sir Lewis Palmer	
6th February 1694	Edward Dunsmoor	Rothwell	Hon. Sarjeant Montague	1717
29th March 1694	Thomas Parker	Rothwell	Sir Erasmus Norwich	1707
1st April 1696	John Pitchley	Rothwell	Sir Justinian Isham	1702
1691	William Gunalls			
February 1697	Jonathan Barker	Rothwell	Francis Lane	1713
12th July 1700	Joseph Saunders	Rothwell	Sir Lewis Palmer	1711
12th December 1700	Richard Storey	Rothwell	Sir William Montague	1708
28th July 1701	John Lockwood	Rothwell	Sir Erasmus Norwich	1706
7th April 1702	John Tongue	Rothwell	Sir Justinian Isham	1703
16th December 1702	John Easton	Rothwell	Lionel Earl of Dysert	1708
22nd July 1703	Edward Marston	Rushton	Sir Lewis Palmer	1706
8th January 1705	Francis Bennett	Rothwell	Hon. Sarjeant Montague	1707
28th May 1706	John Turnsley	Rothwell	Sir Erasmus Norwich	1716
15th December 1706	John Parker	Rothwell	Sir Justinian Isham	1709
13th June 1707	John Gray	Thyndon	Lionel Earl of Dysert	1708

Date Admitted	Name of person Elected & Admitted	Place of Residence	Proposing Governor	Year of Death
17th March 1707	Edward Dolton	Ashley	Sir Lewis Palmer	
1st June 1708	William Inchley	Rothwell	Gefferie Palmer	1718
11th June 1708	William Porch	Orton	Sir Erasmus Norwich	1716
14th June 1708	Henry Knight	Rothwell	Sir Justinian Isham	26th Jan 1733
3rd July 1708	Richard Toseland	Rothwell	Lionel Earl of Dysert	1713
28th February 1709	Richard Chapman	Old	Gefferie Palmer	1713
23rd March 1709	Austine Tee	Dingley	Sir Lewis Palmer	
8th August 1709	Thomas Bosworth	Brampton	Sir Erasmus Norwich	1733
30th October 1709	William Jackson	Dingley	Sir Lewis Palmer	1711
21st December 1710	William Peake	Middleton	Sir Lewis Palmer	1716
23rd July 1711	John Fisher	Rothwell	Sir Justinian Isham	1713
21st January 1711	Thomas Cutbeard	Rothwell	Lionel Earl of Dysert	1725
13th August 1713	Gamaliel Gervis	Wilbarston	Gefferie Palmer	1723
24th September 1713	Edmund Braybrook	Rothwell	Sir Erasmus Norwich	2nd June 1730
30th December 1713	Edward Horner	Rothwell	Sir Gilbert Dolben	1724
4th December 1713	Thomas Brilson	Rothwell	Sir Justinian Isham	1716
16th September 1716	William Belshare	Rothwell	Lionel Earl of Dysert	1722
24th June 1716	James Lovday	Carleton	Sir Gefferie Palmer	21st April 1731
26th July 1716	John Robinson	Rothwell	Sir Erasmus Norwich	1717
27th September 1716	Robert Blaxsley	Hanging Houghton	Sir Justinian Isham	1719
9th May 1717	John Vialls	Rothwell	Sir Gilbert Dolben	31st October 1730
16th February 1717	Nicholas Moor	Rothwell	Earl of Dysert	24th Nov 1728
10th July 1718	William Maydwell	Cottingham	Sir Gefferie Palmer	1718
20th January 1719	William Hassledine	Desborow	Sir Erasmus Norwich	1721

Date Admitted	Name of person Elected & Admitted	Place of Residence	Proposing Governor	Year of Death
30th March 1721	William Joyce's	Rothwell	Sir Gilbert Dolben	1721
14th February 1722	Robert Stratton	Rothwell	Sir Justinian Isham	March 1739
25th June 1722	Walter Lylliman	Rothwell	Earl of Dysert	7th March 1735
20th November 1723	Labeous Driver	Rothwell	Sir Justinian Isham	1726
28th August 1724	Thomas Dexter	Newton	Sir Gefferie Palmer	16th Jan 1728
27th January 1725	John Dexter	Orton	William Washbourne Esq.	26th Aug 1734
Dec (1725?)	Jonathan Bayley	Orton	Sir Justinian Isham	23rd Nov 1743
March 1726	John Loake	Desborough	Earl of Dysert	6th Dec 1729
June 1726	Thomas Sherman	Old	Sir Justinian Isham	5th Aug 1733
24th November 1728	Thomas Cox	Middleton	Sir Jeffrey Palmer	13th Aug 1738
16th January 1728	Francis Taylor	Rothwell	Benjamin Allicocke Esq.	12th Feb 1731
8th December 1729	Joshua Carter	Rothwell	Sir Justinian Isham	1st July 1732
2nd June 1730	Abraham Brightman	Rothwell	John Robinson	30th May 1749
31st October 1730	Edward Humphrey	Rothwell	Sir Justinian Isham	25th June 1751
12th February 1731	George Wignoll	Ashley	Sir Gefferie Palmer	9th July 1736
21st April 1731	Allin Baren	Rothwell	Benjamin Allicocke Esq.	28th May 1734
1st July 1732	John Ayres	Cransley	Rev. Sir John Dolben	8th Oct 1734
26th January 1733	Thomas Buckworth	Orton	John Robinson Esq.	
1st May 1733	Thomas Cooper	Rothwell	Sir Justinian Isham	20th Oct 1736
5th August 1733	Samuel Latimore	Wilbarston	Sir Thomas Palmer	16th Aug 1744
28th May 1734	Jacob King	Desborow	Benjamin Allicocke Esq.	20th Sept 1756
26th August 1734	Henry Brook	Geddington	Rev. Sir John Dolben	1st May 1749
8th October 1734	Henry Walpole	Rothwell	John Robinson Esq.	10th Feb 1755

Date Admitted	Name of person Elected & Admitted	Place of Residence	Proposing Governor	Year of Death
7th March 1735	Thomas Bilton	Rothwell	Sir Justinian Isham	29th Jan 1749
9th July 1736	Robert Sprigg	Cottingham	Sir Thomas Palmer	18th June 1737
20th October 1736	William Lillyman	Cransley	Benjamin Allicocke Esq.	26th Feb 1753
25th June 1737	Philip Mayle	Findon	Rev. Sir John Dolben	27th April 1748
2nd September 1738	John Whittering	Rothwell	John Robinson Esq.	31st July 1759
3rd April 1739	Edward Fletcher	Old	Ernle Washbourne Esq.	5th March 1749
23rd November 1743	George Watson	Wilbarston	Sir Thomas Palmer	6th Feb 1760
16th August 1744	George Baldwin	Rothwell	Benjamin Allicocke Esq.	23rd March 1746
23rd March 1746	Richard Doopup	Rothwell	Rev. Sir John Dolben	31st May 1760
27th April 1748	John Smith	Lamport	Sir Edmund Isham	23rd Jan 1754
1st May 1749	William Tolson or Tolton	Findon	Rev. Sir John Dolben	29th May 1760
30th May 1749	Robert Brian	Rothwell	Sir Thomas Palmer	15th Dec 1760
29th January 1749	Samuel Tarry	Cransley	John Robinson Esq.	23rd May 1765
5th March 1749	John Renold or Rennols	Loddington	Charles Allicocke Esq.	9th Feb 1763
25th June 1751	Thomas King	Rothwell	Sir Edmund Isham	15th Jan 1770
31st July 1752	William Smith	Great Oakley	Wheeler Brooke Esq.	
26th February 1753	William Billing	Carlton	Sir Thomas Palmer	16th Nov 1767
23rd January 1754	Samwell Boal	Rothwell	John Robinson Esq.	3rd June 1754
3rd June 1754	John Dennis	Orlingbury	Charles Allicocke Esq.	6th April 1761
10th February 1755	John Bradshaw	Lamport	Sir Edmund Isham	7th Nov 1758
20th September 1756	John Litchfield	Great Oakley	Wheeler Brooke Esq.	30th Nov 1758
7th November 1758	Thomas Bates	Ashley	Sir Thomas Palmer	4th Sept 1762
30th November 1758	William Goodman	Cransley	John Robinson Esq.	31st Dec 1760

Date Admitted	Name of person Elected & Admitted	Place of Residence	Proposing Governor	Year of Death
6th February 1760	Richard Fisher	Rothwell	Charles Allicocke Esq.	30th July 1770
29th May 1760	Jonathan Tomlinson	Lamport	Sir Edmund Isham	30th June 1761
31st May 1760	Richard Fisher	Great Oakley	Wheeler Brooke Esq.	
10th June 1760	Daniel Brain	Rothwell	Sir Thomas Palmer	26th Aug 1769
15th December 1760	John Willis	Cransley	John Robinson Esq.	22nd April 1765
31st December 1760	Thomas Pellitor	Orton	Charles Allicocke Esq.	
6th April 1761	James Bradshaw	Old	Sir Edmund Isham	13th May 1763
30th June 1761	Thomas Smith	Great Oakley	Wheeler Brooke Esq.	26th July 1762
26th July 1762	Owen Walter	Wilbarston	Sir Thomas Palmer	16th July 1763
4th September 1762	John Skillett	Rothwell	John Robinson Esq.	9th Dec 1767
9th February 1763	Christopher Wallis	Finedon	Charles Allicocke Esq.	29th June 1768
13th May 1763	Samuel Alderman	Rothwell	Sir Edmund Isham	5th July 1771
16th July 1763	William Desborough	Finedon	Sir William Dolben	9th Oct 1767
22nd April 1765	Henry Satchwell or Satchel	Middleton	Sir Thomas Palmer	10th June 1769
23rd May 1765	Richard Cook	Old	John Robinson Esq.	31st May 1770
9th October 1767	William Scott	Rothwell	Charles Allicocke Esq.	6th Feb 1783
16th November 1767	Edmund Smeeton	Desborough	Sir Edmund Isham	18th May 1775
21st June 1775	William Bowers	Browton	Sir John Palmer	26th Aug 1776
26th August 1776	Jonathan Burgess	Old	Justinian Rainsford	12th Aug 1784
22nd May 1777	John Dickenson	Little Harrowden	Allen Young Esq.	15th Feb 1787
10th April 1778	Robert Bowers	Old	Sir William Dolben	12th April 1786
24th September 1781	Samuel Crick	Desborough	Sir William Dolben	29th June 1783
30th November 1781	William Hilton	Middleton	Sir John Palmer	30th Nov 1785

Date Admitted	Name of person Elected & Admitted	Place of Residence	Proposing Governor	Year of Death
28th July 1782	Thomas Tongue	Orton	Allen Young Esq.	
22nd October 1782	Robert Martin	Rothwell	George Hill Esq.	16th April 1796
6th February 1783	Samuel Robinson	Old	John Robinson Esq.	1st April 1784
17th May 1783	John Teer	Broughton	William Dolben Esq.	10th June 1793
29th June 1783	Benjamine Spriggs	Cottingham	Sir John Palmer	27 March 1784
2nd February 1784	Thomas Hankin	Orlingbury	Allen Young Esq.	28th July 1791
27 March 1784	John Humphrey	Rothwell	George Hill Esq.	5th Fe 1791
1st April 1784	Zachary Tomson	Cransley	John Robinson Esq.	
12th August 1784	William Willis	Thorpe Malsor	William Dolben Esq.	24th Dec 1790
30th November 1785	Edward Glithero	Middleton	Sir John Palmer	10th Jan 1787
11th March 1786	Edward Green	Little Harrowden	Allen Young Esq.	21st Fe 1793
12th April 1786	Thomas West	Rothwell	George Hill Esq.	
10th January 1787	John Marshall	Cransley	John Robinson Esq.	
15th February 1787	Daniel Harris	Orlingbury	William Dolben Esq.	10th June 1791
30th November 1788	William Scott	Ashley	John Palmer Esq	
23rd September 1790	Francis Saunders	Finedon	Allen Young Esq.	
24th December 1790	Charles Shortland	Rothwell	George Hill Esq.	
5th February 1791	William Perkins	Cransley	John Robinson Esq.	16th Aug 1791
10th June 1791	James Chester	Loddington	William Dolben Esq.	
28th July 1791	William Freeman	Orton	John Palmer Esq	3rd Feb 1795
29th July 1791	Jacob Butlin	Orlingbury	Allen Young Esq.	24th Aug 1796
16th August 1791	William Threadgold	Rothwell	George Hill Esq.	
2nd February 1793	William Pridmore	Wilbarston	John Palmer Esq	12th Aug 1793
21st February 1793	Jonathan Goldwin	Rothwell	Allen Young Esq.	
10th June 1793	John Howlett	Rothwell	George Hill Esq.	
12th August 1793	William Dickens	Rothwell	Sir Justinian Isham	2nd April 1795

Date Admitted	Name of person Elected & Admitted	Place of Residence	Proposing Governor	Year of Death
3rd February 1795	George Harris	Finedon	Sir William Dolben	
2nd April 1795	Richard Ashwell	Middleton	Sir John Palmer	
16th April 1796	Robert Clark	Orlingbury	Allen Young Esq.	
24th August 1796	Thomas Woodford	Rothwell	George Hill Esq.	
	Frances	Scaldwell		23 Feb 1835
	Thomas Ward			12th April 1835
	William Ditie or Dixie	Stoke Albany	Sir John Palmer	10th March 1836
	Thomas Hatley			4th March 1836
	William Gostick			
27th January 1826	John Smith	Rothwell	Sir John Palmer	
6th July 1826	John Jones	Great Oakley	Thomas Maunsell Esq.	
8th September 1826	William Gibson	Rothwell	Sir Justinian Isham	
13th November 1826	George Thompson	Cransley	John Capel Rose Esq.	9th Dec 1843
17th November 1826	Richard Patrick	Middleton	Sir Richard Brooke	
5th April 1827	William Cooke	Thorpe Malsor	Thomas Maunsell Esq.	5th April 1827
30th April 1827	Robert Waterfield	Middleton	Sir John Palmer	
4th November 1828	Thomas Reeve	Loddington	Sir Justinian Isham	18th Mar 1835
17th August 1829	Richard Garley	Broughton	John Capel Rose Esq.	22nd April 1835
17th August 1829	Joseph Warren	Cottingham	Sir Richard Brooke	
6th October 1829	John Loake	Orton	Sir John Palmer	
7th November 1829	Henry Payn	Rothwell	Thomas Maunsell Esq.	17th June 1856
7th November 1829	Peter Eaton	Old	Sir Justinian Isham	24th Sept 1836
6th September 1830	James Mash	Finedon	John Capel Rose Esq.	
13th December 1830	Francis Ingram	Cottenham	Sir John Palmer	8th March 1840
9th July 1831	Richard Johnson	Rushton	Thomas Maunsell Esq.	12th Nov 1835
16th July 1831	Anthony Barker	Walgrave	A.A. Young Esq.	

Date Admitted	Name of person Elected & Admitted	Place of Residence	Proposing Governor	Year of Death
2nd January 1832	Thomas Holt	Hanging Houghton	Sir Justinian Isham	21st Nov 1842
2nd July 1832	George Grimley	Cransley	John Capel Rose Esq.	1st May 1836
24th August 1832	Joseph Neal	Stoke Albany	Siir John Palmer	14th April 1842
16th February 1833	John Horsly	Rothwell	Thomas Maunsell Esq.	
11th January 1834	Thomas Davis	Rothwell	A.A. Young Esq.	11th Jan 1835
5th May 1834	Robert Cosford	Lamport	Sir Justinian Isham	2th Jan 1837
5th November 1834	Thomas Knibbs	Rushton	John Capel Rose Esq.	
5th January 1835	Samuel Shortland	Rothwell	Sir John Palmer	11th Aug 1839
10th January 1835	Thomas Grainger	Stoke [Albany]	Sir John Palmer	30th Oct 1839
15th January 1835	Joseph Howe	Finedon	John Capel Rose Esq.	1st May 1837
24th January 1835	James Gilbert	Barford	Thomas Maunsell Esq.	8th Nov 1841
10th February 1835	Timothy Madock	Orlingbury	A.A. Young Esq.	9th Dec 1838
14th February 1835	Francis Alderman	Rothwell	Thomas Maunsell Esq.	1st Feb 1838
13th March 1835	Thomas Dickens	Hanging Houghton	Sir Justinian Isham	6th June 1835
27th April 1835	Joshua Barker	Draughton	A.A. Young Esq.	27th April 1835
May 1835	Thomas Fisher	Lamport	Sir Justinian Isham	6th July 1848
May 1835	Samuel Jackes	Cransley	John Capel Rose Esq.	
21st June 1835	John Dams	Middleton	Sir John Palmer	21st June 1835
1st September 1835	Richard Johnson	Thorpe Malsor	Thomas Maunsell Esq.	12th Nov 1835
5th November 1835	John Cunnington	Pytchley	A.A. Young Esq.	4th Nov 1835
20th December 1835	Robert Hill	Thorpe Malsor	Sir Richard Brooke	21st Aug 1835
22nd December 1835	Thomas Wood	Brixworth	Sir Justinian Isham	1st Oct 1845
14th March 1836	John Horner	Rothwell	John Capel Rose Esq.	Buried 16th March 1836

Date Admitted	Name of person Elected & Admitted	Place of Residence	Proposing Governor	Year of Death
9th April 1836	Robert Burbridge	Carlton	Sir John Palmer	9th April 1836
4th June 1836	William Fox	Stoke Albany	Thomas Maunsell Esq.	26th Jan 1839
27th September 1836	John Broughton	Little Bowden	A.A. Young Esq.	13th Dec 1838
4th February 1837	Richard Yeomans	Rothwell	Sir Justinian Isham	22nd May 1850
15th February 1837	Samuel Ginns	Rothwell	John Capel Rose Esq.	2nd August 1841
1st May 1837	Samuel Jaques	Cransley	John Capel Rose Esq.	
7th February 1838	Edward Slow	Rushton	Sr John Palmer	
5th November 1835	John Cunnington	Pytchley	A.A. Young Esq.	4th Nov 1835
20th December 1835	Robert Hill	Thorpe Malsor	Sir Richard Brooke	21st Aug 1835
22nd December 1835	Thomas Wood	Brixworth	Sir Justinian Isham	1st Oct 1845
14th March 1836	John Horner	Rothwell	John Capel Rose Esq.	Buried 16th March 1836
9th April 1836	Robert Burbridge	Carlton	Sir John Palmer	9th April 1836
4th June 1836	William Fox	Stoke Albany	Thomas Maunsell Esq.	26th Jan 1839
27th September 1836	John Broughton	Little Bowden	A.A. Young Esq.	13th Dec 1838
4th February 1837	Richard Yeomans	Rothwell	Sir Justinian Isham	22nd May 1850
15th February 1837	Samuel Ginns	Rothwell	John Capel Rose Esq.	2nd Aug 1841
1st May 1837	Samuel Jaques	Cransley	John Capel Rose Esq.	
7th February 1838	Edward Slow	Rushton	Sr John Palmer	
5th January 1835	Samuel Shortland	Rothwell	Sir John Palmer	11th Aug 1839
1st May 1837	Samuel Jaques	Cransley	John Capel Rose Esq.	
7th February 1838	Edward Slow	Rushton	Sr John Palmer	
14th January 1839	Timothy Joyce	Rothwell	W Maunsell Esq.	
15th February 1839	John Atherston Savage	Isham	A.A. Young Esq.	
31st January 1839	Francis Edgley	Braybrook	Sir Justinian Isham	26th March 1855
19th August 1839	Charles Houghton	Kettering	John Capel Rose Esq.	20th Sept 1847

Date Admitted	Name of person Elected & Admitted	Place of Residence	Proposing Governor	Year of Death
16th November 1839	Henry Eagle	Middleton	Sr John Palmer	16th Nov 1839
26th November 1840	William Shortland	Rothwell	W Maunsell Esq.	
26th November 1840	Samuel Francis	Lamport	Sir Justinian Isham	17th Jan 1849
15th June 1841	Jonathan Tye	Rothwell	A.A. Young Esq.	19th April 1851
2nd August 1841	George Craddock	Great Harrowden	John Capel Rose Esq.	11th Feb 1852
8th November 1841	John Cooper	Cottingham	Sr John Palmer	
4th January 1842	George Hodson	Orlingbury	A.A. Young Esq.	6th May 1846
14th April 1842	Thomas Cross	Rothwell	Sir Justinian Isham	11th Sept 1856
21st November 1842	John Chester	Loddington	John Capel Rose Esq.	26th Feb 1846
9th December 1843	Robert Stanyon	Cottingham	Sr John Palmer	8th Sept 1849
3rd June 1845	Thomas Kilsby	Rothwell	T. P.Maunsell Esq.	
8th July 1845	Samuel Ashby	Kettering	A.A. Young Esq.	
1st October 1845	Thomas Scott	Kettering	Sir Arthur de Capel Brooke	4th May 1849
26th February 1846	George Loake	Rushton	Geoffrey Palmer	7th Aug 1847
6th May 1846	Benjamin Hipwell	Middleton	Sir John Palmer	22nd Feb 1854
18th August 1846	John Bosworth	Rothwell	T. P.Maunsell Esq.	
26th February 1847	William Brown	Loddington	A.A. Young Esq.	8th Sept 1854
7th August 1847	Randall Payne	Pipwell	Sir Arthur de Capel Brooke	6th April 1848
20th September 1847	John Blisset	Wilbarston	Geoffrey Palmer	18th Oct 1849
6th April 1848	Thomas Perkins	Ashley	Sr John Palmer	
6th July 1848	Thomas Perkins	Barford	T. P.Maunsell Esq.	
17th January 1849	Thomas Butlin	Orlingbury	A.A. Young Esq.	
4th May 1849	Thomas Chambers	Middleton	Sir Arthur de Capel Brooke	
8th September 1849	Samuel Jones	Rothwell	Geoffrey Palmer	
10th September 1849	George Baker	Carlton	Sr John Palmer	8th May 1854
18th October 1849	Christopher Valentine	Thorpe Malsor	T. P.Maunsell Esq.	10th Jan 1853
22nd May 1850	John Horner	Broughton	A.A. Young Esq.	11th Dec 1851

Date Admitted	Name of person Elected & Admitted	Place of Residence	Proposing Governor	Year of Death
19th April 1851	William Canon	Lamport	Sir Arthur de Capel Brooke	
26th May 1851	Thomas West	Middleton	Geoffrey Palmer	
21st July 1851	John Serjeant	Rothwell	Sr John Palmer	
11th December 1851	Hugh King	Rothwell	T. P.Maunsell Esq.	17th May 1855
11th February 1852	Thomas Blakesley	Old	A.A. Young Esq.	14th Dec 1881
13th November 1852	John Dickson or Dixon	Great Oakley	Sir Arthur de Capel Brooke	
10th January 1853	William Coles	Faxton	Geoffrey Palmer	25th Feb 1857
22nd february 1854	Joseph Baxter	Rothwell	T. P.Maunsell Esq.	19th Nov 1869
8th May 1854	John Wykes	Little Cransley	A.A. Young Esq.	
8th September 1854	John Hobbs	Loddington	Sir Arthur de Capel Brooke	
26th March 1855	Thomas Horam	Rothwell	Geoffrey Palmer	
17th May 1855	John Deaper	Rothwell	Sr John Palmer	
7th January 1856	William Chamber	Rothwell	T. P.Maunsell Esq.	21st April 1856
21st April 1856	William Levis	Isham	A.A. Young Esq.	
17th June 1856	John Walker	Rothwell	Sir Arthur de Capel Brooke	22nd May 1857
11th September 1856	James Murton	Rothwell	Geoffrey Palmer	
25th February 1857	John Harris	Rothwell	Sr John Palmer	
22nd May 1857	William Bradshaw	Rothwell	T. P.Maunsell Esq.	
8th January 1858	Thomas Ward	Little Har-rowden	A.A. Young Esq.	2nd Sept 1861
11th May 1858	William Tibbut	Pytchley	Sir Arthur de Capel Brooke	
18th September 1858	Joshua Benford	Cransley	Geoffrey Palmer Esq.	
24th February 1859	Wiiliam Corby	Draughton	Sir John Palmer	11th May 1865
24th February 1859	William Greene	Rothwell	Thomas Maunsell Esq.	
21st March 1859	William Leach	Brixworth	A.A. Young Esq.	18th May 1861
11th November 1859	Eagle Maydwell	Middleton	Geoffrey Palmer Esq.	
29th March 1860	Thomas Towell Sen	Geddington	W. J Rose Esq.	

Date Admitted	Name of person Elected & Admitted	Place of Residence	Proposing Governor	Year of Death
15th October 1860	John Rowe	Thorpe Malsor	T. P. Maunsell Esq.	
December 1860	John Burditt	Wilbarston	Sir John Palmer	14th Aug 1865
December 1860	Timothy Lee	Little Harrowden	A.A. Young Esq.	
18th May 1861	Samuel Bamford	Lamport	Sir T. H. Palmer	
25th May 1861	Joseph Morris	Orlingbury	W. J Rose Esq.	18th March 1873
2nd September 1861	Abraham Cox	Rushton	Geoffrey Palmer Esq.	16th Nov 1863
24th May 1864	George Watkins	Rothwell	T. P. Maunsell Esq.	12th Jan 1865
10th January 1863	Thomas Hodson	Pytchley	A.A. Young Esq.	25th March 1873
6th June 1863	Richard Barrand	Stoke Albany	Geoffrey Palmer Esq.	
25th July 1863	[Torn off]	Rothwell	Sir John Palmer	
16th November 1863	William Rockleys	Thorpe	T. P. Maunsell Esq.	
31st July 1864	William Smith	Harrington	A.A. Young Esq.	14th April 1870
12th September 1864	Samuel Cursley	Middleton	Geoffrey Palmer Esq.	
15th October 1864	Joshua Freeman	Draughton	W. J Rose Esq.	
11th January 1865	John Green	Carlton	Sir T. H. Palmer	5th Feb 1873
12th January 1865	John Perkins	Rothwell	T. P. Maunsell Esq.	
27th April 1865	William Denton	Orlingbury	A.A. Young Esq.	1st Jan 1876
11th May 1865	Charles Wilford	Draughton	G. Palmer Esq.	
14th August 1865	Samuel Shortland	Weekly	H. S. Rose Esq.	
6th September 1865	George Church	Rothwell	T. P. Maunsell Esq.	
20th March 1866	Henry Knapp	Orton	A.A. Young Esq.	
2nd June 1866	Robert Fletcher	Middleton	Sir G. Palmer	
11th June 1866	William Lenton	Broughton	W. J Rose Esq.	
11th June 1866	John Perkins	Rothwell	Rev G. E. Maunsell	17th March 1875
21st December 1867	Robert Turner	Geddington	Sir W. Capel Brookes	
2nd December 1868	John Errington	Wold	A.A. Young Esq.	
25th May 1869	Thomas Chambers	Middleton	Sir G. Palmer	
11th November 1869	Thomas Kilborn	Geddington	W. J Rose Esq.	

Date Admitted	Name of person Elected & Admitted	Place of Residence	Proposing Governor	Year of Death
12th November 1869	William Davis	Thorpe Malsor	Rev G. E. Maunsell	
14th April 1870	William Ward Timson	Cransley	Sir W. Capel Brookes	2nd May 1892
31st March 1871	John Gibson	Walgrave	A.A. Young Esq.	
15th September 1871	Charles Hoofis	Middleton	Sir G. Palmer	
11th November 1871	Samuel Chester	Loddington	W. J. Rose Esq.	
5th February 1873	Robert Wykes	Thorpe Malsor	Rev G. E. Maunsell	24th April 1886
25th March 1873	William Tye	Rothwell	Sir W. Capel Brookes	17th March 1888
18th March 1873	Joseph Woolston	Broughton	A.A. Young Esq.	
5th May 1873	Thomas Jackson	Middleton	Sir G. Palmer	15th Sept 1880
14th October 1873	[Torn] Smith	Broughton	Rev G. E. Maunsell	
3rd November 1873	[Torn] Walker	Rothwell	Sir W. Capel Brookes	
31st May 1874	[Torn] Turland	Faxton	A.A. Young Esq.	
19th November 1874	[Torn] Ginns	Pipewell	Sir G. Palmer	Surrendered his place
24th November 1874	[Torn] Dawkins	Rothwell	W. J Rose Esq.	
17th March 1875	Unreadable	New Bottle	Rev G. E. Maunsell	
12th August 1875	Thomas Burditt	Loddington	Sir W. Capel Brookes	2nd Aug 1881
6th September 1875	Richard Underwood	Harrington	A.A. Young Esq.	18th Nov 1879
3rd December 1875	William Cranford	Middleton	Sir G. Palmer	2nd July 1881
1st January 1876	John Heeps	Old	W. S. Rose Esq.	
26th February 1876	James Matthews	Rothwell	Sir Charles Isham	
19th June 1876	John Remington	Rothwell	Sir W. Capel Brookes	16th Aug 1881
11th July 1876	William Bird	Orlingbury	A.A. Young Esq.	14th July 1884
2nd September 1876	Samuel Tebbutt	Rothwell	Sir G. Palmer	9th Nov 1885
6th February 1877	Joseph Penn	Old	W. S. Rose Esq.	31st March 1879
10th April 1877	John Humphrey	Great Oakley	Sir W. Capel Brookes	7th Jan 1880
13th April 1877	Robert Wright	Arthingworth	Sir Charles Isham	16th June 1897

Date Admitted	Name of person Elected & Admitted	Place of Residence	Proposing Governor	Year of Death
22nd June 1877	Thomas Holman	Walgrave	A.A. Young Esq.	16th April 1884
31st July 1877	Charles Pinnock	Rothwell	Sir G. Palmer	29th Dec 1879
7th August 1877	John Butlin	Rothwell	W. S. Rose Esq.	13th April 1882
3rd October 1878	John Waters	Geddington	Sir W. Capel Brookes	22nd February 1881
19th November 1878	Shadrack Taylor	Rothwell	Sir Charles Isham	7th March 1896
31st March 1879	Hugh Efram	Thorpe Malsor	A.A. Young Esq.	25th Feb 1881
18th November 1879	Thomas Tyrell	Middleton	Sir G. Palmer	26th May 1884
29th December 1879	Joseph Gibson	Walgrave	W. S. Rose Esq.	11th Jan 1888
7th January 1880	George Cross	Rushton	Sir W. Capel Brookes	
15th September 1880	Samuel Bollard	Harrington	Sir Charles Isham	6th Sept 1886
22nd February 1881	Francis Wallis	Orlingbury	A.A. Young Esq.	
25th February 1881	Samuel Cockin	Rushton	W. S. Rose Esq.	14th Jan 1888
1st March 1881	Benjamin Dawkins	Rothwell	Sir W. Capel Brookes	4th June 1888
2nd July 1881	William Tye	Rothwell	Sir Charles Isham	
2nd August 1881	Joseph Morriss	Broughton	A.A. Young Esq.	9th April 1890
16th August 1881	Thomas Coles	Cottingham	Sir G. Palmer	7th Aug 1887
22nd December 1881	William Tebbutt	Pytchley	W. S. Rose Esq.	14th June 1889
17th January 1882	William Cox	Middleton	Sir W. Capel Brookes	
13th April 1882	William Bugby	Old	Sir Charles Isham	
9th November 1885	Thomas Oram	Orlingbury	A.A. Young Esq.	
16th April 1884	William Thorpe	Middleton	Sir G. Palmer	
26th May 1884	John Sharman	Rushton	W. S. Rose Esq.	23rd Dec 1896
14th July 1884	James Cox	Middleton	Sir W. Capel Brookes	9th Oct 1888
9th October 1884	John Clements	Brixworth	Sir Charles Isham	11th March 1890

Date Admitted	Name of person Elected & Admitted	Place of Residence	Proposing Governor	Year of Death
15th October 1885	George Efram	Thorpe Malsor	A.A. Young Esq.	15th April 1897
24th April 1886	William Woodcock	Wilbarston	Sir G. Palmer	
6th September 1886	Frederick Wiford	Draughton	Sir Charles Isham	26th Aug 1894
15th January 1887	Thomas Humphrey	Great Oakley	Sir W. Capel Brookes	3rd March 1888
29th July 1887	William Chambers	Rothwell	Captain B. Tibbitt	14th March 1902
7th August 1887	Timothy Gamage	Walgrave	A.A. Young Esq.	24th Dec 1902
11th January 1888	George Hunt	Harrington	Sir G. Palmer	25th May 1899
14th January 1888	James Howlett	Old	Sir Charles Isham	
3rd March 1888	Henry Sharman	Rothwell	Sir W. Capel Brookes	
17th March 1888	George Stevens	Old	Captain B. Tibbitt	9th May 1889
31st May 1888	Frederick Thompson	Little Harrowden	A.A. Young Esq.	
4th June 1888	William West	Cottingham	Sir G. Palmer	10th March 1903
26th June 1888	John Bradley	Old	Sir Charles Isham	
9th October 1888	John Bradshaw	Cottingham	Sir W. Capel Brookes	21st Feb 1899
14th June 1889	Edward Remington	Loddington	A.A. Young Esq.	1st July 1895
18th November 1889	William Tye	Rothwell	Sir G. Palmer	
10th January 1890	George H Durham	Scaldwell	Sir Charles Isham	8th Jan 1903
11th March 1890	William Cannon	Middleton	Sir W. Capel Brookes	
9th April 1890	Thomas Taff	Rothwell	Captain B. Tibbitt	
16th January 1891	John Ward	Little Harrowden	A.A. Young Esq.	5th March 1901
24th August 1891	Charles Timpson	Middleton	Sir G. Palmer	19th Nov 1896
29th March 1892	Thomas Latimer	Lamport	Sir Charles Isham	11th Oct 1901
2nd May 1892	John Andrew	Thorpe	Sir W. Capel Brookes	14th June 1903
26th August 1894	George Chamberlain	Isham	Captain B. Tibbitt	

Date Admitted	Name of person Elected & Admitted	Place of Residence	Proposing Governor	Year of Death
1st July 1895	Frank Harris	Rothwell	G. H. Watson Esq.	
3rd July 1895	William Linnett	Rushton	Sir Charles Isham	9th July 1896
17th July 1895	Sidney Remington	Rothwell	R. Booth Esq.	
7th March 1896	Thomas Henry Willis	Rothwell	Captain B. Tibbits	14th July 1897
9th July 1896	Richard Joyce	Rothwell	C. Thornhill Esq.	
19th November 1896	William Willis	Rothwell	G. H. Watson Esq.	
23rd December 1896	C. W. Dominic?	Walgrave	Sir Charles Isham	
15th April 1897	Charles Stanley	Rothwell	R. Booth Esq.	
16th June 1897	Charles Woodford	Rothwell	Captain B. Tibbits	6th Nov 1900
14th July 1897	Joseph Taylor	Rothwell	J. L. Watson	
21st February 1899	John Patrick	Orlingbury	Sir Charles Isham	
25th May 1899	William Freeman	Rothwell	Rev. C. Maunsell	
19th July 1900	J. W. Hobbs	Cottingham	Sir W. Capel Brookes	
16th November 1900	Carpenter York	Rothwell	Captain B. Tibbits	
5th March 1901	George Bradley	Rothwell	Rev. C. Maunsell	
2nd June 1901	Benjamine Cursley	Middleton	Sir W. Capel Brookes	
27th August 1901	John Richardson	Rothwell	Captain B. Tibbits	
11th October 1901	Jerry Cooper?	Isham	Rev. C. Maunsell	
14th March 1902	George Foster	Rothwell	Sir W. Capel Brookes	
24th December 1902	John Oram	Rothwell	Rev. C. Maunsell	

Glossary

Almshouse	A house founded by charity (Alms), offering accommodation for poor people.
Armiger	A Knight, a person entitled to use a coat of Arms
Bessum	A Broom or sweeping brush.
Commission of Oyer & Terminer	In law, courts oyer and terminer were commanded to make diligent inquiry into felonies and misdemeanors specified in the commission
Court of Chancery	A division of the high court of justice. Its head was the Lord Chancellor.
Demesne	Land reserved to the Lord of the Manor, providi g food for his table.
Enfeoffment	To entrust land in a person or persons in return for their service.
Feoffee	A trustee invested with a freehold estate to hold in possession for a purpose, typically a charitable one.
Final Concord	A final concord, or 'fine', was the product of a 'collusive action', or a fake legal procedure. The word 'concord' means 'agreement'. The legal procedure usually took place in the Court of Common Pleas.
Hilary Term	The sitting of Parliament beginning in January.
Idiotism	Someone with a mental health problem, similar to an imbicile, but probably includes a person with dementia.
Imbicile	A fool or halfwit.
Impropriate Rector	A lay owner of a rectory
Lady Day	25th March. This was New Years Day prior to 1753.
Messuage	A house
Michaelmas	Religious Festival falling on 29th September.
Modus	A private arrangement between an impropriate rector or a vicar and another person for the commutation of tithes to a cash payment.
Moiety	An half share.
Recusancy	A Catholic. After 1581, recusancy became an indictable offence, In that year the fine for missing an Anglican service was twenty pounds per month, and being a recusant became a treasonable offence. A fine of 100 marks and a year in prison was imposed on those hearing mass.
Recusant	One who neglected to attend the services of the Church of England, and/or openly professed their Catholic faith.
Seisin	Possession of land by freehold.

Terrier	A document detailing the land owned by a manor.
Tithes	A portion of everything produced given to the church to support the clergy
Verderer	A judicial; officer of a royal forest
Vouchers	Small invoices, receipts and notes
Yardland	An area of land of variable size, but usually 20-30 acres

Bibliography

Primary Sources

JHR 1 & 2	Feoffment made between Owen Ragsdale, Thomas Morgan, Thomas Tresham, George Gascoigne, Ferdinand Poulton and Oliver Farren for the use of Owen Ragsdale's estate to endow the hospital. (10th November 159)
JHR 3	The articles annexed to the feoffment.
JHR 4	Copy of the will of Owen Ragsdale.
JHR 5	1837 copy of the Letters Patent.
JHR 6	An enrolled feoffment of 3rd September 1600 transferring estate to new governors.
JHR 7	An account of Owen Ragsdale's life. By Ferdinand Poulton late 16th or early 17th century.
JHR 8	An un-dated copy of the statutes of the hospital.
JHR 9	A 17th century copy of the statutes
JHR 10 & 11	Two copies of the statutes including three additional statutes established between 1685 and 1705.
JHR 12	Orders of the governors regarding the conduct of residents.
JHR 13	An order of the governors relating to default of rents, dated 16th August 1709.
JHR 14	A Book containing Abstracts of the Statutes of the Hospital, with details of subsequent Orders 1870-1929.
JHR 15	An undated and fragmentary note of the foundation and title deeds of the hospital.
JHR 16	Twenty-one items relating to admissions, acceptances and resignations to the office of governor between 1670 and 1817.
JHR 17	An undated (18th century) memoranda from the hospital records regarding Governors, Assistants and Principals for the period 1670 – 1731.
JHR 18	An undated (18th century) memoranda from the hospital records regarding Governors, Assistants and Principals for the period 1670 – 1731.
JHR 19	A note made sometime between 1811 - 1814 regarding the present Governors and Assistants.
JHR 20	Twenty four items regarding admissions, acceptances, resignations etc. for the office of Assistant, 1612 – 1749.
JHR 21	Applications (2) to the post of Principal and bonds for that office, 1670 – 1814.
JHR 22	18th century document regarding the Principals of JHR between 1670 and 1727.
JHR 23	One hundred and six letters, mostly regarding admission to the hospital. 1671 – 1776.
JHR 24	Notebook containing details of admissions 1826 – 1837 with one part of a page regarding deaths of individual residents.
JHR 25	Book of admissions to the hospital covering the period 1838 – 1858, with details of deaths of residents in the period and names of staff.
JHR 26	Book of admissions to the hospital covering the period 1858 – 1956, with details of deaths of inmates 1858 – 1961.
JHR 27	Late 17th century document regarding the complaints of "the hospitall men" regarding stoppages of money and what they should have.
JHR 28	A promise from a poor man, John Fisher, dated 2nd June 1711, to conform to the rules of the hospital, in particular to attend prayers regularly and to wear the blue coat.
JHR 29 -34	Account books for the period 1671 – 1889.

JHR 35	An abstract of accounts, statements of accounts and rents which includes accounts of repairs over 5/-. 1683 – 1695.
JHR 36	An undated note of revenues of the hospital covering the period 1725 – 1730.
JHR 37	A statement of accounts for 1759 when Sir T Palmer was treasurer.
JHR 38	A collection of letters mostly written between A. Young, treasurer of the hospital and Messrs. Hoares, solicitors concerning finances. The period covered is 1783 – 1823.
JHR 39 a & b	A receipt for £400 reduced annuities, part of the investments of the hospital, with a letter from Sir W. Dolben Treasurer to Messrs. Hoares.
JHR 40	An account of yearly income and outgoings of the hospital. 8th June 1789.
JHR 41	A note of income and expenditure, c1780.
JHR 42	Letters from the Office for Taxes to A. E. Young, Treasurer, concerning the financial affairs of the hospital, 1809 and 1819.
JHR 43	A Letter of 26th December 1809 from Samuel Hafford (later Principal) to persons unknown, concerning a £5 note of the Bank of Messrs. Marriot & Co. of Northampton, which he has had returned, despite assurances of the Bank's respectability.
JHR 44	Correspondence concerning Property Tax paid by JHR and the claims for recovery of Property Tax (includes letter from Nicholas Vansittart. Chancellor of the Exchequer, (1812-22).
JHR 45	Statement of account, Messrs. Hoare and Co to the Governors, 1854-7, 14 Oct. 1857.
JHR 46	Power of attorney, Governors to Giles Groocock of Desborough, husbandman, to collect Hospital rents 23 March 1612/13.
JHR 47 a & b	a) Letter, Henry Goode (son of William Goode, Principal) to Francis Lane, at Glendon, regretting his (Gocde's) inability to meet Lane and Sir Justinian Isham, to pass Wm. Goode's accounts; b) enclosing letter - Lane to Sir Justinian Isham, deferring the meeting between them. 30 October, 1696.
JHR 48	Declaration by Wm. Hammond and Richard Greay that they will provide a sufficient quantity of wood and faggotts for the Hospital 6 March, 1780.
JHR 49	Letter, W. Dolben to A.E. Young, concerning a meeting at JH. 6 Sept. 1809.
JHR 50 a & b	2 letters. W. Dolben to A.E. Young concerning dividends and the transfer of the Treasurer to Young. 13 January 1810; 8 March 1810.
JHR 51	Letter, W. Dolben to A.E. Young, concerning power of attorney to receive dividends on behalf of JHR 4th May 1810.
JHR 52	Draft letter, unfinished [W. Dolben] to Revd. Dr. Atteribury at Cork, concerning dividends received by JHR and the trustees receiving ssrue, W.D. having relinquished the office of Treasurer. 14th May 1810.
JHR 53	Letter, Hugh King of Rothwell, tailor to the Hospital to Governors of JHR, asking for an increase in the allowance of 4/- per suit.
JHR 54	Letter, Samuel Hafford (Principal) to A.E. Young (Treasurer) at Orlingbury concerning repairs to the fences of JHR land, 19 February 1816.
JHR 55 a & b	2 letters, A.E. Young to Sir Richard Brooke, Bart., concerning dividends and dealings with Messrs. Hoare. 29 July 1818; 17 August 1818.
JHR 56 a & b	Letters, A.E. Young to Sir Richard de C, Brooke, Bart., 4 June and 11 June 1819.
JHR 57 a-c	3 letters from Charity Commissioners re JHR land and registration of it etc. (and accounts) 1857 - 1858.
JHR 58	Charity Commissioners Order concerning proceeds for sale of a house and buildings

in High Street, Rothwell belonging to JHR. 8th March 1898.

JHR 59   Draft, incomplete, complaint by Governors of JHR that Rothwell Church is in need of repair and that the parish does not carry out the repairs but charges the Hospital therewith. Not dated, but early 17th century.

JHR 60   A bundle of vouchers, accounts etc. for the Hospital buildings, land and sheep tithes, dating from 1764 – 1771.

JHR 61-88 Bundles of vouchers from1766 to 1827

JHR 89   A Bill for materials for blue coats from 5th Dec 1687.

JHR 90 a & b a)   Receipt for Crown Rents, payable out of land in Old of 1788. b)   Receipt for purchase of Crown Rents, 1789 1 January 1795.

JHR 91   Receipt by Samuel Hafford and Daniel Daulby of £25.

JHR 92   3 miscellaneous vouchers: 1785 - 98.

JHR 93   20 July, 34 Elizebeth I (1592) Bargain and sale. Sir Thomas Tresham of Rushton, knight and his son Francis to Morgan, Gascoigne, Tresham, Pulton and Farren. Tenement and croft in Rothwell adjoining churchyard, between Manor House of Rothwell, the occupied by Mary Ragsdale, widow of Owen on west, and the messuage or tenament of William Kenwarden (formerly tenement of Thomas Brathat alias Tylor) on east. Protection against Wm. Tresham, 3rd son of Sir Thomas Tresham. Power of attorney to Thomas. Vavasour, Philip Pulton, gents, and Thomas. Walker, yeoman. 100 marks. On the back, later endorsment as for "place where the Hospital is built".

JHR 94   8 October, 1612 Quitclaim. William Tresham one of the younger sons of Sir Thomas Tresham of Rushton deceased to the 5 original Governors of JHR. Premises etc. as JHR 93.

JHR 95 a & b 2 copy letters dated 11 June, 1819, 14 June 1819. a)   Governors JHR to Hon. Mrs. Cockayne Medlycott, requesting to have removed the obstruction placed in an ancient roadway to the Orchard and back premises of JHR through the Homestead of Abraham Walter, her tenant. b)   Sir R. Brooke to Hon. Mrs. CM. enclosing and explaining (a) above.

JHR 96   15 June [1819] Letter Mrs. B. Cockayne Medlycott at Rushtcn Hall, to Sir Richard Brooke at Gt. Oakley, saying that the land over which the Governors claim a road in Rothwell has always been open part of the year.

JHR 97   23 September, 1819. Depositions (3 on 1 sheet) of Inhabitants of Rothwell remembering the road and JHR's freedom to use it.

JHR 98   12 July, 1817. Estimate for new gates at JHR.

JHR 100   8 July, 18 Henry VIII (1526).Quitclaim. Richard Wall, one of the sons of Thomas Wall formerly of Rothwell, deceased, Roger Cowper, clerk, Vicar of Rothwell, Henry Burdon, Wm. Cowper and George Sheryff, all of Rothwell, yeomen, to Edward Nyxson of Rothwell, yeoman, 1 messuage and land in the Leather fair, Rothwell. Obtained 6 Sept. 17 Henry VIII (1528) from William Hazilrigge of Gt. Bowden, Leicestershire gent. and Eleanor his wife, formerly widow of Thomas Wall, to use of Richard during life of Eleanor.

JHR 101   1 May, 1648. Bargain and sale. Richard Humfrey of Rothwell, yeoman, and Anne his wife to George Murffin the elder of Rothwell, roper, and Anne his wife. Messuage in the common street of Rothwell etc. with all gates, doors, windows, fences etc. thereto belonging.

JHR 102   1 Feb. 1681/2. Release. Ann Murfin of Rothwell, widow of George M. the elder of Rothwell, to George Murfin, her grandson, of Rothwell, roper. Premises etc. as preceding.

JHR 103 a & b 10 Feb. 1681/2. Marriage settlement (bargain and sale 10 Feb. 1681/2. 1) George Murfin of Rothwell, roper, to 2) Thos. Ponder of Rothwell, gent., and John Bilton

	of Orton, yeoman; 3) Anne wife of George Murfin., one of the daughters of Wm. Barrett late of Orton, deceased. In trust for lives of George and Ann and the longer liver etc. provision to sell in case George needs money. Premises as preceding.
JHR 104 a & b	20 May, 2 Win. & M. [1690]. Mortgage, George Murfin as above to John Norman of East Farndon, yeoman. Property now called the Five Bells, Rothwell. Bond to perform covenants Murfin to Norman.
JHR 105	20 May, 2 Win. & M. [1690]. Mortgage, George Murfin as above to John Norman of East Farndon, yeoman. Property now called the Five Bells, Rothwell. Bond to perform covenants Murfin to Norman.
JHR 106	30 May, 1693. Assignment of mortgage, Hanna Norman of East Farndon, widow of John Norman (see JHR 104) to Samuel Ponder of Thorpe Underwood, yeoman. 5 Bells, Rothwell.
JHR 107 a-c	18, 19 May, 1704. Conveyance (1 & r) George Murfin of JHR 104 to Samuel Ponder of JHR 106. Premises as JHR 106. 20 May 1704 Release of equity of redemption etc.
JHR 108 a & b	24, 25 October 1728. Conveyance (1 & r) Samuel Ponder to Thomas York of Rothwell, yeoman. 5 Bells, Rothwell and 2 messuages adjoining the School House.
JHR 109	6 January 1728/9. Mortgage. Thomas York as prec. to Henry Dent of Kettering, mercer and draper. Premises as JHR 108.
JHR 110 a & b	6 July, 1732. Assignment of mortgage. Henry Dent as preceeding to William Watts of Kettering, flaxdresser. Bond to perform covenants 6 July 1732 York to Watts. Premises as JHR 109.
JHR 111	26 March 1738. Assignment. Sarah Watts of Kettering widow and sole executrix of William Watts as JHR110 to Thos. Chapman of Rothwell, yeoman, as trustee for the Governors of JHR (for the residue of the term of the mortgage to protect the freehold they have purchased from Thomas York (see JHR 108), and with consent etc. of said Thomas York. Premises 5 Bells, Rothwell.
JHR 112	Not dated, but c. 1740. Abstract of title deeds of the 5 Bells, Rothwell, 1648-1738.
JHR 114	16 Jan. 28 Chas. II (1677). Bargain and sale, Joshua Ayre of Rothwell, yeoman and Eliz. Surges alias Bridges of the same, widow to Nicholas Smith of R, mercer. Easton's ½ yardland in Rothwell. Terrier indented attached.
JHR 115	17 June, 1725. Agreement for sale (1) Thos. Munn the younger of Rothwell, gent. , Robert Balderson of R, gent and Robert Dexter of Desborough, gent, to (2) Robert Peake of Rothwell, weaver. Messuage in Rothwell, formerly occupation John Buckby deceased, who devised it to Munn.
JHR 116	29 Sept. 1725. Bargain and sale. Judith Buckby of Rothwell, widow of John Buckby of Rothwell, weaver, deceased and parties in JHR 115. Messuage in Brigg Street Rothwell, Mortgage paid off.
JHR 117	Undated but c. 1742. Abstract of title deeds of 2 cottages in Rothwell, one called the Sun, mortgaged to the Governors of JHR; 1723-42.
JHR 118	7 June, 1653. Bond to perform covenants;. Henry Archer of Wisbech, Cambs., gent, to John Archer the younger of Rothwell, yeoman.
JHR 119	11 July, 1812. Letter, Thomas Marshall, Clerk to the Rothwell Inclosure Commissioners, to A.E. Young (Treasurer, JHR) informing him of a meeting to be held to receive claims to the Commissioners by those who have neglected to claim, JHR being one of these.
JHR 120	15 July, 1812. Letter, Sir John Palmer to A.E. Young agreeing to the nomination of Mr. Hodgson as solicitor for JHR in the matter of claims to the Inclosure

	Commissioners as Mr. Marshall is also Mrs. Medlicot Cockayne's solicitor.
JHR 121	1 August, 1812. Rothwell Inclosure: Printed Book of Claims.
JHR 122	28 March, 1813. Rothwell Inclosure. Bill for £4.15.0, JHR's share of the rate towards defraying expenses of Act etc., and note that JHR's allotment in lieu of tithes is found at the expense of the Proprietors.[5]
JHR 123	18 April, 1813. Letter, H. Palmer to A.E. Young conveying Sir John Palmer's recommendation of John Stiles as a fit person to he a tenant of JHR.
JHR 124	17 December, 1813. Notice of Land Tax charge to John Stiles for the Inclosure Allotment in Rothwell belonging to the Hospital.
JHR 125 a & b	2 Letters dated 17 January & 20 October 1815, from Samuel Hafford (Principal) to A.E. Young (Governor) at Orlingbury concerning the land held of JHR by John Stiles, who has no money and is likely to be distrained upon; Hafford is willing to be tenant in Stiles' place.
JHR 126	1815 - 1818. Small bundle of accounts and correspondence: Messrs. Hodson and Burnham of Wellingborough, solicitors, with the Governors, concerning the occupation of a house and land in Rothwell, property of the Hospital, by John Stiles, an insolvent.
JHR 127	1767 - 1771. Bundle containing lists of sheep and lambs in Rothwell Fields, with the tithe payable.
JHR 128	12 January, 1773. Account of sheep in Rothwell, liable for tithe to JHR.
JHR 129	1780 - 1783. Accounts of sheep and lambs in Rothwell liable to JHR for tithe, also wood for JHR; lambs 1780, sheep 1781, wood and lambs 1781, sheep 1783, wood and lambs 1783.
JHR 130	10 January, 1814. Letter (fragmentary) J. Meadows to (?) concerning Land Tax on land at Rothwell.
JHR 132	1 December, 29 Elizabeth I [1586/7]. Mortgage (and counterpart) John Lucas of Old, yeoman, to Edward Lucas of London, gent, and Thomas Lucas of Newington Blossomfield, Bucks., yeoman. Recites Thomas Spencer of Everdon, esq., leased, 4 March 1574, the Manor of Old, with the Manor House etc. to the said John Lucas for 60 years at 50s. p. a. Now: John Lucas assigns remainder of the lease to Edward and Thomas Lucas in return for a promise to pay John's debts of £220 to John Cope of Everdon. gent., proviso of redemption: full payment to Edward Lucas at his house in Red Cross St., Cripplegate, London, on 30 Sept. 1587. Endorsed: 1) note of proviso of redemption (probably contemporary) 2) note, not dated, of contents and that the estate has since been cleared for the use of Jesus Hospital, Rothwell
JHR 133	1 August, 29 Elizabeth I [1587]. Release of the mortgage. (JHR 132) Endorsed as a mortgage Lucas and Lucas for £200.
JHR 134	29 Elizabeth I [1586/7]. Lease (unexecuted). Hugh Hare of Inner Temple, London, esq., John Cope of London, gent and William Spencer of Everdon, esq. to John Waman of Old, labourer. Tenement etc in Old in occupation said Waman (except all oak, ash and elm trees and other trees). 12 years at 5/- p.a. (plus 8d. p.a. for sheep commons). The document also contains a repairs clause.
JHR 135	27 August 29 Elizabeth I [1587]. Bargain and sale. Hugh Hare of Inner Temple, London, esq., John Cope of London, gent., and William. Spencer of Everdon, esq. to Owen Ragsdale of Rothwell, gent. Manor of Old, etc. (sold by William Spencer to Hare and Cope 6 Feb. 1587) and also a windmill and maltmill in Old in tenancy of John Lucas and also tenement or cottage in Old in tenancy of John Waman and also 16s. 6d. in chief rents in Old (recited) £180 consideration. 2 endorsements of note of contents.
JHR 136	27 August 29 Elizabeth I [1567]. Bond to perform covenants William Spencer to Owen Ragsdale.
JHR 137	29 August 29 Elizabeth I [1587]. Assignment of residue of term, John Lucas to George Gascoigne of Little Oakley, Ferdinando Poulton of Bourton, Bucks,

	Thomas Tresham of Newton and George Poulton of Desborough, esquires. Lesse and lands of lease of 4 March 1574 (recited in JHR 132). £500 consideration.
JHR 138	30 August 29 Elizabeth I [1587]. Deed to suffer a recovery. Parties: 1) Owen Ragsdale of Rothwell, gent., and Henry Lucas of Old, yeoman, 2) Robert Seeley of Rothwell, yeoman and John Ellis of Lt. Oakley, gent., 3) William Spencer of Everdon, esq. , Thomas Spencer of Lincolns Inn, Middx., esq. Hugh Hare of Inner Temple, London, esq. , and John Cope of London, gent. Manor of Old, including 4 messuages, 2 mills, 1 dovehouse, lands and 20s. rent in Old and Scaldwell.
JHR 139 a & b	Michaelmas, 29 Elizabeth I [1587].Final concords (2). Owen Ragsdale, gent. and Henry Lucas querent and William Spencer, knight, and Elizabeth his wife, Thomas Spencer, knight Hugh Hare, knight, and John Cope, gent. Manor of Old, 4 messuages, 3 tofts, 2 mills, 3 orchards and various lands in Old and Scaldwell, as JHR 138.
JHR 140	21 November, 30 Elizabeth I [1587]. Recovery. Ellis and Seeley versus Ragsdale and Lucas. Premises etc. are the same as those in JHR 138.
JHR 141	1 June 34 Elizabeth I [1592]. Release: Trustees of JHR to John Johnson of Old, husbandman. Recites: 1) Bargain and sale 14th May 1587, 2) JHR 135, 3) Covenant, Manor of Old to use of Ragsdale, 4) covenant premises to the use of Johnson, 5) fine to Johnson, 6) recovery to Johnson. Johnsons ½ yardland etc. considered part of Manor of Old. Ragsdale agreed it was not, but died before a deed could be drawn up, hence present deed, ½ yardland in Old, formerly belonging to a tenement called Smetons, occupation Henry Lucas.
JHR 142	1 June, 34 Elizabeth I [1592]. Release. Trustees of JHR to Thomas Warren of Old, husbandman.½ yardland in Old, as JHR 141. Recitals, etc. as JHR 141.
JHR 143	1 June, 34 Elizabeth I [1592]. Release. Trustees of JHR to Robt. Cannell of Old, husbandman. Messuage and I yardland in Old. As JHR 141.
JHR 144	1 June, 34 Elizabeth I [1592]. Release. Trustees of JHR to Henry Petiver of Old, yeoman. 1 messuage, 1 yardland in Old. Recitals etc. as JHR 141.
JHR 145	20 Sept. 40 Elizabeth I [1598]. Assignment of term, Anne Dalleson of Cransley, widow, to Oliver Farren of Molesworth, Huntingdonshire, gent. Mansion house in Old, formerly occupation of Owen Ragsdale, and all lands in Old of Mary, widow of Ragsdale. she leased the property for 50 years to John Sheppard of Old, gent. on 19th January 1593. Sheppard granted 24th January 1593 to Dalleson for the remainder, in return for Dalleson's being bound for Sheppard to Mary Ragsdale. Farren bought out Dalleson for £40. (Except this year's crop to Dalleson.)
JHR 146 a & b	5th November 1660. Lease (counterpart) Governors of JHR to Richard Tresham, of Old, gent, Spencers Manor in Old formerly leased to William Tresham, father of Richard (except the farm and cottage in occupation of widow Cooper) and lands in Town Fields of Old. 21 years at £30 p. a, A terrier of the lands in the Town. Fields is described as annexed. This was presumably annexed to the lease. Bond to perform covenants.
JHR 147 a-c	31st October, 1676. Lease (counterpart) Governors of JHR to Richard Tresham of Old, gent. As JHR 146, John Cooper in occupation of all except farm, etc. 25 years at £30 p.a. Attached: Terrier indented of lands in Fields. Endorsement, not dated. that Richard Tresham is dead, and John Chapman of Old, Richard's executor, is now tenant. b) Bond to perform covenants. c) Copy terrier made 30 Sept. 1689.
JHR 148	Not Dated, 17th century. Substance of the lease, (JHR 147), "breviated for my Lord Chiefe Baron Mountagues perusall".
JHR 149 a & b	29th September, 1692. a) Lease (counterpart). Governors JHR to John Chapman of Old, gent. Spencers Manor in Old (except cottage etc. occupied by John Cooper) 21 years at £30 p.a. Terrier indented attached. b) Bond to perform covenants.
JHR 150	Draft agreement. Since the old windmill, part of Spencer's Manor, was accidentally burnt down, and John Chapman has put up a new one, the new one shall be in lieu of a fine for the lease, and shall revert to JHR on determination of the lease.

| JHR 151 | 30 December, 1709. Lease (counterpart). Governors of JHR to Elizabeth Chapman of Old, widow, and John Chapman of Old, husbandman (one of the sons of Elizabeth Chapman). Spencers Manor in Old and cottage and Lanes Barn formerly occup. John Cooper, little close on the Green and 1 yardland. 21 years at £44, p. a. Terrier indented attached Bond to perform covenant. |

JHR 151   30th December, 1709. Lease (counterpart). Governors of JHR to Elizabeth Chapman of Old, widow, and John Chapman of Old, husbandman (one of the sons of Elizabeth Chapman). Spencers Manor in Old and cottage and Lanes Barn formerly occup. John Cooper, little close on the Green and 1 yardland. 21 years at £44, p. a. Terrier indented attached Bond to perform covenant.

JHR 152   4th September, 1759. Bargain and Sale. Governors of JHR to John Cleaver of Old, miller. Windmill in open fields of Old and custom of grinding thereunto belonging. £68 consideration. Also in same deed: Lease to John Cleaver by Governors Ley of ground in Old 21 years at 2s. 6d. p. a.

JHR 153   20th May, 17 Henry VII (1502). Grant, Thomas Stowe of "Wynyn", Bucks, yeoman, and Ann his wife (heir of John Lane formerly of Old, deceased) to Thomas Lodyngton of Northampton, pewterer. All lands etc. in Old which once belonged to John Lane. Power of attorney to deliver seisin to Thomas Cawight otherwise called Thomas Webber of Old and Thomas Clark of Old. 2 seals, one with "S".

JHR 154   20th May, 23 Henry VII [1508]. Grant, Thomas Lodyngton of Northampton, pewterer and Margaret, his wife, to John Garad of Old and Alice his wife. All the lands of JHR 153 above, and also a messuage and ¼ arable in Old. Livery of seisin given. Endorsed that Sir Thos. Tresham delivered these two deeds (JHR 153, 154) to Francis Bowden, 10 March 1628/9.

JHR 155   26th November, 14 Elizabeth I [1571]. Lease for a life. Henry Lucas of Old, yeoman, to Elizabeth Garrett of Old, widow. 1 messuage, 3/4 land in Old now or late in tenancy or occupation of Robert Corbye. 1 barn and a close, commonly called Lanes Barn in Old, in the tenancy or occupation of Corbye. 1 little close on the Green at Old and lands thereto belonging. 1 cottage called Spencers House and a close, in the tenancy of Henry Warren. For the natural life of Elizabeth Garrett and 2 years after her death. 1d. p.a. during life and 1st year after death and 20s. for 2nd year. Seal missing. Repairs clause (great timber and spars excepted).

JHR 156   Easter Term, 14 Elizabeth I [1572]. Final Concord, Henry Lucas, querent , Thomas Fyssher and Agnes his wife, deforcant 1 messuage, 1 cottage and lands etc. in Old.

JHR 157   4 August, 32 Elizabeth I [1590]. Bargain and sale. Henry Lucas of Old, yeoman, to Owen Ragsdale of Rothwell, gent. Messuage in Old late ten. Robert Corby, 3 quatrons, 1 barn (Lanes barn), 2 closes, cottage called Spencer House (abutments for all) £50. Bond to perform covenants attached.

JHR 158   6 August, 32 Elizabeth I [1590]. Feoffment. Lucas to Ragsdale. Property as JHR 15.

JHR 159   Hilary, 33 Elizabeth I [1591]. Final concord. Owen Ragsdale, gent., querent and Henry Lucas and Anne his wife, deforcants 1 messuage, 1 cottage, 1 garden, 1 orchard and lands in Old.

JHR 160 a& b   12 September, 9 James I (1611). a) assignment of term. James Cowper of Old, husbandman, and John his son and heir, to William. Cowper of Old, husbandman, second son of James recites: 1) assignment of residue of term of part of JHR 155. 2) lease, 27th December 1597. Governors JHR to James & Elizabeth Cowper for 96 years. Premises as JHR 155 plus a ¼ yardland lately purchased of Thomas Chapman by Governors (JHR 168). b) 9th March 1598/9. Terrier indented. Dwelling house and lands etc. of James and Elizabeth Cowper, Lanes barn, occupied by William Corbie, cottage and close in occupation of Steven Chambers. 3/4 yardland and 1/4 yardland in the fields of Old. Gives numbers of bays of housing, abutments etc.

JHR 161   Undated, 17th century. Substance of the lease, 27 Dec. 1597; JHR to James Cooper (recited in JHR 160).

JHR 162   20th August, 1657. Terrier indented. Messuages, lands etc. in Towne fields of Old which James Cooper held by lease of the feoffees of JHR (see JHR 163).

JHR 163   n.d., 17th century terrier, being a copy of JHR 162. Additional information that the lands are those of lease as in JHR 161.

JHR 164 a-c	25 March, 1689. a) Lease. Governors of JHR to John Cooper, senior, of Old, husbandman. Farmhouse in Old, with 1 yardland and 1 little tenement (formerly Lanes Barn) 21 years £11.10s. 0d p. a. Terrier indented attached, b) Bond to perform covenants, c) Draft bond, 1693, to perform covenants Thomas son of John Cooper to Governors of JHR, John. Cooper having passed over his interest and term of years of the lease.
JHR 165	18th January, 1689/90, Terrier of "*John Coopers land in Old*". Witnessed.
JHR 166	6th March, 1 Henry VI [1423]. Quitclaim. John Elyot son of John Elyot of Scaldwell to John Elyot the father and Emma his wife. Piece of ground and 5 arable in Old, which John Elyot senior and Emma had from Hugh Geronde of Faxton.
JHR 167	16th December, 32 Elizabeth I [1589]. Feoffment. Euseby Isham of Braunston on the Hill, knight, to Thomas Chapman of Old, yeoman, 1 quatern in the fields of Old, in tenancy of Agnes Corby. Warranted against William Catesby, knight, David Owen, knight, deceased, John Owen, knight, deceased, Gregory Isham, father of Euseby. Attorney to Stephen Dexter of Old, yeoman.
JHR 168	31st October, 34 Elizabeth I [1592]. Bargain and sale (and counterpart) Thomas Chapman of Old, yeoman, to Trustees of JHR ¼ yardland in Old, formerly in occupation Agnes Corby, now occupied by James Cowper, except 2 leys claimed by Alex Ibbs the parson of Old and allowed to him by an award, dated 21st May 1592, by Euseby Isham and Owen Ragsdale.
JHR 169	n.d.. Abstract of the title of the Manor and lands in Old belonging to the Hospital, 1580-1592.
JHR 170	n.d. but c.1760. Notes of title deeds to the Old property (1587 - 1760).
JHR 171 a & b	1801. a) Map of an estate at Old, belonging to the Hospital, surveyed in 1801 by J. Crutchley. 140 acres, references, field names, compass points. Parchment, good. 16" x 12". b) 1804 Survey (and valuation) of an estate at Old belonging to JHR in occupation of Thomas Norton. By — Watson (from the endorsement). Identical lands to JHR 171.a.
JHR 172	15th January, 1822. A survey of land in Old in the occupation of Mr. Norton. 132 acres. By Mr. Walter (from endorsement). Some names similar to JHR 171 a & b but acreage's different.
JHR 173	6th December 1805. Letter (copy) (W. Dolben to Mr. Norton, tenant of an estate of JHR at Old, concerning an increase of the rent, and giving Norton first refusal.
JHR 174	14th August 1823. Letter, Richard Stephens to J. Rose concerning the wish of Dr. Dean of Old to exchange a cottage at Old belonging to him for a cottage opposite the Rectory at Old belonging to JHR.
JHR 175 1 & 2	2 Valuations dated 6th December 1827 and 22nd March, 1828. 1) Valuation of an estate at Old belonging to JHR, 6th December 1827. 2) Valuation of a Farm and House, Bakehouse at Rothwell belonging to JHR, house etc. in occ. Robert Hafford. 22nd March 1828.
JHR 176	20th April, 8 Eliz. I [1566]. Assignment of term. Sir Thomas Nevell of the Halt, Leicestershire, Knight. to Nicholas Burbage of Stanwick, yeoman. Recites: Letters patent, 3rd December 1565, Elizabeth I to said Thomas; lease of tithe barn etc. in Orton and Thorpe, part of Rothwell, all tithes of corn and wool of Orton and Thorpe Underwood, ½ tithes of lambs, tithes of the mills sometime held by Richard Alderman. All which were possessions of the late monastery of Cirencester in county of Gloucestershire (except woods, mines and quarries).
JHR 177	12th March, 22 Elizabeth I [1580]. Bargain and sale enrolled. Edward, Earl of Lincoln and Christopher Gowff of West Horsley, Surrey, gent. to William. Swayne of London, gent, and Edward his brother. Property as in JHR 176, which was granted to Earl of Lincoln and Gowff by queen Elizabeth by letters patent of 11th March 1580.
JHR 178	23rd March, 22 Elizabeth I [1580]. Bargain and sale enrolled. William and Edward

Swayne to Kenelm Watson of Liddington, Rutland, gent, and John Herdson of London, gent. Property as JHR 176, 177.

JHR 179   26th April, 23 Elizabeth I [1581]. Bargain and sale. Watson and Herdson to Edward Watson, senior, of Rocklngham, armiger. Property as JHR 176 – 178.

JHR 180   8th Nov., 25 Eliz. I [1583]. Assignment of term. John Dyve of Ridlington Park, Rutland, esq., Thomas Waldrara of Easton, Leicestershire, gent., and William Bolton of Dunsby, Lincolnshire, clerk, executors of John Kellam of Bradley, Leicestershire, gent, deceased, to Edward Watson the younger of Bringhurst, Leicestershire, esq. Recites JHR 176 and recitals therein; Nicholas Burbage died and left to Isabel his widow, and Robert, son, who assigned to Kellam, 7th August 1580. Consideration £35.

JHR 181 a & b   2nd November, 27 Elizabeth I [1585]. a)   Bargain and sale. Ed. Watson of Rockingham, esq. to Owen Ragsdale of Rothwell, gent. Property as in preceding. b)   Bond to perform covenants, Watson to Ragsdale.

JHR 182   2nd November, 27 Elizabeth I [1585]. Deed of covenant Edward Watson of Rockingham, esq. to Owen Ragsdale of Rothwell, gent., Watson to assign to Thomas Hampden of Rothwell, gent, on whomever Ragsdale shall appoint. Recites: JHR I76 - 180 etc.

JHR 183   3rd November, 27 Elizabeth I [1585]. Assignment. Watson to Hampden, as agreed in JHR 182.

JHR 184   3rd November, 27 Elizabeth I [1585]. Quitclaim, Watson to Ragsdale. Property as in JHR 181.

JHR 185   26th September, 1732. Lease. Governors of JHR to Thos. Yorke of Rothwell, gent., Orton tithes for 3 years at £80 p.a.

JHR 186   2nd April, 1755. Agreement. Governors of JHR to Daniel Daulby of Rothwell, yeoman. Lease of tithes in Orton for 3 years at £80 p.a.

JHR 187   n.d. but 17th century. Abstract of title, Orton and Thorpe Underwoode tithes, 1565-1591.

JHR 188   n.d. but 17th century. Note on the findings of the Commission on the Statute for Charitable Uses, held at Rothwell, 13th October 1681, concerning the ownership of lands in Thorpe Underwood etc.

JHR 189   10th September, 1690. Bond to perform covenants. Thomas Ponder of Rothwell gent., to Governors of JHR. Lease missing, but cf. JHR 191.

JHR 190   5th October, 1693. Interrogatories and depositions of witnesses in Chancery case concerning the great tithes of Orton and sheep tithes in Rothwell; Thomas Louder, gent., complainants, Edward Hill et al, defendants.

JHR 191   19th April, 1694. Arbitrator's award. By Francis Lane of Glendon, esq., in Exchequer case; Thos. Ponder of Rothwell, tenant of JHR, for tithes in Orton and Rothwell, versus Edward Hill, esq., Nathan Hill, gent., William Stephens, Thomas Shortland, Christopher Mold, all of Rothwell and Ralph Palmer of Orton, for tithes due, 1690-1693. Ponder to have the 3 years tithes due as tenant to JHR to whom tithes belong. Endorsement of production in Chancery 1761.

JHR 192   6th July 1745. Case for opinion of counsel and opinion, concerning Orton tithes etc.

JHR 193   n.d. c.1745. Copy opinion of counsel in case above.

JHR 194   n.d. but c.1746. Draft case for Governors of JHR in case above.

JHR 195 a & b   22nd April 1746. a) Copy answer of Peach in case above. b) Terrier of the lands in Orton taken from Peach's answer (Not dated) 1746.

JHR 196   24th June, 1746. Copy of Chancery decree, ordering Peach to pay arrears. [As part of letter L. Oliver to Charles Allicock 26th July 1746].

JHR 197   16th June, 1748. Copy of interrogatories entered before a Chancery Master by Peach. [Part of letter L. Oliver to John Aldwinckle, attorney].

JHR 198   13th October, 1753. Copy answer of Peach and others (his tenants). Case concerning costs and setting out of lands.

JHR 199	25 July, 1754. Letter, Richard Palmer to John Aldwinckle concerning the probably successful outcome of the case for JHR.
JHR 200	26th March, 1755. Copy receipt for arrears paid to JHR.
JHR 201	15th October, 1755. Summons to attend a commission for setting out JHR lands in Orton.
JHR 202	11th December, 1759. Bond of Peach and his tenants to attend the Chancery Court to answer a charge of contempt.
JHR 203	11th May, 1758, exhibited 28th December, 1761. Notice from Thomas Peach to Daniel Daulby (JHR's tenant) to restore Orton tithes received and to demand no more.
JHR 204	1745- 1762. Bills, costs etc. in above case (8 items).
JHR 205	1765 - 1787 Papers concerning the agreement and Act of Parliament to vest the tithes at Orton in Thomas Peach, as above: a) statement of case concerning Orton tithes by J. Robinson. b) note concerning the tithes. c) abstract of title 1564-1667 (1765 ?). d) petition for a Bill 18 Feb. 1765. e) draft articles of agreement 1765. f) draft Bill n.d. g) Note of income etc. of Thorpe and Rothwell tithes not dated, but c.1764-5. h) copy correspondence and correspondence re lengthy dispute about costs 1770-1774, copies etc. 1786-1787 (8 items). i) 2 receipts for costs of Act and letter Sept-Oct. 1787.
JHR 206	27th January, 1659/60. Agreement for sale, Ralph Munn of Rothwell, yeoman, to Edmund Baron the elder, gent. The Principal JHR Munn to sell to Governors JHR 1 acre in Church Field, Orton.
JHR 207 a & b	4th August, 1660. Bargain and sale. Munn to Governors JHR. As JHR 206.
JHR 208	Easter, 16 Charles II [1664]. Final concord. John Parsons, querent and Simon Dix and Elizabeth his wife, deforcants 7 acres land, 2 acres meadow and 3 acres pasture etc. in Orton.
JHR 209	1st May, 19 Charles II [1667]. Bargain and sale. John Ellis of Orton, yeoman, and Anne his wife, Elizabeth Dix wife of Simon Dix, deceased, of Ratliffe, Middlesex, and John Nutton of Ratliffe and Hannah his wife, sole daughter and heir of Simon and Elizabeth Dix to Governors of JHR. ¼ yardland in Orton, in occupation of the said Ellis. Bond to perform covenants 1st May 1667 Final concords (2) Trinity, 1667.
JHR 210	31st October, 1667. Receipt, John Ellis has received consideration money as in JHR 209.
JHR 211	9th September, 1600. Power of attorney. John Band to his son Ferdinand, to act as tenant of the Rectory of Orton for the unexpired term of the lease thereof.
JHR 212	1st February, 1705/6. Note of measurement of two pieces of land in Orton Field, by Henry Dormer.
JHR 213	1739. Terrier of fields and furlongs in the Manor of Orton, belonging to the Hospital before the inclosure: by George Nunns (mentions a plan being made).
JHR 214	29th October, 1755. Terrier of land in Orton belonging to JHR. Surveyed by Francis Jannels of Wilbarston.
JHR 215	22nd December, 1809. Letter, T. Samwell from Dingley Hall to Sir John Palmer, Bart., at Carlton, concerning Property Tax on the Orton Estate.
JHR 217	[11 October, 1774]. Copy stamped 29.12.1843 - 19.1. 1844. Conveyance (lease and release, lease missing), to, 1) James Haughton Langston of Mincing Lane, London, esq., and Sarah his wife and, 2) Chris. Smyth of Northampton, gent., 3) Reverend. Edmund Smyth of Gt. Linford, Bucks., clerk, manor of Thorpe Underwood and 2 pews in Rothwell Church; lands in Rothwell and East Haddon and Harrington; ⅓ of the advowson of Rothwell; ⅓ of the advowson of East Haddon; bought by Langston from William. Henderson. To Edward Smyth for use etc. of Christopher Smyth Charges on property 4d. p.a. to Harrington Church 6s. 4d. p.a. to JHR, £4 p.a. to Vicar of East Haddon; lease Henderson to John Knighton, 1st Jan. 1755 for 21 years; Lease, Henderson to William White, 19th June 1758, 21 years; Part of the Manor of Thorpe Underwood. Copy Final Concord, Smyth v Langston.

JHR 218 a & b [26th January 1826]. Copy 16.10. 1843 - 19.1.1844 of deed of partition to 1) Revd. Wm. Smyth the elder of Gt. Linford, Bucks, clerk and Susanna his wife. 2) Wm. Tyler Smyth of Northampton, esq. and Ann his wife. 3) George Rubbra of Northampton, gent.

JHR 219 a & b 11th & 12th July 1837. Conveyance (lease and release) Reverend. W. Smyth of Gt. Linford, Bucks., clerk and William Tyler Smyth of Lt. Houghton, esq. to Revd. William Smyth the younger of Lathbury House, Bucks., clerk and Henry Locock of Cornhill, London, silicitor, as trustee for William Smyth the younger. $1/3$ advowson of Rothwell.

JHR 220 31st January, 1844. Conveyance. 1) Revd. Wm. Smyth of South Elkington, Lincolnshire, clerk. 2) Revd. Edmund Smyth to 3) Governors of JHR. Manor of Thorpe Underwood and land in Thorpe, Harrington and Rothwell (plan attached).

JHR 222 a & b 7th, 8th March 1893. Letter (and copy reply) Fisher and Son, land agents, Market Harborough, to A. A.Young, concerning the rent of the farm at Thorpe Underwood owned by the Hospital and rented by Mrs. Hall.

JHR 223 24th November 1914. Lease, Governors of JHR to Stanton Ironworks Co. Ltd. Ironstone under the Hospital Farm, Thorpe Underwood (plan). 21 years. Authorisation by Charity Commission, sealed, 29th September 1914.

JHR 225 21st August 1926. Lease for term of 40 years. Governors of JHR to Stanton Ironworks Co. Ltd. Ironstone under part of the Hospital Farm, Thorpe Underwood (plan). Authorization of Charity Commission, sealed, 20th April 1926, endorsed.

JHR 228 13th January, 3 James I [1606]. Bargain and sale. William Crowe of Welford, shepherd to John Dunckley of Welford, shepherd. Part of Crowe's Close in Welford. Sometime parcell of the possessions of the Late hospitall or Priory of St. Johns of Jerusalem in England now dissolved". Dunckley to mound and fence 3 parts of the hedges etc. and to make the division between the two parts of the close, i.e. to maintain 3 foot of the said fences throughout and Crowe to make and so maintain 2 foot of the said fences throughout.

JHR 232 a & b 25th February, 1655/6. Bargain and sale. John Day of Little Bowden, tailor and Anne his wife to John Coles of the same, husbandman. Cottage in Little Bowden in occupation said John Day and pasture for 1 cow etc. Bond to perform covenants. Day to Coles.

JHR 233 10th May, 1659. Marriage settlement. John Coles of Little Bowden, husbandman [Edward Middleton of Lubenham, Leicestershire, weaver] to Thos. Mawson of Little Bowden, yeoman and James Middleton of Lubenham, weaver, as trustees. Marriage to be between John Coles and Elizabeth daughter of Edward Middleton. To use of John and Elizabeth Coles, and their heirs, or those of the survivor. Property as JHR 232.

JHR 234 12th April, 1670. Final concord. Abraham Walter and John Coles quer. and John Day deforciants. 2 messuages, 2 gardens, 3 acres land, 1 acre meadow, 4 acres pasture etc. in Little Bowden, Leicestershire.

JHR 235 c.1725. Abstract of title deeds of JHR property in Rothwell, Welford, Little Bowden, Faxton, 1423-1725.

JHR 236 25th August, 1711. Assignment of mortgage, Edward Halford of Kettering, apothecary, to John Bletso of Gt. Bowden, Leicestershire, esq. and Thomas. Massey of Harborough, Leicestershire, gent (as trustee) Mortgage 11th November 1708. Joshua Darlow of Great Bowden, miller, to Halford, of 1 acre in Great Bowden, being ½ Jenkinsons Close, and the Windmill in South Field, in occupation Darlow, with utensils etc. for the management, thereof. Halford transfers to Massey as trustee.

JHR 237 22nd July, 1697. Conveyance (Lease and release, lease missing), William Jenkins of Bodenham, Herefords., yeoman to Matthias Jenkins of Hackney, Middlesex, gardener. 2 messuages, 1 dovehouse, 2 gardens, 1 orchard, 140 a. arable, 40 a. pasture, 12 a. meadow in Bowley parva, Bodenham, Herefords.

JHR 238 24th April, 1736. Bond: Samuel Meadows of Kettering, butcher, to Anne Brown of

Rothwell, widow. Meadows to pay Anne Brown £2.15.0 p.a. during her life for the reversion of a moiety of a cottage etc. in Bakehouse Hill, Kettering, of which Samuel Meadows and Anne Brown at the moment are tenants in common.

JHR 239   7 September, 1703. Appointment of trustees of Rothwell Free School (under Decree of the Commissioners for Charitable Uses, 8 Feb. 1683/4); Earl of Dysart, Sir Erasmus Norwich, Sir Lewis Palmer, Bart., Gilbert Dolben, Wm. Washbourne, John Allicock, Edward Saunders and Henry Bacon; in place of Viscount Cullen, Sir Roger Norwich, Bart., and Andrew Lant, esq. Deceased.

JHR 242   17th April, 1772. Account of the rents which pay the School Salary.

JHR 243   n.d. but c.1809-10. Note on the Governors of JHR and Trustees of the Free School. Numbers of pupils, income etc. (Incomplete or unfinished).

JHR 247   8th December, 1690. Draft lease. Trustees of Rothwell Free School to Richard Dixon of Rothwell, fuller. Cottage in Rothwell, in occupation said Richard Dixon 50s. p. a. , no term written in. Repairs clause, a no subletting without licence clause. Note of the Decree of the Commissioners for Charitable Uses, 8th Feb. 1683/4, appointing Trustees of Rothwell Free School. Note by William Goode (Principal of JHR) to Andrew Lant regarding the draft and other tenants' rents.

JHR 248   8th December, 1690. Lease (unsigned, draft?) Parties as JHR 247. Recites: Decree of Commissioners for Charitable Uses, 8th February 1684, that St. Mary's Chapel in Rothwell should be used as a Free School, and the £3.4s.11d. p. a. with which Queen Elizabeth I endowed the said chapel should be paid to the use of the Free School, together with rents, etc. of the messuages in Rothwell and Geddington with which Owen Ragsdale endowed the Free School: and appointed as Trustees, Viscount Cullen (deceased), Sir John Egerton, Sir Justinian Isham, Sir Roger Norwich, Bart., and Andrew Lant, esq. Property etc. as JHR 247, lease for 7 years.

JHR 249 a & b   8 December, 1690. Lease (and counterpart). Trustees Rothwell Free School to Samuel Cooke of Rothwell, shepherd. Little cottage in Rothwell where Cooke lives. 16s. p. a. for 7 years.

JHR 250   8th December, 1690. Lease (counterpart). Trustees of Rothwell Free School to Elizabeth Norton of Geddington, widow. Little cottage in Geddington where Elizabeth Norton now lives. 20s. p. a. for 7 years.

TNA Prob 11/79/26
TNA Prob 11/147/369
TNA Prob 11/443/214
TNA C78/253
TNA SP 12/183, f.143.
Lincolnshire Archives, Fac. 9/59.

Secondary Sources

Aston, N. (2004) 'Dolben, Sir John, second baronet (1684–1756)', Oxford Dictionary of National Biography, Oxford University.

Bailey, B. (1988) Almshouses. Robert Hale Ltd, London.

Brown, A. E. (2004) 'Bridges, John (bap. 1666, d. 1724)', Oxford Dictionary of National Biography, Oxford University Press.

Browne, Willis (1755) The History and Antiquities of the Town, Hundred, and Deanery of Buckingham.

Bull, F. W. (1924) Jesus Hospital, and its founder, Owen Ragsdale, Northamptonshire Architectural Society.

Calendar of the Cecil Papers in Hatfield House; Volume 1, 1306-1571.

Clay, Rotha Mary (1966) The Medieval Hospitals of England, Frank Cass & Co Ltd, London.

Gotch, J.A. (1883A complete account, illustrated by measured drawings, of the buildings erected by Sir Thomas Tresham in Northamptonshire, between 1575 and 1605. Taylor & Son Ltd.

Habakkuk, J. (1955) Daniel Finch, 2nd Earl of Nottingham: His House and Estate. In J. H. Plumb, ed. Studies in Social History .

Hayton, D., Cruickshanks, E. and Handley, S. (2002), The History of Parliament: the House of Commons 1690-1715, Cambridge University Press, Cambridge.

Henning, B. D. Ed, (1983) The History of Parliament: the House of Commons 1660-1690, Boydell & Brewer.

HMSO (1865) Calendar of State Papers Domestic: Charles I, 1625-49.

HMSO Charity Commission (1831) Reports of the Commissioners. Vol 3.

Isham, G. (1962) Two Local Biographies: Owen Ragsdale and Sir John Robinson. Northamptonshire Past and Present. Vol.III.

Isham, J. Parish Register extracts, Being Extracts from the Lost Registers of Barby, Maidwell, Pytchley and Rothwell in Northamptonshire and from the Register of Stonely in Warwickshire.

Jefferies, F. (1835) The Gentlemans Magazine, Vols 158 – 159

Jones, J. (1988) 'Balliol College: a history, 1263–1939'. Oxford University Press.

Jordan, W.K. (1959) Philanthropy in England: 1480 – 1660. George Allen and Unwin Ltd. London.

Lee, J.M. & McKinley, R.M. (1964) Victoria County History: A History of the County of Leicester Vol 5.

Lobel, M. D. and Crossley, A. (1969), Victoria County History: A History of the County of Oxford. vol 9.

Macnair, M. (2004) 'Hill, George (c.1716–1808)', Oxford Dictionary of National Biography, Oxford University Press.

Melville, Lord (1899) 'Lathom Hospital'. Journal of the British Archaeological Association. Second series, 54.

Montgomery-Massingberd, H. eds. (1976), *Burke's Irish Family Records.* Burkes Peerage Ltd, London, U.K

Namier, L. & Brooke, J. eds. (1964) The History of Parliament: the House of Commons 1754-1790.

Neil, S.R and Leighton, C. eds. (2007) Calendar of Patent Rolls 38 Elizabeth I (1595-1596). C66/1443-1457. List and Index Society. Vol 317.

Page, W. (1930) A History of the County of Northampton: Volume 3.

Pevsner, N., Cherry, B. ed. (1995) The Buildings of England, Northamptonshire, Penguin Books.

Sedgwick, R. Ed. (1970) The History of Parliament: The House of Commons 1715-1754.

The Record Society (1896) Royalist Composition Papers, Vol 35 (2S), No 757.

Wake, J. & Rev. H. Isham Longden (1935) Montague Musters Book, Northamptonshire Record Society, Vol VII.

Warner, A. R. (1952) The Records and Collections of the College of Arms.

Wedgwood, J. C. (2002) The House of Commons 1690 – 1715 Cambridge University Press.

Whalley, Rev. Peter (1791)'The history and antiquities of Northamptonshire: Compiled from the manuscript collections of the late learned antiquary John Bridges, Esq'. Vol ii

Wood, A. (1721) Athena Oxonienses:An Exact History of All the Writers and Bishops who Have Had Their Education in the Most Ancient and Famous University of Oxford, from the Fifteenth Year of King Henry the Seveth, A.D. 1500, to the Author's Death in November 1695. Vol.1. R. Knapdock, D. Welwinter and J. Tonson.

Yorkshire Archaeological Society (1890) Feet of Fines of the Tudor Period: Part 3, 1583-1594. Leeds.

Index